THE EXPERIMENTER'S DILEMMA

HARPER'S EXPERIMENTAL PSYCHOLOGY SERIES

UNDER THE EDITORSHIP OF H. PHILIP ZEIGLER

THE EXPERIMENTER'S DILEMMA

JOHN JUNG
California State College
Long Beach

HARPER & ROW, PUBLISHERS

NEW YORK · EVANSTON · SAN FRANCISCO · LONDON

TO MY STUDENTS

CONTENTS

PREFACE

This volume is directed to students who are currently taking or have recently completed a course in experimental methodology. There are many problems associated with experimentation on humans which the student will eventually encounter when he conducts his own experiments. Even if he does not advance to this stage but remains a consumer of information from psychological laboratories, it will be useful for him to face some of the issues about experiments to be raised in this volume.

The attitude toward experimentation presented in the following pages is critical, if not negative. In a sense, this commentary will be seen as antiexperimental. Yet, the writer is an experimental psychologist and believes that the scientific approach is a, *not the,* method of great value for studying psychology. Perhaps my critical tone is assumed in order to counteract the attitude that many experimentalists have that their method is the only one. My goal is not to reject the experimental method but rather to call attention to some of the limitations of both the method and the manner in which it is commonly employed in research. My hope is that awareness of these issues and problems will help prepare students to plan better experiments, to execute them in ways which avoid some of the current problems, and to see experiments in a more proper perspective than as a panacea.

I have been fortunate to have the permission of the authors of the reprinted articles and their publishers to include their work here. I wish to thank these authors, not only for this permission, but for their ideas which have provided the inspiration for this project.

I also owe a word of thanks to Rod Wong for a critical reading of an early draft and to Gil Padilla and his experimental psychology class for "serving as *Ss*" and giving the manuscript a road test. Their comments and encouragement are appreciated, especially since it has helped me to see the manuscript from the viewpoint of its intended audience.

Finally, I wish to thank George A. Middendorf, of Harper & Row, for his support and interest in this project. I would also like to thank H. Philip Zeigler for his encouragement and advice on this project.

JOHN JUNG

THE EXPERIMENTER'S DILEMMA

1

WHAT IS THE EXPERIMENTER'S DILEMMA?

Experimental psychologists have traditionally stressed the virtues and advantages of the experimental method and have assigned it a central role in the development of a scientific psychology. Only in recent years have we increasingly realized that along with its advantages, the experimental method, especially when used with human subjects, has a number of limitations and disadvantages whose implications require us to reconsider our traditional views regarding the role of the experimental method in psychology. It is to such a reconsideration that the present book is primarily addressed.

First, what are the advantages of experimentation? The principal virtue of the experimental method resides in the fact that it makes possible *controlled* observation. Thus, the experimenter *(E)* can manipulate conditions so as to eliminate alternative explanations of his results. For example, if one wants to study the effects of marijuana, one must be able to sort how how much of the observed effect is due to the process of smoking, the age or sex of the subject *(S)*, his expectations about the effect of marijuana, his previous experience with drugs, the social environment in which smoking occurs, the purity of the drug, and so forth. If it is suspected that all of these factors may play a role, each must be studied separately and in specified combinations before any valid conclusions about drug effects can be reached.

In contrast, uncontrolled observations permit tentative conclusions at best, because alternative explanations cannot be ruled out as all antecedent conditions involved in producing the events requiring explanation cannot be identified. The strong preference for the experimental method depends primarily on the fact that it provides control and permits valid inferences about the causes of observed effects.

Nevertheless, the procedure necessary to achieve control has a variety of effects, particularly when used with humans, which may not be obvious but which seriously compromises, detracts from, or diminishes the usefulness of the experimental method. These disadvantages will be discussed at length in the remainder of the book. At this point, it might be useful to preview some of these problems with a few examples.

1. THE REACTIVE NATURE OF EXPERIMENTATION

Subjects are generally aware that they are being experimented upon and, being human, may modify their "normal" behavior. Some may try to please the E by trying to do what they think he wants; others may behave in whatever ways they think will make themselves "look good"; finally, some will try to confound and frustrate E, either to just be "ornery" or to prevent themselves from feeling manipulated. One could try to solve this problem by observing Ss in natural rather than laboratory settings so that they would be unaware that they were being observed. However, the more natural the situation, the less control attainable.

2. THE "UNIVERSALITY" OF EXPERIMENTAL FINDINGS

Since human subjects, unlike albino rats, cannot be kept in cages awaiting the pleasure of E, they must be obtained by some selection method. The validity or generalizability of results can be affected by the selection method if it favors the inclusion of certain types of Ss to the exclusion of other types. The most readily available Ss may not be the most representative of the larger population whose behavior is being studied. Thus, selection on the basis of convenience conflicts with E's goal of developing laws of behavior which are valid for humans as a species. Convenience is a major factor in the widespread preference for college sophomores and albino rats as Ss, but how representative are they of humans as a species or mammals as a zoological class?

3. EXPERIMENTER "BIAS" AND SUBJECT BEHAVIOR

Experimenters generally have a considerable emotional and intellectual investment in their research such that certain experimental outcomes may be more desirable than others. A growing body of evidence indicates that the expectancies, hypotheses, or biases of Es may be communicated in some fashion to their Ss. Although such communication is unintentional and neither *E* nor *S* may even be aware of it, this source of bias seriously reduces the validity of the experimental findings. One possible solution to this problem would be to replace *E* with a "neutral" tape recording made by someone who did not know the *E*'s hypothesis about the outcome of the experiment. But while such a change might solve one problem, it could create others such as reducing the motivation of the *S*.

The experimental psychologist is thus in a dilemma, i.e., a situation requiring him to choose between equally undesirable alternatives. Every alternative that diminishes the problems raised by experimental procedures also diminishes the advantages provided by those procedures. As we shall see, psychologists have responded to this dilemma in a variety of ways, ranging from a further refinement of the traditional experimental method to suggestions that we should abandon these procedures and adopt a more "human" approach to psychology. One aim of this book is to stimulate a thoroughgoing discussion of these problems and to suggest some courses of action that may extricate us from the experimenter's dilemma.

IDEAL VERSUS ACTUAL EXPERIMENTS

Many of the choices and decisions that *E* must make are not considered in textbooks describing the conceptual nature of the experimental method. There one learns about ideal experiments or the nature of what an experiment is in principle, and not what it is like to actually perform an experiment. Let us examine briefly the nature of the typical textbook account.

First, one learns about independent and dependent variables. The variables whose effects one wishes to ascertain are the independent variables while the behavioral responses one observes are the dependent variables. Although one is taught the definitions of these concepts, one does not learn about some of the factors which determine the *E*'s choices of particular independent and dependent variables, i.e., "Why these and not those?"

Then, the concept of experimental control is introduced and explanations of various experimental designs for achieving control are provided. One learns how to form equivalent groups of *S*s by random sampling or matching procedures. One learns that we are looking for differences in behavior under conditions where the independent variable is operative and those where it is not. Thus, the experimental group receives some value of independent variable *X* while it is withheld from the control group. Finally, any differences between these groups on the dependent variables are attributed to X.

So much for ideal experiments! Friedman (1967) has challenged the myth of the "standardized experiment" which is sometimes fostered by textbook explanations about the nature of experiments. In these accounts, one gets the impression that there are accepted standards which are adhered to in the conduct of experiments. However, based on filmed experimental sessions using a task devised by Rosenthal and Fode (1961) which will be described in detail in Chapter 4, Friedman has obtained objectively analyzable records of what most of us have suspected all along; namely that there is substantial uncontrolled variability in the manner in which experiments are actually conducted by Es.

Even the social interaction between S and E when S shows up for the test session varies considerably, and there is reason to suspect that the nature of this interaction could very well affect the results of some experiments. More seriously, perhaps, is the lack of standard procedures within the experiment proper, starting with the giving of instructions, to the administration of stimuli, recording of responses, and dismissal of Ss. During this period, the amount of social interaction and conversational small talk also varies. Some Es are formal and professional, others are more casual and nonchalant about uniformity of procedures for all Ss. The pace and style of stimulus presentation vary with different Es, as do the accuracy and conscientiousness for recording S's responses. Most experimental reports have some description about S's characteristics and his behavior in the experiment, but rarely, if ever, does one find descriptions of E's traits and behavior reported, unless, of course, these factors are being studied systematically as independent variables in themselves. Even the verbal interchange at the conclusion of a session varies. Although such differences could not possibly affect the Ss' behavior in the just completed session, it well might influence their attitudes and performances in future experiments.

Friedman emphasizes the social nature of psychological research. Unlike the physical sciences, which psychology has emulated as a model, the interaction between S and E in an experiment is similar to other forms of dyadic situations. Whereas chemicals do not respond differently as a function of the personality of E, human, and also animal Ss to some degree, respond differently in some situations to different types of *E*s. In addition to the differential effect of different *E*s, the fact that *S* knows he is being studied can, in itself, alter his behavior. The attempt by *E* to measure behavior can distort the behavior of interest.

Accepting the fact that wide differences exist among *E*s in the way in which they run their *S*s, just how serious is this lack of standardization? How do we know that such procedural variations actually influence the results or conclusions of an experiment? If evidence which is positive is available, just how widespread is the problem? Even if it can be shown that procedural variations can alter the findings in one type of task or situation, that is no guarantee that it will also modify those in a different type of experiment.

Furthermore, could not lack of standardization even be a virtue? Thus, if the same results occurred with different data collectors in one experiment or in several different experiments despite wide procedural differences, this situation would ensure us more confidence in the generalizability of our findings. On the other hand, if results cannot be replicated under altered conditions either in the same laboratory or in different ones, we know there are some limits to the generality of our findings which can be studied in additional experiments. If standardization were the first rule, we might never discover other variables affecting the behavior under study. On the other hand, if test conditions are allowed some variability in different experiments, we can worry about standardization only when results can no longer be reproducible under differing conditions. However, if the results can be repeated under varying conditions, then we have gained generalizability. We would still not know exactly how much the variations among *E*s affect the behavior of *S*s; all we would know is that despite any possible *E*-variable effect, the influence of other variables are even greater and still occur. This issue is another aspect of *E*'s dilemma.

EXPERIMENTS AS SEEN BY *E*s

Another aspect of experiments creating problems for *E* is the fact that the perception of an experiment is not the same for *E*s and *S*s since the goals are not similar for both parties. For the *E,* the experiment is a powerful method for obtaining answers to questions which he is studying. He wants to understand, control, and predict behavior. Use of the experiment allows *E* to draw conclusions about causal relationships.

As a result, his attitude toward the S can be quite impersonal since the S is a guinea pig, a number, or a piece of data. As Lyons (1964) observed,

> The experimenter keeps looking for the perfect servant—who will carry out the master's wishes with understanding and intelligence yet not go beyond them; who will accede without obsequiousness and cooperate without being servile; who will be independent and unrestricted yet neither negativistic nor resistive; and who will never cut through the entire master-servant relation, and thereby destroy it by seeking to put himself in the master's place, for example, by trying to know as much about the experiment as does the experimenter himself [p. 105].

Thus, the experimental situation is one in which E does not trust S and has to keep him as naive and ignorant as possible about the purposes of the experiment.

EXPERIMENTS AS SEEN BY Ss

In contrast, the S is not primarily interested in the problem under attack by E, although he may have some curiosity about it. He is generally cooperative so that he can learn something about himself and others. To a lesser extent, or as a fringe benefit, he is "aiding science." Sometimes, however, he is pressured into volunteering by requirements for his psychology course, by his instructor, or by his friends. Other times, he is lured into the experiment either by being paid, by curiosity, or by challenge-seeking. The exact motives for participating probably depend on whether S volunteered or was "drafted" into service. In any case, once he gets into the experiment, he is not a passive organism but a very active one who attempts to decipher the secret purpose or true meaning of the experiment. Such an attitude is quite natural but can create difficulties for E such as when different Ss have different hypotheses about the purpose. Or in studies where deception is necessary, the validity of E's findings are at stake if S can see through to the real purpose. Lyons (1964) realized that E must deal with the very persons he wants to find out things about, so he can never reveal the true purpose to his Ss.

There is variation among Ss in their attitudes toward experiments, but most of them are either in fear, awe, or respect of E, who after all is a psychologist. And everyone, thanks to the popular magazines, movies, etc., knows what psychologists can do! "Being-experimented-on" feelings lead many Ss to be docile, subservient, and obedient to virtually any request imposed upon them while under the power of E. Compliance, however, is not necessarily without hostility toward E and attempts to outwit him (Jourard, 1968, see Selection 1).

From the preceding description of the experiment, as seen from two disparate views, that of E and that of S, we can see that there is not much agreement between the two parties. Nonetheless, they do participate in a social interchange when placed together in an experiment. A number of psychologists have been stressing the social nature of human experiments (Friedman, 1967; Orne, 1962; Riecken, 1962; Rosenthal, 1966). What implications does this conception of the psychological experiment—as opposed to the model based on the experiment in the physical sciences—have for the psychologist? What new problems does it present for psychological research? The goal of the present book is to discuss these aspects of psychological experiments in the light of the new emphasis on their social nature.

Chapter 2 will discuss in greater detail some of the different attitudes and perceptions of experiments on the part of Ss. We will examine how such differences can affect research results and their interpretation by investigators. Chapter 3 is concerned with how research might be affected by the types of Ss generally used, the manner in which they are recruited, the role of prior experience, and differences between volunteer and drafted Ss. The influence of E on the outcomes of experiments will be the topic in Chapters 4 and 5. First, there will be evidence presented and evaluated about the role which the expectancies or hypotheses of Es has on the outcomes of experiments. Then will follow a discussion of other attributes of Es, such as age, sex, or hostility, which can influence results.

In Chapter 6 there will be a discussion of some ethical aspects of the use of human Ss, in particular the use of deception. In addition, concern about informed consent, invasion of privacy, and safety from harm will be discussed. Finally, Chapter 7 provides an overview of the E's dilemma and considers the relationship between experimental and naturalistic methods of investigation.

2

HOW DOES *BEING-EXPERIMENTED-ON* AFFECT THE BEHAVIOR OF *Ss*?

There has been increased concern in the past decade about the attitudes which *Ss* have toward the experiments in which they participate. The behavior of *Ss* is markedly affected by the perceptions they have of experiments. Although the issue was raised some time ago (Rosensweig, 1933), it has only been recently that serious experimental investigation has been proposed and conducted on this issue (e.g., Orne, 1962; Riecken, 1962; Rosenberg, 1965).

There is a variety of views held by psychologists as to the nature of these attitudes, ranging from conceptions of docile and cooperative *Ss* to defiant and hostile ones. First, we will summarize the major formulations, some of which will be described in detail shortly.

1. Riecken (1962): The *S* wants to "put his best foot forward" and tries to figure out the purpose of the experiment so he can appear in the best possible light by concealing or disclosing, emphasizing or belittling those qualities which he thinks will be positively and negatively evaluated in the experiment.

2. Orne (1962): The *S* is cooperative and eager to be a "good" *S* so as to please *E.* He attempts to determine the purpose of the experiment and acts in accord with various cues or demand characteristics of the situation which tip him off as to what is the correct behavior.

3. Rosenberg (1965): The *S* is anxious about the impression he makes since he assumes he is being evaluated in an experiment. This apprehension leads him to behave in whatever manner he believes will put him in the best light. This tendency may be greater in some conditions of an experiment than in others.

4. Fillenbaum (1966): The *S* is "faithful" and follows the instructions religiously, without attempting to second-guess or outsmart *E.*

5. Masling (1966): Sometimes, *S* will resist the attempts of *E* to study him; he may even be uncooperative or deliberately behave in unusual ways.

6. Argyris (1968): The *S* may resist, become hostile or apathetic, or even fail to show up because experiments contain unintended side effects due to their rigorous control of the situation.

7. Sigall, Aronson, and Van Hoose (1970): The *S* is primarily concerned about his own image, not the goals of *E*. Sometimes the goals of *S* and *E* are compatible but other times they are not. In the latter situation, *S* will behave in his own self-interest.

8. Dulaney (1962): The *S* will do what he thinks *E* wants him to do, *provided S* wants to do it.

Although a large number of conceptions of *S*'s reactions to *being-experimented-on* have been presented, it should be clear that there is similarity among many of them. Even different views can be simultaneously correct; it is possible for *S* to be both cooperative and apprehensive of evaluation. Or it may be such apprehension is the antecedent of uncooperative behavior such as when *S* adopts a defensive strategy to prevent *E* from discovering the *S*'s "true" personality.

Regardless of the particular attitude of *S* towards experiments, the fact that *S* knows he is in an experiment may modify his behavior from what it is like in real life, sometimes changing it one way and sometimes another. Some *Ss* act in more socially desirable ways, knowing that they are being observed, while others act in defiant directions. Some *Ss* become more flamboyant while others become more restrained and subdued. Being in an experiment is rather like being on a TV camera. Some people keep looking at the camera, others wave and smile at it, and still others become self-conscious and nervous.

Campbell (1957) refers to this aspect of experimentation as *reactive arrangements* and sees it as a limiting factor on generalizations of findings to behavior outside of experimental situations. Awareness of being-experimented-on may produce either negative or positive reactions. Negativism may occur in *Ss*, but it is more likely that cooperative behavior will result, often producing pseudo-confirmation of *E*'s hypothesis.

The danger of methodological artifact stemming from reactive arrangements is by no means a new threat or one unique to psychological research. Shapiro (1960) has documented the history of the use of placebo conditions in medical and drug research. It was recognized long ago that the power of suggestion often led to dramatic effects. The ingestion of placebos, or pills consisting of innocuous ingredients, has sometimes produced changes equal to those caused by actual medicines. The doctor's patient is not different from the experimental S when it comes to being influenced merely because one is being observed.

Sommer (1968) has examined a similar effect which has come to be known as the *Hawthorne effect*, after the Hawthorne industrial studies (Roethlisberger & Dickson, 1939). No matter what environmental changes were created, worker production seemed to always show improvement, much to the surprise of the investigators who were trying to identify optimal working conditions. What was happening was that workers were responding to the observation process itself and behaving in ways atypical of work under natural conditions. Sommer points out that the term Hawthorne effect has negative connotations, for when it is present it suggests that the experimental results may be artifacts. However, Sommer points out that it is a pervasive feature of most field research because persons are usually aware when they are being studied as research Ss.

The importance of knowledge of the psychological effects of experimentation upon S cannot be underestimated. To the extent that behavior is altered by S's awareness of participation in an experiment, E has limited generalizability of his findings to the real world. This problem is one to which we shall return later but it is an issue which should be kept in mind. We will now examine in detail some of the major views of S's attitudes toward experimental participation.

RIECKEN'S *PUTTING-HIS-BEST-FOOT-FORWARD*

Perhaps the most influential contribution toward generating interest in the study of interaction between E and S has been the work of Riecken (1962, see Selection 2). He regards the experimental context as one in which S tries *putting-his-best-foot-forward.* However, since he does not usually know the purpose of the experiment, especially at the outset, it is no easy matter for him to identify the type of behavior most likely to achieve this goal. However, as the experiment progresses, S eventually forms working definitions to the experiment's purpose. As the experiment continues, such hypotheses may be revised in the light of more information.

From E's perspective, however, the success of the experiment depends upon S's naiveté as a subject. Therefore, he must keep the true purpose of the experiment unknown to S, and resort to elaborate deceptions, if necessary, to keep him naive. Thus, S's tendency to formulate hypotheses about the true purpose of the experiment creates problems for E. If S discovers the true hypothesis, he may behave in ways atypical of his normal behavior. Even if he does not identify the actual purpose which E intends in his experiment, S's false hypotheses will still guide his behavior. Furthermore, since different Ss may form a variety of hypotheses, it becomes all the more difficult for E to understand and interpret his results.

In view of these considerations, it is obvious that if he cannot prevent S from forming hypotheses about the experiment, E must at least determine what these hypotheses were so that he can take them into consideration in interpreting S's behavior in the experimental situation. Riecken suggests that the use of careful interrogation can reveal the nature of preconceptions of experiments held by S. One can also evaluate the interpretations formed by S of the actual procedures in an experiment by use of a postexperimental inquiry. Similar suggestions were made by Orne (1962), whose work we will now examine.

ORNE'S *DEMAND CHARACTERISTICS*

Another important analyst of the E-S interaction has been Martin Orne. Orne (1962, see Selection 3) maintains that the S who agrees to serve in an experiment comes with a favorable attitude and is highly cooperative, to the point of blind obedience. Since he has formed a tacit contract to play the role of experimental subject or "guinea pig," he endeavors to discover the hidden purpose of the experiment so that he can behave in ways to fulfill E's hypotheses. According to Orne, every experimental situation contains numerous cues, which Orne collectively terms *demand characteristics* and which serve to provide hints to S as to what behavior is expected on his part. Other sources of demand characteristics include rumors or gossip about the experiment received outside of the laboratory before S participates.

In an attempt to demonstrate the role of demand characteristics, Orne (1959) instructed one group of Ss to behave as if they were under hypnosis and attempt to "fool" a different E who had to test them as well as a group of actually hypnotized Ss. The fact that E

was unable to distinguish between actual and simulated hypnosis led Orne to infer that behavior under hypnosis may sometimes be due to the demand characteristics of the situation, not to hypnosis per se. In other words, the S acts the way he thinks hypnotized persons act, even if he is not really hypnotized. This conclusion does not imply that hypnosis may not have genuine effects; what Orne is doing is to raise the possibility that "hypnotic" effects may sometimes be elicited by the demand characteristics of the situation rather than any special properties of the hypnotic procedure.

Orne's more general point, of course, is that it is important to assess the demand characteristics perceived by S in a given experiment since the behavior displayed by S may be wrongly attributed by E to the effects of some independent variable whereas in fact it is due entirely to S's perception of what his behavior should be.

A striking example of the role which demand characteristics can play is provided by a study by Orne and Scheibe (1964). Previous studies (e.g., Bexton, Heron, & Scott, 1954) had demonstrated that sensory deprivation could produce severe psychological malfunctioning. Confinement to small quarters in the absence of variations in visual, auditory, and other sense modalities led to impairment of cognitive, perceptual, and motor abilities. Such results made common sense in the light of the usual conceptions of solitary confinement, brainwashing, etc.

Yet, Jackson and Pollard (1962) suggested that some of the experimental results could have stemmed from the power of suggestion. Consistent with this view is an experiment conducted by Orne and Scheibe (1964) to determine how much of the sensory deprivation effect was attributable to demand characteristics of the experimental task. After all, the Ss do know that they will be isolated for long periods of time and may have some preconceptions as to what should happen to them psychologically. Is it possible that some, if not all, of the effects ascribed to the sensory deprivation are due to the demand characteristics of the situation?

An experimental and a control group each was subjected to four hours of isolation in a room with a window. Paper and pencil was available on a table, which they could use. These conditions are not nearly as extreme as those usually employed in sensory deprivation studies. Before isolation the experimental group received an extensive physical examination, signed a release form, and was reassured that if at any time in the experiment they could not "take it any more," they could press a "panic button" in order to be rescued. In addition, they were "assured" that there was no danger in the presence of an emergency medical tray full of drugs and syringes. In contrast, control group *Ss* did not undergo this phase of the study but were simply informed that they were control *Ss* for a sensory deprivation study before being isolated.

Despite the fact that the isolation treatment was identical for experimental and control groups, there were marked differences on a battery of perceptual, cognitive, and motor skills tests which showed impairment in the experimental group. Orne and Scheibe attributed this poorer performance to the demand characteristics of the situation, the medical exam, the concept of the panic button, etc., which led experimental group *Ss* to expect bizarre effects. Orne and Scheibe conclude that similar processes could have operated in previous studies which obtained sensory deprivation effects. This is not to say that sensory deprivation has no effects of its own but that demand characteristics may produce effects similar to them.

How can *E* determine the nature of demand characteristics in a given experimental situation? All experiments have such features, although they may not always undermine the validity of the experimental results. In his more recent analysis of the problem, Orne (1969) discusses three methods, which he calls "quasi-controls," by which one can evaluate the demand characteristics.

First, one can learn a lot about *S's* task perception by simply asking him in a postexperimental inquiry session (Orne, 1962; Riecken, 1962). However, such procedures can be not only time-consuming but invalid. The verbal report can be inaccurate, either deliberately so or due to lack of awareness by *S*. Furthermore, even the postexperimental inquiry has its own demand characteristics. Orne (1959) described the *pact of ignorance* which might exist during such inquiry. The *S* who has caught on to the deception is reluctant to admit it because he realizes he may be disqualified from the experiment. This consideration is also undesirable for *E* and may prevent him from probing too deeply with his interrogation. The technique is well worth using, but it must be carefully planned if valid information is to be obtained.

A second procedure (Orne, 1959; Riecken, 1962) for identifying demand characteristics of a particular experimental task is the pre-inquiry or nonexperiment. The experiment is conducted on a *dry-lab* basis with the equipment and procedures shown to *Ss* just as if they were to receive the independent variable treatment. They would then receive the same tests and questionnaire as the experimental group and their task would be to behave as if they had actually received the treatment. It is assumed that the task perceptions by Ss in the non-experiment are the same as those of Ss in the actual experiment. If the results are identical it would suggest, but not prove, that the results of the real experiment could have been due merely to the demand characteristics of the task. On the other hand, different results in the quasi-control, preinquiry condition and in the actual experimental condition would tend to rule out the possibility that the real results are due only to demand characteristics, but rather must be attributed to the independent variable.

Finally, the use of simulators (Orne, 1959) may aid in identifying demand characteristics. This technique has been described earlier in the context of Orne's study of the demand characteristics of hypnosis. It is important to note that Orne (1969) holds that quasi-controls do not

> permit inference to be drawn about the effect of the inde-
> pendent variable. They can never prove that a given finding in
> the experimental group is due to the demand characteristics of
> the situation. Rather, they serve to suggest alternative explana-
> tions not excluded by the experimental design employed [p.
> 160].

ROSENBERG'S *EVALUATION APPREHENSION*

Riecken's pioneering paper stressed the tendency of *S putting-his-best-foot-forward* as a source of increased random variability but did not explicitly examine the possibility that this factor could systematically alter results so that false confirmation or disconfirmation of hypotheses could occur. Rosenberg (1965) placed the emphasis upon this consequence of such tendencies of *S*. In accord with Riecken, he pointed out that *S* tries to look good so as to gain approval and avoid scorn from *E*. He is apprehensive that *E* is trying to assess his mental health. This *evaluation apprehension,* as Rosenberg terms it, could conceivably operate in all *S*s equally. However, Rosenberg's significant contribution is to examine evaluation apprehension in experiments where it is aroused to different degrees in different experimental conditions. He proposes that *S*s in treatments which arouse greater evaluation apprehension will be more likely to interpret instructions and procedures of the experiment as means to evaluate them. As a result, they will seek more strongly to win positive and avoid negative evaluation than will *Ss* in other experimental conditions.

An example of a research area where evaluation apprehension may exist differentially is that of *cognitive dissonance*. Some studies have claimed that when *Ss* are required to argue in favor of a position opposite to their true convictions, their attitudes will be changed toward that argument—more when they are offered small rather than large monetary rewards as justification. The task of publicly supporting a view contrary to one's own for little justification is assumed to produce greater cognitive dissonance than if large justification is provided. Dissonance theory predicts that one way by which the aversive state of dissonance can be reduced is for *Ss* to change their attitudes. Therefore, the low-justification *Ss* (with greater dissonance) should show more attitude change.

Although Festinger and Carlsmith (1959) and Cohen (in Brehm & Cohen, 1962) have provided experimental evidence supporting the preceding prediction, Rosenberg has questioned the validity of the dissonance-theory explanation. He suggests that the *Ss* with high justification (low dissonance) are more likely to become suspicious that they are being evaluated. (After all, if you are offered $20 to tell the next *S* that a boring experiment had been fun or to write an essay arguing a position against your own beliefs, wouldn't you be suspicious of such a large reward for such little work?) Such *Ss* might possibly perceive the experiment as a test of their honesty and feel that the offer was in essence a bribe. Such perceptions might lead to resistance on the part of high-justification (low-dissonance) *Ss* to any attitude change. On the other hand, low-justification (high-dissonance) *Ss* would be less likely to feel that they were being bribed and would not resist showing attitude change. The net result would be more attitude change in the low-justification (high-dissonance) condition. The same results are predicted by dissonance theory and by Rosenberg's evaluation-apprehension theory. However, Rosenberg's explanation is not in terms of differential cognitive dissonance, but rather in terms of differential evaluation apprehension.

Rosenberg regards the existence of evaluation apprehension as a contaminant in research findings which makes valid interpretation difficult. One way of reducing such apprehension in dissonance experiments would be to employ two different *Es*, one for the dissonance arousal and one for the assessment of attitudes, so that *S* thinks he is in two different and totally unrelated experiments. Rosenberg (1965) repeated the Cohen experiment with this procedural innovation. Since the high-justification (low-dissonance) Ss did not have their attitudes measured by the *same* E who had them express views contrary to their own on some issue, they were unlikely to have much evaluation apprehension when tested for their attitudes. By reducing evaluation apprehension in this manner, the results failed to support the dissonance-theory prediction that high-justification Ss would show little attitude change; in fact, they showed the most change, a result in line with a different theory of attitude change held by Rosenberg which need not be discussed here.

Further research by Rosenberg (1969) on evaluation apprehension has attempted to delineate factors which can arouse and cue the occurrence of evaluation apprehension. It is important to conduct studies to determine what factors arouse or reduce evaluation apprehension according to Rosenberg, because he thinks it contaminates research over a broad range of psychological research. For example, telling Ss that the task involves the measurement of their personalities is a powerful method of arousing evaluation apprehension. However, such explicit instructional sets are not necessary, although they may enhance the effect. Merely providing hints as to the nature of "normal" or "mature" responses will be sufficient to bias Ss to behave in such a manner.

Rosenberg's work has important implications for psychological research. When controversies arise regarding the interpretation of results because it is suspected that the original data were contaminated by evaluation apprehension, it is possible to conduct what Rosenberg calls an *altered replication.* An example has already been provided by Rosenberg's (1965) study of dissonance theory and attitude change in which he reduced the likelihood that evaluation apprehension would arise and obtained different results.

One can also reduce the influence of evaluation apprehension by defining the experiment in certain ways for S so as to lead him to feel that E is not so much interested in the results of individuals as he is in the differences between groups. In addition, even if he is being evaluated, Rosenberg suggests that S could be given the impression that the purpose of the experiment is about a technical or "dry" matter and not about some aspect of personality.

Finally, in agreement with Masling (1966), Rosenberg acknowledges that not all Ss are concerned about how they will be evaluated by *E*. Some *S*s will seemingly try to wreck the experimental outcome by producing bizarre or unpredictable behavior. Actually, Rosenberg points out that evaluation apprehension may be at the root of behavior which does not seem aimed at making a favorable impression. Thus, taking the experiment as a joke could serve as a defensive ploy against the threat of being evaluated. In line with Argyris's (1968) notion that rigorous control may inadvertently lead to resistance and rebellion, Rosenberg also recognizes that anger and resistance may stem from overly strong evaluation apprehension.

Thus far, we have emphasized the major views about the nature of *S*'s perception of the experimental situation. At times it seems as if the views of Riecken, Orne, and Rosenberg are similar and at other times they seem quite different. All three conceptions emphasize the *S*'s desire to look good; but whereas this goal is the main one for Riecken and Rosenberg's *S*, it is only an intermediate goal for Orne's *S*. Orne's conception depicts an *S* eager to cooperate mainly so that he can help *E* and contribute to science. Orne (1962) does recognize that *S* worries about how he will be evaluated but he feels that "nonetheless, they seem even more concerned with the utility of their performances [p. 778]."

A RECONCILIATION OF VIEWS?

The apparent contradiction in these major conceptions of *S*'s primary motives is interpreted by Sigall, Aronson, and Van Hoose (1970) as due to the fact that in some situations the goals of *E* and *S* are compatible but not in others. Like Riecken and Rosenberg, they suggest that *S* is primarily interested in looking good. In order to achieve this goal, he often appears cooperative because his behavior supports the *E*'s predictions. This is coincidental rather than genuine cooperation. However, if the experimental situation were one in which *S* would look foolish or ridiculous in order to support *E*'s hypothesis, Sigall *et al.* predict that cooperation would not occur. Instead, *S* would behave in a manner which would give the best self-presentation, even though it did not support *E*.

Sigall *et al.* tested their analysis by pitting the motive to please *E* and the motive to make themselves look good in one condition, and allowing them to coincide in two other conditions. The task involved copying a long list of telephone numbers. Regardless of whether *S*s were led to expect that their performance should increase or decrease, the results showed that Ss improved the amount copied as compared to a control condition. Thus, even if they knew E was predicting a decrease, Ss copied even more because such performance would make them look good, even though it did not fulfill E's hypothesis. However, in another condition in which E told Ss that their performance would decrease, they were also instructed that good performance on this task was a symptom of obsessive-compulsive tendencies. Under this situation, their performance showed a marked decrease. However, Sigall et al. attribute the drop as motivated by the desire to avoid appearing obsessive-compulsive, and not as due to the wish to fulfill E's alleged hypothesis.

Silverman and Shulman (1970) have also attempted to reconcile the contradictory views of Orne and Rosenberg regarding the primary motives of S. They agree with Sigall et al. that whenever S is in a conflict between complying with the demand characteristics of the experiment and promoting one's own image in a favorable light, he will protect himself, even if at the disadvantage of E.

Silverman and Shulman (1970) based their analysis of experiments on research done in the specific area of attitude change. In these studies, S usually is aware that his attitudes are being assessed, and in many cases it is clear that attitude change is being measured. Under such conditions, it is not always obvious how S will react. If he allows himself to be persuaded, he may appear weakminded and malleable; if he resists propaganda, he might appear independent. On the other hand, being persuaded may appear to indicate flexible openmindedness whereas resistance might reflect rigidity and dogmatism. Clearly, S faces considerable conflict in attitude-change studies in deciding whether to comply with demand characteristics.

Silverman and Shulman (1970) make several predictions about S's behavior in such situations. In accord with Sigall et al., they predict compliance when there is an absence of evaluation apprehension. However, when evaluation apprehension is present, S will act in a manner to maintain favorable self-presentation, regardless of whether this is consistent with demand characteristics. Furthermore, if the demand characteristics are too strong, S will intentionally act counter to them, possibly to avoid giving the bad impression of being easily manipulated.

A final view which illustrates the complexity of motives which S brings with him into the experiment is provided by Dulaney (1962).

In his discussion of some aspects of awareness in verbal conditioning experiments, he concluded "that a human subject does what he thinks he is supposed to do if he wants to . . . [p. 109]." Thus, in accord with Orne's view, Dulaney allows that S is capable of cooperating but adds the intriguing proviso, i.e., "If he wants to." Dulaney is suggesting that although S often knows what E expects him to do, for one reason or another, he behaves in a different manner. For example, an S in a learning experiment may become bored once his performance is perfect on a given trial. Even though E is assuming that he would continue to perform at a high level on additional trials, the boredom may lead to a drop in his performance. In some cases S seems to be testing E by observing the reactions of the latter as various forms of unpredicted behavior are emitted. In the jargon of today, one could say that some Ss just prefer "doing their own thing." They are not "hung up" with evaluation apprehension and find no need to try to behave in ways to please E.

IMPLICATIONS OF REACTIVE ARRANGEMENTS

The fact that many Ss act differently when they are aware that they are serving in an experiment can create questions of interpretation for some types of experiments, depending on the type of task involved.

A useful distinction was made by Riecken (1962) between *task-ability* and *self-quality problems*. With the first type, the task is presented or perceived as one involving ability, skill, or capacity. The mental set of S is likely to lead to behavior which appears cooperative. The task is well-defined and it is clear how one can look good, namely do one's best on the experimental task.

On the other hand, self-quality problems are seen as measuring attitudes and beliefs or reactions to negative experiences such as insult or frustration. In a sense, personality is being evaluated. In such situations, there is ambiguity as to which self-image is the most favorable one to project. Depending on how he thinks E will appraise certain behavior, S will either inhibit or display that behavior.

The knowledge that one is in an experiment may affect behavior on task-ability and self-quality tasks in different ways. With the former variety, Ss will probably try harder because they know they are being evaluated. Furthermore, they know what constitutes "good" performance. But with self-quality tasks, it is more difficult to predict exactly how the behavior will vary as a result of observation. All we can say is that it will be influenced, but we cannot specify in what manner unless we know how S perceives the task.

Experimental situations which involve the use of deception are especially prone to difficulties stemming from the reactive nature of experiments. For example, consider studies in the area of stress, harm, and danger which require that Ss be convinced of the authenticity of the threat. Of course, in laboratory studies, the E is limited in what he can do and there is no real physical harm that can happen to Ss. Instead, E must resort to cleverly contrived situations in order to deceive Ss into thinking that some harm is potential. But just how credible are such deceptions?

When Ss participate in an experiment, they assume (sometimes erroneously, perhaps) that the investigator is bound by certain ethical codes. He is regarded as a responsible and trustworthy professional person. The possibility that genuine harm can occur to them as part of the experiment is perceived to be quite remote.

With this attitude on the part of most Ss, what problems of interpretation can this create for experiments which attempt to induce fear and stress in Ss via deceptions? Would not such an attitude attenuate the effectiveness of any deceptions aimed at creating stress? In fact, many Ss who are familiar with psychological research know that much deception is practiced. When they are then in an experiment which apparently involves danger, their assumption that Es are trustworthy in terms of any adverse consequences increases their tendency to be suspicious of the alleged procedures within the experiment. Nowadays, Ss are not so naive as to trust Es as to the cover stories provided about the experiment, but they do assume that Es are restricted when it comes to doing things which could actually harm Ss.

For example, Rowland (1939) had two deeply hypnotized Ss pick up a large rattlesnake. Even though one S attempted to do so, he was prevented from actually endangering himself by invisible glass. Other dangerous behavior such as throwing acid at other persons also occurred when instructed to do so under hypnosis. These antisocial behaviors under hypnosis have been replicated by Young (1952).

But Orne and Evans (1965) have questioned the validity of these dramatic demonstrations. They replicated Young's experiment successfully. However, they also added a control group of nonhypnotized Ss. Even these Ss displayed the antisocial behavior, suggesting to Orne and Evans that such behaviors were not really judged as dangerous when performed in the context of an experiment. Interviews with *Ss* revealed that although some of them felt uncertain about some of the tasks, "they were quite convinced that they would not be harmed *because* the context was an experimental one, presumably being conducted by responsible experimenters [Orne & Evans, 1965, p. 199]." In short, knowledge that they were being experimented on allowed *Ss* to engage in what otherwise would be considered very dangerous activity.

A similar objection has been made by Orne and Holland (1968, see Selection 10) to the widely cited study of obedience by Milgram (1965). Pairs of *Ss* (one a stooge) served in a study alleged to deal with the effects of punishment on learning. The real *S* always ended up by "chance" as the teacher and the stooge served as the learner. The task of *S* was to administer increasingly painful shocks to the learner each time he made a mistake. The stooge's behavior was rigged so that he made more and more errors, requiring *S* to give increasingly stronger intensities of shock. Although the learner was in another room, *S* could hear the moans, grunts, and screams of the apparently tormented learner. Milgram's purpose was to demonstrate the blind obedience of *Ss* to authority even when ordered to cause severe pain for a fellow human.

Orne and Holland (1968) question the plausibility of this situation. They note, "Despite the movie image of the mad scientist, most *Ss* accept the fact that scientists—even behavioral scientists—are reasonable people [p. 287]." It is possible that many of the obedient *Ss* simply did not think anyone was really being shocked. If this were the case, the obedience would simply stem from the demand characteristics of the situation.

In another contrived situation, Darley and Latané (1968) studied some factors which influenced helping behavior in emergency situations. They recruited *Ss* to come to the laboratory for a group discussion of personal problems. Each *S* was told that since some individuals are embarrassed by such discussions, he would be tested in a private cubicle equipped with intercoms connecting the rooms where other *Ss* were housed. In the middle of the discussion, one of the other *Ss* went through an epileptic fit which was heard over the intercom. The experimental question was how long would it take before the *S* would report this emergency to *E* who was in another room.

Of course, the emergency was faked by a confederate whose

seizure was tape recorded. How well were the Ss deceived by this manipulation? Darley and Latané do not report any attempt to determine the credibility of the deception. While it is plausible that most Ss would have been totally surprised by the occurrence of the apparent emergency, it is possible that some Ss just did not believe it was "real" because they knew they were in an experiment.

Similar questions could be raised about many experiments. As long as S is aware that he is in an experiment, we cannot ignore the possibility that he is prepared to regard virtually any event—however unlikely—to be part of the experiment; and if it's only an experiment, it's safe.

ARE Ss REALLY DECEIVED?

Yet, psychologists have been prone to ignore the question of whether or not deception actually works. Stricker's (1967) survey of 390 published articles showed that only 24 percent of the 88 studies using deception bothered to measure or report the efficacy of their deceptions. Furthermore, in studies where assessments were made of S's perceptions of the experiment, Stricker maintains that the criteria for judging awareness were not always sound.

He also notes that the dynamics of the assessment tend to produce underestimates of the amount of detected deception. As in Orne's (1959) concept of the pact of ignorance, neither S nor E wants to let on or find out about the deception. For S does not want to "ruin" the experiment nor does E want to have to discard his data. On the other hand, it is also possible for overestimations of the amount of awareness to be obtained. Some Ss may be generally suspicious about experiments and report feeling deceived in a given study without actually being able to identify the particular deception in a given experiment.

Add to this situation the countless studies *without* actual deception in which Ss think some deception is present and the analysis becomes quite complex. This perception would not be detected since E would not bother to ask as no deception was actually used. Finally, studies with deception which is readily seen through by many Ss usually do not get submitted for publication.

What are the causes of suspicion? Stricker, Messick, and Jackson (1969, see Selection 11) report that little is known about the factors producing suspicion. Two possible reasons which they offer are prior experience with deception and hearsay about deception from

3

WHO SERVES AS Ss IN PSYCHOLOGICAL EXPERIMENTS AND ARE THEY REPRESENTATIVE?

It sometimes seems as if psychology experiments are almost always done with either albino rats or college sophomores taking introductory psychology courses. Both types of Ss are convenient and relatively inexpensive. However, the cost of limiting ourselves to these types of Ss may be rather high in the long run because our generalizations may be quite limited. Few studies are done primarily because of interest in albino rat or psychology student populations.

Beach (1950) examined the studies reported in every alternate year of the *Journal of Comparative and Physiological Psychology* (and its predecessor, the *Journal of Animal Behavior*) through 1948. He found a trend towards greater use of the albino rat in animal studies over the years. He criticized this situation, calling for use of a larger variety of organisms. He also recognized that for some research topics, human Ss were the only acceptable type of S. Beach, as well as Lockard (1968), reports that the adoption of the albino rat as the dominant organisms studied in many laboratories was largely an historical accident. From force of habit, psychologists have continued to make this indefensible choice, and Lockard predicts the rat data will receive only a few paragraphs from future historians of psychology.

Turning now to human Ss, a similar tabulation of published research was done by Smart (1966) on a smaller scale. He found that 73 percent of the articles in the 1962–1964 *Journal of Abnormal and Social Psychology* and 86 percent of those in the 1962–1964 *Journal of Experimental Psychology* used college students as their subjects. Furthermore, a disproportionate number of these subjects were male. A more recent survey (Schultz, 1969) of journal articles showed high agreement. Similar evidence of the overwhelming reliance on college students as Ss was obtained by this author (Jung, 1969, see Selection 4) who found that 90 percent of human Ss used other sources. The first factor will be discussed in Chapter 3. As for the possibility that Ss who are themselves naive about deception becoming suspicious due to tip-offs and gossip from other students, there is contradictory information. Wuebben (1967) found that 64 percent of his debriefed Ss divulged their secrets to others, whereas Aronson (1966) found that few Ss violated their pledge to secrecy.

Such differences could be due to a number of factors. On the one hand, the different investigators may have differed in their rapport with their Ss. But it is also possible that the degree of confession to E—that they broke their promises—varies without the skill of interrogation. Evidence is available which shows that tipped-off Ss are highly reluctant to admit to such knowledge. Levy (1967) and Golding and Lichtenstein (1970) had confederates tip-off Ss as to the nature of the deception. Despite this advance information, very few Ss admitted possessing it when later interrogated.

Finally, as discussed earlier, Ss are generally suspicious of experiments. When they know that they are being-experimented-on, they expect deception to be involved frequently. This situation has led many psychologists to wonder who is really being deceived—the S or the E. Seeman (1969) observes that soon we will "no longer have naive subjects but only naive experimenters [p. 1026]."

Regardless of the particular factors leading an S to become suspicious, what are the consequences of such wariness on behavior? Stricker *et al.* (1969) think the effects will ". . . be extremely varied, depending upon the subjects' perceptions and motivations connected with the study [p. 347]." Thus, knowing that an S is suspicious is insufficient for predicting his reaction to such doubts. The type of experiment, as well as S's personality, may determine whether S goes along with the deception, resists manipulation, or vindictively tries to sabotage the whole enterprise.

by academic psychologists were college students. In fact, 80 percent of all human Ss were from introductory psychology courses.

One does not need statistical information to be convinced that college students are not typical of the general population. They differ in intelligence, age, and social-class background. Furthermore, they do not hold the same patterns of attitudes, values, and interests that noncollege populations typically have (Bereiter & Freedman, 1962; Sternberg, 1955). In addition, there may be differences among students as a function of size, location, or prestige of their colleges.

Within the college population, one would expect differences to exist among students majoring in different fields. Introductory psychology courses probably consist more of psychology majors than of students enrolled in other introductory courses.

Results of studies performed with college students—mostly introductory psychology students—are frequently applied to other populations which differ substantially in a variety of dimensions. For some types of phenomena, these generalizations may hold, but for many other processes, we may expect different findings for college and noncollege populations. It appears urgent that psychologists make greater efforts to utilize Ss other than introductory psychology students. Although they are less convenient to use than college students, there are other sources of large captive audiences such as hospital patients, prison inmates, and military personnel which might be used as Ss more frequently.

But such changes will not come easily because it will be costly both in terms of time and money. Probably as long as psychologists can justify or rationalize the required participation of psychology students as Ss, there will be little headway made toward studying other types of people. One incentive for changing present sources of Ss might be the demonstration in numerous studies of empirical differences in results between college and noncollege Ss.

This pessimism is reinforced by an anecdote reported by Argyris (1968). He reported that some students had speculated about the possibility of creating a source of Ss similar to the Manpower Supply of Business Help. Through such a union, students who served as Ss might get paid, be better treated by Es, and receive more thorough feedback about the study than they could by serving as Ss for course requirements. Argyris described the reactions of some psychologists to this idea as ". . . similar to the reactions of businessmen who have just been told for the first time that their employees were considering the creation of a union [p. 189]." There was also nervous laughter and scorn. It appears that human experimental psychology may continue to be the psychology of the college sophomore for many years to come!

METHODS FOR RECRUITING COLLEGE Ss

Among the ranks of college students who constitute the major source of human Ss, there are subvarieties of populations in terms of the manner in which they are recruited. Most Ss are quasi-volunteers or draftees who are fulfilling psychology course requirements, some are paid participants, and there are even a few truly "voluntary" Ss.

Most Ss coming from psychology courses are drafted into service by a course requirement, course option (serve in experiments or write essays, etc.), or extra credit on a course grade. A small minority of psychology students are either paid or gratis participants, whereas almost all of the few Ss from nonpsychology courses truly volunteer in this manner. In fact, less than 7 percent of all human Ss—psychology or nonpsychology—are paid or gratis participants (Jung, 1969).

In most universities, the scheduling of appointments and the selection of experiments is largely left to the initiative of Ss (Jung, 1969). They sign up for the time and experiment of their choice. This procedure can allow certain types of bias. There may be differences between participants who are early birds and late-comers in motivation or interest in experiments. Persons who sign up for different types of experiments may differ in ability or personality.

An alternative procedure is for the investigator and his data collectors to arrange the sign-ups. This method restricts possible bias due to S choosing his own type of experiment and the time during the semester when he is to participate. Unfortunately, this method is used to account for only 11 percent of all college Ss (Jung, 1969). In view of the variety of procedures for obtaining college Ss, it is possible that conflicting results could occur for similar experiments done at colleges using different recruiting methods.

VOLUNTEER Ss

One factor that might affect the results of experiments is whether or not the Ss volunteered. But as one might gather from the preceding discussion, true volunteers are rare since most research utilizes draftees—Ss who are pressured into "volunteering." The true volunteer S is primarily a mythical creature or one fast becoming extinct. Many published experiments describe their Ss as "volunteers" whereas in fact they are not, except in the sense that they may have selected one experiment over another. In other research situations such as polls or surveys, however, the distinction between volunteers and nonvolunteers is more valid. Participation here is often optional and respondents are frequently different from nonrespondents. In addition, polls and surveys usually involve wider sampling of the general population than is the case with laboratory experiments.

Most studies attempting to identify differences between volunteers and nonvolunteers have employed intact groups such as classroom settings. This procedure is different from that usually employed in obtaining Ss for most experiments. An appeal is made for volunteers; a comparison is then made of various personality variables between volunteers and nonvolunteers using results of tests given before the appeal. Usually, there is no attempt to compare them on actual performance of some subsequent task since, by definition, the nonvolunteers do not wish to participate in the experiment.

For example, Lasagna and von Felsinger (1954) compared volunteers and nonvolunteers for a drug experiment. The main concern was a comparison of differences in the personal histories between the two groups, which indicated more severe maladjustment among the volunteers. However, there was no attempt to compare their actual performance on the fictitious drug experiment.

Yet, in order to compare the characteristics of volunteers and nonvolunteers it is sometimes necessary to require the nonvolunteers to fill out questionnaires and personality tests. One must wonder whether some of the observations of personality differences obtained in such studies stem from the annoyance or hostility which nonvolunteers may feel when pressured to fill out these tests just after they have refused to be in an experiment.

One of the few studies (Rosnow & Rosenthal, 1966) comparing volunteers and nonvolunteers which actually required participation on a task subsequent to the appeal for volunteers involved attitude change. First, pretest measures of attitudes toward fraternities were taken. Then, a pitch was made for volunteers for a fictitious perception experiment in order for E to identify volunteers and nonvolunteers. Finally, a week later, persuasive communications were

presented for or against fraternities and posttest measures of attitudes were made to see if any change had occurred.

It should be noted that in this study, and others like it, the experiment for which volunteers are recruited is *not* the same one that all
Ss are later subjected to for purposes of comparing volunteers and
nonvolunteers. The problem is that we cannot assume that an S's
attitude toward one type of study is the same as toward another
type. An S who refuses to be in an experiment on perception may
eagerly volunteer for an attitude study.

Keeping these considerations in mind, let us examine some of
the findings obtained when comparing characteristics of volunteers
versus nonvolunteers. Bell (1962, see Selection 5) has reviewed
studies of this type. In addition, there are several other analyses of
these studies (Rosenthal, 1965; Rosenthal & Rosnow, 1969; Rosnow
& Rosenthal, 1970). Although the support for each conclusion varies,
the overall evidence is suggestive of such differences as:

> Volunteers are higher in need for social approval.
> Volunteers, especially males, are more intelligent.
> Volunteers tend to have more unconventional personalities.
> Volunteers more often tend to be first-borns.
> Volunteers for certain experiments are less well adjusted.
> Volunteers tend to have higher need for achievement.

The difficulty in arriving at clear-cut conclusions may be due to
the fact that not all volunteers elect to be in experiments for the
same reasons, and not all nonvolunteers choose to decline participation for the same reasons. Some volunteers are primarily interested in testing themselves or in learning more about psychology,
others may be seeking excitement or challenge, and still others may
be trying to please the instructor or responding to peer pressure.
Among nonvolunteers, some may simply not be interested, others
may be overly anxious, and still others may just not find the time
convenient.

The type of experiment may also influence the rate of volunteering
(Martin & Marcuse, 1958). More students volunteered for studies
in personality and sex attitudes than for learning experiments.
Martin and Marcuse also found that the manner in which volunteers
and nonvolunteers differed from each other was not the same for
all types of experiments.

One factor creating difficulty for investigators comparing volunteers and nonvolunteers is what Rosenthal and Rosnow (1969) term *pseudo-volunteers.* These *Ss* are the *no-shows* who sign up or agree to serve, but fail to show up, thus tormenting and frustrating data collectors who wait in vain. It is possible that some persons volunteer in public situations half-heartedly, perhaps because they do not wish to appear uncooperative. Later, when the scheduled experiment is due, these persons would not feel as much pressure to participate so they do not show up. This analysis is plausible in view of Gustav's (1962) study of attitudes of students toward required participation in experiments. The results suggested more irritation and apathy on the part of students than most psychologists think exists.

Based on a comparison of personality differences among volunteers who are *shows* and *no-shows* by Leipold and James (1962) and by Levitt, Lubin, and Brady (1962), it seemed conclusive to Rosenthal and Rosnow that these pseudo-volunteers may be more like nonvolunteers. Classifying them with the volunteers, as is usually done, may serve to mask the true extent of differences between volunteers and nonvolunteers.

On the other hand, it does not appear reasonable to consider all no-shows as pseudo-volunteers, because a variety of reasons ranging from forgetfulness to accidents can prevent *S* from fulfilling his intention to participate.

It should be apparent that it is difficult to evaluate the nature of differences between volunteers and nonvolunteers and the influence of such differences on the outcome of experiments. First, we must establish what personality differences exist between them. Next, we need to compare their performances in a variety of experimental situations. These studies are necessary because if differences can be found here, limits can be placed on the generalizability of results obtained with volunteer *Ss.*

Of course, in order to conduct the research outlined above, we need some way of identifying volunteers and nonvolunteers, usually by making some fictitious appeal for volunteers. Then we are faced with the dilemma of having to force the nonvolunteers to be tested so that we have measures of their personality and experimental performance for purposes of comparison with that of volunteers.

Lest we become too discouraged by this complex situation, it should be restated that the problem is not as real for experiments with college students from psychology courses as it is for research such as polls or surveys done with other populations. For there are very few truly voluntary Ss among psychology students who are, after all, the supply of 90 percent of all human Ss tested by academic researchers. Since these Ss are required to participate, the matter of whether or not differences exist among volunteers and nonvolunteers is irrelevant.

However, as we recruit more and more Ss from noncollege populations, the problem of volunteer-nonvolunteer differences becomes more important, because we have little means of forcing most noncollege populations to serve as Ss. Ironically, while this procedure creates one problem, it simultaneously reduces another one—namely the limited generalizability of results based almost entirely on college students.

DEGREE OF EXPERIMENTAL SOPHISTICATION

Usually, the E attempts to use only Ss who are naive about experimentation, especially with respect to the purpose and expected results of his own experiment. Such Ss are often hard to come by since word gets around the campus dormitories about many experiments, especially the ones with unusual aspects. Even if some Ss fail to catch the gossip about particular studies, they may acquire some degree of sophistication about experiments in general since introductory psychology students in most schools must serve in several different studies. Thus, even though most Ss are rather anxious about their first experiment, they may become more relaxed in subsequent experiments. Behavior of experienced Ss has been found to differ from that of naive Ss in verbal conditioning (Holmes, 1967). He found that Ss who had been in greater numbers of experiments were more cooperative.

In learning experiments, it is possible for more experienced Ss to benefit from learning-to-learn which would enable them to perform better in subsequent experiments. But whereas positive transfer would accrue from *general* factors such as learning-to-learn, it is possible for negative transfer to stem from the *specific* learning in previous experiments. In a classic study, Underwood (1957) compared the amount of forgetting in a number of experiments as a function of the amount of prior participation in similar learning situations. He found that forgetting was greater, the higher the number of lists memorized in previous studies. Interference with the memory of the most recent list was occurring for Ss who had learned many prior lists so that they forgot more than naive Ss who were learning their first list.

But experience as an S per se may not be the main factor. Holmes and Applebaum (1970) have reported that the kind of previous experimental experience, positive or negative, can affect the likelihood of future participation in experiments. Positive histories lead to a higher total of future volunteered participations.

Another consequence of prior experience in experiments is greater suspicion of deception. As pointed out earlier, in many psychological experiments S is deceived about various aspects of the study. He is misled about the true purpose of the study, about the nature of his own performance, about that of other Ss, or about the apparatus. Deception is even resorted to by Es to give Ss the impression that they will receive some material gain in the experiment. Thus, Festinger and Carlsmith (1959) promised participants either $1 or $20, while Valins (1966) promised slides of nude Playboy models. After the experiments, however, Es did not fulfill their promises.

It is possible that prior experience of this sort will make S suspicious in subsequent experiments that some deception is involved. Perhaps it is not even necessary for S to have firsthand experience with prior deception in order for him to be suspicious of psychologists. Most students have friends who have been in experiments or they have read about psychological research.

But being suspicious is no guarantee that S can see through the deception; after all, Es can be quite clever and devious. To be suspicious may only mean that S does not believe everything E tells him; but this suspicion is not equivalent to knowledge of what is the true state of affairs.

A number of studies have been conducted to determine if there is any support for the hypothesis that previous experience with deception will enhance Ss' future suspicion of deception. Fillenbaum (1966) conducted two studies to assess the influence of prior deception. In Experiment I, Ss first were given an impression-formation task in which they had to write paragraphs describing their impressions about the nature of some hypothetical persons described briefly to them by E.

After this task, E informed Ss in the experimental group that they had been deceived as to the purpose of the task. This was not necessary in the control group which was not deceived. Then an incidental learning task was given to both groups in which Ss had to cancel and underline words in a passage according to a complex set of rules. They were not told to try to memorize the content of the passage, but when they finished, E did test them on the content of the passage.

It was assumed that experience of prior deception might enhance the suspiciousness of experimental group Ss, which would lead them to doubt the alleged purpose of the second task. They might attempt to memorize the passage, for fear that the true purpose of the task was a memory test. Yet, since there was no difference in favor of the experimental group, Fillenbaum concluded that prior deception had no effect and that Ss are "faithful" in that they religiously follow the instructions—even those who were suspicious but did nothing in line with their suspicions.

In Experiment II, both the experimental and control groups were instructed in such a way as to maximize suspicion by telling them that the true purpose of experiments is not always what E tells Ss. Both groups were deceived on the first task. Then *debriefing* was provided in which the fact that deception had been employed was revealed to S's. The results still showed no differences in incidental learning on the second task.

Brock and Becker (1966) employed a much more dramatic situation than Fillenbaum's deception. After serving on three mental tasks in Experiment I, Ss were debriefed and told that they had been deceived as to the true purpose. Then another E asked them to serve in a different experiment. In Experiment II, a motor learning task was required in which S had to press buttons to light and then unlight some bulbs on a panel in front of him. During the course of this task, due to a rigged setup, one button press "caused" either low (a "pop") or high damage (a "bang" and clouds of smoke) to the apparatus. The purpose of this treatment was not to study motor learning, as S was told, but to see if S felt guilty for apparently damaging the equipment. It was predicted that Ss who apparently created high damage would be more willing to sign a petition requesting the university to increase tuition to improve the university than those causing low damage.

The fact that some Ss had been debriefed about deception in Experiment I had different effects on compliance, depending on the similarity of Experiments I and II. Debriefed Ss did not differ in petition-signing from those without debriefing when the two experiments appeared to be unrelated. However, when the two tasks were perceived as part of the same study, those Ss who were completely debriefed showed much less compliance.

Silverman, Shulman, and Weisenthal (1970) deceived and debriefed one group of Ss on subtests from an intelligence test while another group was given a memory task without deception. Then, in a second study common personality tests were used for both groups. Differences were obtained, with the previously deceived Ss tending to give favorable self-presentation and lowered compliance with demand characteristics. It was suggested that prior deception sensitizes Ss to look for ulterior purposes of experiments and increases evaluation apprehension.

Instead of examining the effects of direct past experience with deception, Golding and Lichtenstein (1970) assessed the influence of tip-offs about deception on behavior in a deception task. Some Ss were made suspicious by a stooge who warned them that "There's something fishy about that experiment," while others were fully tipped off about the nature of the deception in which fake heart rates were heard by S as he viewed slides of nudes from *Playboy*. The hypothesis, based on Valins (1966), was that Ss would prefer the nude models associated with rapid changes in heart rate.

The results showed the effect found earlier by Valins (1966); however, there was no difference between a noninformed control group and the tipped-off groups. Although the latter groups were suspicious due to having been tipped off, their behavior did not differ from the naive Ss. This fact raises doubts as to the validity of Valins's interpretation of his data and suggests that demand characteristics may have been responsible for the higher ratings for slides of nudes associated with heart rate changes.

Examination of a few studies attempting to determine the influence of past deception and suspicion of deception yields no clear-cut answer. Undoubtedly, the type of deception, the type of task, as well as the personalities of the Ss can produce different reactions to experimental deception. The problem is a complex one but one well worth further investigation because of its implications for the conduct of experiments.

4

CAN *E*s UNINTENTIONALLY BIAS OUTCOMES OF EXPERIMENTS?

In most sciences, there is little danger that the *E*s can inadvertently bias the behavior of the objects under investigation. However, in psychological experiments there has been growing concern that *E*s may somehow unintentionally bias the results of their observations. In psychology, the act of observation may itself have an effect on the behavior being studied. This reactivity of organisms to being studied is greater with human *S*s, although it exists also for many lower forms of organisms.

Experiments are usually undertaken by *E*s to test their carefully formulated hypotheses and predictions. In other words, *E*s do not conduct experiments without usually also having some expectancies or preconceptions as to what the outcomes will be. An experiment is designed to obtain an answer from nature for the questions posed by *E*s. This aspect of science is quite proper but yet may lead to difficulty in the area of psychological research. A major dilemma exists for psychology if the *E*'s hypotheses not only guide the type or research he undertakes but also bias the behavior of the organisms under study, especially if the bias is in favor of his predictions.

Most published research consists of so-called *positive results*, findings which more or less support the predictions proposed by *E*s. (This fact should not be interpreted to mean that *E*s are so clever that most of their predictions are supported in most of their experiments. For one thing, journal editors usually do not publish *negative results*. In view of this policy, and for other reasons as well, *E*s who obtain negative results may not even bother to submit such findings to journals for consideration.) Still, what are we to make of the volumes of journals mostly full of positive results? Are we able to safely conclude that at least for these studies *E*s were sufficiently wise and knowledgeable about psychology and were able to make valid predictions? Certainly we would like to be able to think so, for these "facts" are generally accepted as "truth."

However, one unpleasant, possible alternative basis for such successful predictions is that the expectancies or hypotheses of *Es* have managed to bias the results in favor of these hypotheses. Such bias, it should be clear, is assumed to be unintentional. We are not concerned with forms of cheating or misrepresentation. Most *Es* are honest and scrupulously attempt to avoid bias. However, despite such noble intentions, some recent investigators—notably Robert Rosenthal and his colleagues—have been suggesting that *Es* somehow unintentionally transmit their expectancies to *Ss*.

If we make the additional assumption that most *Ss* are cooperative and wish to be "good *Ss*" as noted by Orne earlier, or even if they only appear to be cooperative (Sigall *et al.*, 1970), we can see that any subtle cues produced by *E* during the experimental session might well influence an *S*'s performance in the direction desired or expected by *E*. The typical *S* is highly motivated and eager to serve as an *S*, either to learn something about himself or to figure out the hidden purpose of the study. As he performs, some of his responses will be those expected by *E*. Although *E* attempts to be objective, and doubtless believes he is, it is possible that he gets a bit excited or smiles a lot whenever predicted behavior occurs while he may frown whenever behavior inconsistent with his prediction occurs. Such unintentional cues could serve to reinforce *S* to continue making such responses expected by *E*.

A fascinating example of an actual case of such unintentional bias is the story of Clever Hans, the remarkable horse who apparently could solve mathematical problems. His answers were made by tapping with his hoof. Careful scrutiny of this incredible behavior, however, led Pfungst (1911) to conclude that Hans was reacting to unintentional cues provided by observers. What was happening was that as Hans approached the correct answer, the questioner would expectantly look up to see if Hans would stop tapping. Of course, this unintentional cue functioned as a signal for Clever Hans to stop tapping. Astonished observers, however, attributed mathematical skills to him.

Thus far, we have speculated on the quite plausible possibility that the results of psychology experiments may be affected by unintentional cues produced by *Es*, which guide behavior of *Ss* in ways that fulfill *Es*' hypotheses. We have also assumed that *Ss* can, in varying degrees, discern such cues. Finally, if the *Ss* are also cooperative to the demand characteristics of the situation, we will obtain what Rosenthal terms variously as *E-bias* or the *E-expectancy effect*.

Despite such speculation, it was not until relatively recently that

Rosenthal began his systematic program of experiments designed specifically to assess E-bias. Rather than conjecture that such bias occurs, Rosenthal and his associates set out to demonstrate and measure such biases in a clever experimental situation.

THE ROSENTHAL PARADIGM

The basic paradigm or experimental situation adopted by Rosenthal is an *experiment within an experiment* (Rosenthal, 1963b, see Selection 6). Student Es are assigned to test Ss on a so-called test of empathy, in which they have to look at a series of 20 photographs of individuals for 5 seconds each and rate them as to the extent to which the persons in the photographs have been experiencing success or failure. A scale ranging from $+10$ (extreme success) to -10 (extreme failure) is employed for the ratings.

Actually, the photographs have a mean rating of zero, indicating neutrality, according to a prior standardization test administered to other students. Therefore, from what we have just stated, *our* expectation in this study would be that the mean rating of Ss should also be zero. However, Rosenthal usually attempts to differentially bias his real Ss—namely the student Es—by instructing half of them to expect their Ss to produce a mean rating of $+5$ while telling the other half to expect a mean rating of -5. Student Es are told that such expectancies are based on well-established findings of past studies which they are to replicate. In some studies, the expectancies are based on alleged personality tests which had been given to Ss.

Student Es are told to read the instructions provided by Rosenthal to Ss but not to say anything else other than "Hello" and "Goodbye." The importance of secrecy was stressed to the student Es since one goal of the study was to be able to replicate "well-established" findings, just as "students in physics are expected to do."

To summarize, two different groups of student Es are led to expect opposite types of ratings from their Ss. Since the Ss are assigned at random to Es, and since the pictures have been standardized earlier as being neutral with respect to success or failure, there should be no difference in the mean ratings of the two groups of Ss, *if* there is no E-bias. However, to the extent that the expectations of Es influence the results of their Ss, one group of Es should obtain ratings above zero while the other group should get ratings below zero. Such an experiment was done by Rosenthal and Fode (1961) and the results supported the prediction that E-bias occurs.

Since that initial experiment, this basic person-perception task has been used extensively by Rosenthal and other investigators. According to Rosenthal (1969), it has been the experimental task in 57 out of 75 studies of *E*-bias involving the use of human *S*s. Only a few of these studies were primarily concerned with demonstrating the occurrence of *E*-bias; most of them were performed to identify variables which modify the degree of *E*-bias. Such variables include personality traits of *E*s and *S*s such as anxiety or need for approval, sex of *E*s and *S*s, and characteristics of the physical setting of the laboratory, to name a few. In addition, using both subjective reports of *S*s and objective records such as filmed and tape-recorded sessions, analyses have been made of the characteristics of the manner in which *E*s run their *S*s. Factors such as degree of professional-like conduct of the session, extent of interpersonal rapport between *E* and *S*, amount of kinesic communication by *E* (such as signals from the head and leg regions), and amount of paralinguistic communication by *E* (such as tone of voice) are the main aspects of *E*'s behavior examined.

Other studies of *E*-bias using human *S*s are much fewer in number. They have employed a variety of tasks ranging from projective tests such as the Rorschach Inkblot Test to psychophysical judgments, reaction time, and structured laboratory interviews. Although the overall results of these 85 studies cited by Rosenthal (1969) represent mixed support for the *E*-bias effect, half of them have produced results which could have occurred by chance less than 10 times out of 100. This level of statistical significance is not as infrequent as that (5 times out of 100) usually demanded by psychologists before they will accept evidence as supportive of an experimental hypothesis. However, the large number of findings taken as a whole cannot be disregarded even if most of the studies examined individually do not meet the conventional statistical criterion, which after all is an arbitrary rather than a magical criterion.

In addition, nine studies using animal *S*s have been done. Most of them tested the performance of rats which had allegedly been selectively bred for maze-brightness versus maze-dullness. The overall evidence showed strong *E*-bias effects on both maze and Skinner-box performance.

GENERALIZABILITY OF *E*-BIAS EFFECT

The *E*-bias effect has received extensive study in a large number of experiments. As of 1966, Rosenthal (1966, Chapter 17) stated that over 350 different Es, mostly male students who majored in a variety of areas, have been used. Most of the Es have been volunteers, although sometimes students enrolled in a class have served as Es, and most of the Es have been paid for their services.

Over 2000 human Ss have been tested, with about 60 percent being female students from a variety of majors, although most came from introductory psychology courses. Most Ss did not receive pay but were volunteers or were enlisted by their instructors to participate.

However, despite the large sample of Es and Ss, the primary task has been the person-perception photo-rating task, although other tasks have also been used occasionally. According to Rosenthal (1969, p. 228), the strongest evidence for E-bias has not occurred with this widely used task.

Yet, according to some views, ambiguous tasks such as the person-perception task might be most likely to yield evidence of E-bias. As noted by Barber and Silver (1968), E-bias has not occurred on structured tasks such as the Wechler Adult Intelligence Scale or Taylor Manifest Anxiety Scale and may be limited to ambiguous tasks such as the widely used person-perception task. Barber and Silver conclude: ". . . effects of the experimenter's expectancies on the results of his research (may) vary directly with the ambiguity, lack of structure, or nonfactualness of the experimental task [p. 26]."

Bias or expectancy in the real world can operate in a manner similar to that shown by Rosenthal in the laboratory. Kenneth Clark (1965) has noted how ghetto schoolchildren have been doomed to failure by the expectations by their teachers that they are not intelligent. This is an example of a self-fulfilling prophecy—one that is likely to be fulfilled, because its proponents will act in ways which enhance its fulfillment.

An experimental demonstration of how such factors might operate was done by Rosenthal and Jacobson (1968) in a fascinating study of how teachers' expectations can influence children's school performance. Teachers were told by Es that about 20 percent of the children were intellectually superior, according to a nonverbal IQ test. The particular children alleged to be superior were selected at random and their names were given to teachers in the experimental group who were led to expect large gains in academic ability from these kids. Followup tests were given several times over the next two years on the same test. The results showed that the kids who were thought to be more intelligent by their teachers showed bigger gains on the IQ tests than control group children.

It is possible that the teachers' expectations of the allegedly brighter kids led teachers to treat them preferentially or in some such way as to motivate them to higher actual performance. There are some ethical problems with such a study. However, it does demonstrate that self-fulfilling predictions can come true.

UNDERLYING MECHANISM FOR *E*-BIAS

As we shall see later, not all psychologists have accepted Rosenthal's evidence as support for the existence of *E*-bias. Such critics do not mean that there is no such phenomenom as *E*-bias but rather question whether or not it has been unequivocally demonstrated by Rosenthal's work. For the time being, let us accept Rosenthal's contentions and turn next to a discussion of the obvious questions: Just how is the *E*-bias transmitted?

Honest errors committed by *E* in the process of recording data or reading instrument panels can occur. However, such honest errors should be random, some in a direction favoring and some in a direction opposing *E*'s hypothesis. Nonetheless, it is possible that a constant error or errors in a given direction can occur supporting *E*'s hypothesis. Rosenthal (1966, p. 12), however, describes a study done by his colleagues which suggests such errors of recording as well as computational errors committed during data analysis are infrequent and trivial in effect. Furthermore, studies which are filmed and tape-recorded show less than 1 percent discrepancy between the records of *Es* and those made by independent judges (Rosenthal, 1969, p. 247).

Rosenthal (1963b) examined evidence for an operant conditioning type of explanation for some of the *E*-bias findings. According to this view, *E* subtly reinforces *S* whenever he happens to make a correct response—that is, a response consistent with expectation. Such reinforcement was assumed to be verbal in nature, such as those used in studies of verbal conditioning (Krasner, 1958; Spielberger, 1965). These verbal responses of *E* were not assumed to be as explicit as "That's right," but were thought to be more subtle such as "Mmh hmm," "OK," or "Good." If the *E* made one of these utterances each time *S* made a correct response, it would be possible for *E* to bias his results in his favor.

However, Rosenthal concluded that verbal conditioning was not a necessary mediator for the E-bias effect. Of course, it could occasionally operate but it seems that E-bias can still occur even when verbal conditioning is not possible, such as when tape recordings serve as Es (Rosenthal, 1969, p. 249).

In addition, if verbal conditioning were a major factor, E-bias should not occur with the very first photo in the series since verbal conditioning requires a number of trials. Yet, Rosenthal reports such instant bias. Furthermore, rather than increased bias as the trials continue—as one might expect if verbal conditioning were involved —the bias actually diminishes over the series of 20 photos.

It should also be noted that verbal conditioning could not be responsible for the E-bias demonstrated in animal studies. Apparently the mechanism involved here, according to Rosenthal and Fode (1963), is differential handling and treatment of allegedly maze-bright and maze-dull rats. The former received gentler and greater amounts of handling than the latter, according to the reports of the Es themselves after the experiment.

Returning to human studies, Rosenthal (1968, 1969) suggested that since the very first response of Ss can sometimes be influenced by E-bias, some of the mediation may occur during the period prior to the actual testing during which E greets, seats, and instructs his S. Rosenthal suggested that auditory cues alone may be sufficient to produce E-bias, according to an unpublished study by Adair and Epstein (1967). In this study, Es with opposed expectancies tape-recorded the instructions. There were differences in performance consistent with the bias of the E who taped the instructions suggesting that some type of vocal intonation or paralinguistic cue may have served to bias Ss. Other studies suggest that the visual channel may also serve to bring about E-bias. Rosenthal cited an unpublished study by Kennedy, Edwards, and Winstead (1968) in which E-bias effects were obtained when there was face-to-face interaction between E and S, but not when S could receive no visual cues from E. Thus, it is possible that some type of kinesic cues such as facial expression or body posture mediates E-bias.

Despite this suggestive evidence, Rosenthal (1969) noted: "For all the hundreds of hours of careful observation, and for all the valuable things learned about experimenter-subject interaction, no well-specified system of unintentional cueing has been uncovered [p. 254]." Similarly, Rosenthal (1966) lamented: "Perhaps the knowledge of interpersonal influence processes is a tacit knowledge [p. 301]."

In view of the inability of Rosenthal to identify how E-bias occurs, he must wonder how do the student Es know how to produce it. The answer Rosenthal (1969) comes up with is, "Perhaps they do not know, but perhaps within the context of the given experiment, they can come to know [p. 254]." What he is suggesting is a learning process quite different from the verbal conditioning explanation which involves more interaction between the responses of E and S. In verbal conditioning, E does the "teaching" or reinforcing by giving a verbal reinforcer each time S makes the correct response. Under this alternative explanation, it is S who does the "teaching," not E. The E himself is probably unaware that such training is even occurring. Rosenthal speculates that when S first happens upon the correct response, the probability increases that E will repeat any covert unintentional cues he happened to be emitting just prior to S's correct response. With future Ss, E is likely to be more efficient at emitting unintentional cues which produce the E-bias effect. What we have in the E-S dyad is a type of interpersonal learning situation with the behavior of E being shaped by S.

One of the difficulties in clearly identifying the mediating mechanism may be that the processes vary for different tasks. As Barber and Silver (1968) pointed out, the paralinguistic and kinesic cues may operate in the ambiguous situations such as the person-perception task but not in situations which are more structured such as paper-and-pencil tests.

Unfortunately, we will have to leave the question of just how E-bias occurs an open one for the time being.

METHODOLOGICAL IMPLICATIONS

Although the exact extent to which E-bias occurs in psychological research and the method by which it is mediated can be debated, there appears to be enough evidence to maintain that some E-bias does occur in certain types of research.

What can be done to minimize such bias? Obviously, to the extent that such bias operates, it undermines the validity of conclusions drawn from psychological experiments.

One obvious solution would be for the psychologist who is the principal investigator on a project to employ research assistants or data collectors who themselves are not informed of the investigator's hypotheses. It should be pointed out that most published research is based on data collected by such assistants, and not by the principal investigator(s). It is not as clearly known how frequently these assistants actually know of the investigator's hypotheses, but the suggestion under consideration is that they not be informed about the expected outcomes. It would still be possible, however, for assistants to act just like Ss and attempt to formulate their own hypotheses about the purpose and expected outcomes of the experiment. There is no guarantee that there will be no E-bias merely if the data collectors are not officially informed of the investigator's hypotheses.

In one study by Rosenthal, Persinger, Vikan-Kline, and Mulry (1963), an assessment was made of the possibility that the principal investigator's hypotheses could still influence the results of research assistants who were *not* informed of the investigator's hypotheses. Student Es were given different expectancies about their Ss' performance on the person-perception task. Then, these student Es were given research "grants" to hire their own research assistants to run additional Ss. The student Es were instructed that their assistants should obtain similar results; however, they were not allowed to actually instruct their assistants as to what results to expect. Thus, the student Es were biased to expect their assistants to obtain results similar to their own; yet the assistants were not explicitly biased by the student Es. Nonetheless, the results indicated that the research assistants obtained results which corresponded with the expectancies of the persons who trained them.

There is some ambiguity about the procedure of this experiment. Just how did Rosenthal *et al.* (1963) convey to student Es the expectation that their assistants would obtain results similar to those they got from their Ss? All they say is, *"Es*, however, were subtly led, by their printed instructions, to expect their As (assistants) to obtain data of the same sort they had themselves obtained from their earlier run Ss [p. 314]."

Assuming, however, that expectancies of assistants can conceivably affect results, it would appear that E-bias elimination would eventually depend on the use of automated administration of experimental sessions. There is already substantial automation in the presentation of stimuli and the recording of responses in many areas of research. The instructions are often tape-recorded. However, even in these experiments, there is a human E who greets Ss, goes through the session with Ss, and dismisses them at the end of sessions. By eliminating the use of human Es, we could minimize E-bias.

Rosenthal (1966) suggested a number of other ways of coping with the problem of E-bias. If we only use one or two different Es in an experiment, as is the case with most experiments (McGuigan, 1963), any biases that these Es have may influence the results in a systematic direction. However, if we randomly sample Es just as we do Ss, thus using several different Es within a single experiment, there is a chance that biases of different Es might cancel each other out. There is still opportunity for biases of individual Es to operate, but overall it is assumed that the effect of E-bias will be cancelled out.

The use of a larger number of Es per experiment may also serve to control bias by reducing it, not merely cancelling it out. Rosenthal (1966, Chapter 19) notes that for a given number of Ss in an experiment, there would be fewer Ss tested by each E as we increase the number of Es. The advantages of this situation would be to reduce the opportunity for Es to learn how to bias, lessen the chances that Es would figure out which Ss are members of which experimental treatment, and minimize the effects of trends in early returns from biasing the expectancies Es would have for subsequent Ss. All of these benefits would reduce E-bias; in addition, we would acquire a bonus in gaining greater generalizability of results.

It is interesting to note that Rosenthal's recommendation of having less experienced Es contrasts with present procedures based on the assumption that more objectivity would be obtained with highly experienced Es.

Another approach to reducing E-bias suggested by Rosenthal is the careful observation of E's behavior during the experimental sessions either by subjective or objective means. The knowledge that observers are watching may reduce the operation of E-bias.

Reduction of E-bias may also be achieved by the use of blind contact. In most psychological studies, the Es know which treatment is being received by Ss; if, however, he did not or was "blind" to information about which treatment a given S was receiving, it would not be possible for his expectancies about the effects of the treatments to influence how he interacted with individual Ss. Studies using safeguards are rare, except in the area of psychopharmacology but Rosenthal suggests that they be more widely used.

A final procedure proposed by Rosenthal is the expectancy control group. This method should not be equated with a no expectancy control where *E*s are given no expectancy. In the expectancy control procedure, all *E*s are given expectancies such that half of the *E*s for each experimental treatment have opposite expectations. The strategy is not to eliminate *E*-bias but to assess it by giving opportunity for it to operate in opposite directions in the very same experiment.

Consider a simple two-group experiment, involving an experimental group and a control group aimed to evaluate the effects of a stimulant Drug X on alertness. The experimental group which is administered the Drug X would be expected by *E* to be more alert than the control group which receives a pharmacologically harmless placebo.

As a control for expectancy bias, Rosenthal suggests that two additional groups be added to the experimental design for which the *E*s would have expectancies opposed to those described above. Thus, a third group would also receive stimulant Drug X but their *E*s would be misled into expecting lowered alertness. Similarly, a fourth group would receive the placebo, but this time their *E*s would be misled to expect higher alertness.

One possible drawback to this procedure is that E-bias effects may not be symmetrical. Thus, in the person-perception task, for example, it may be easier to bias *S*s toward positive than toward negative ratings.

Although Rosenthal is concerned about the ethical problem of using deception on his *E*s and *S*s, he concludes that this is a small cost relative to the gain achieved in being able to better assess the effects of the independent variable, free from *E*-bias. It may be argued that some areas of research do not need the use of expectancy controls, which after all, involve more planning and work. However, Rosenthal (1966, p. 402) maintains that we cannot specify in advance which areas do not need such controls. The purpose of using them, in the first place, is to identify those problem areas which can afford to be studied without worry of contamination from *E*-bias.

CRITICAL EVALUATION

The strongest critics of Rosenthal's work purporting to show *E*-bias have probably been Barber and Silver (1968). On the one hand, they have charged that the statistical analyses of the results in many of the studies claiming *E*-bias have been weak or inappropriate. The details of this criticism are complicated, as is Rosenthal's (1968) refutation of these attacks. Many of the issues under dispute are not easily resolved since as Rosenthal (1968) noted, "The conclusions one wants to draw from an array of data are a matter of taste and judgment [p. 37]." Furthermore, as shown by Rosenthal (1969, p. 35), there is considerable disagreement among statisticians as to the proper use of statistics.

In addition, Barber and Silver attack Rosenthal's work on methodological rather than statistical grounds. They suggest that intentional bias has not been entirely ruled out in many *E*-bias studies. Even the actual fudging or doctoring of data cannot be ruled out in some cases. Obviously if these methods are the processes by which *E*-bias is manifested, the phenomenon is not particularly interesting. All we would have would be an additional situation where dishonesty or cheating was operative. What makes Rosenthal's work intriguing is the possibility that it demonstrates bias via some form of unintentional influence. Barber and Silver suggest that before we can worry about the mechanism of unintentional influence, we must first be sure that no intentional forms of influence are being employed by *E* on the results.

In response to Rosenthal's (1968) countercharge that no proof was given by Barber and Silver of cheating or intentional biasing, they responded that, ". . . the burden of proof is upon those who wish to claim that, in these studies, the student experimenters unintentionally and subtly biased their subjects' responses; the burden of proof is not upon reviewers who point out that alternative explanations have not been rigorously excluded [Barber & Silver, 1968b, p. 61]."

In terms of their evaluation, Barber and Silver (1968b) concluded that *E*-bias occurred in only 12 of the 31 studies available at that time. Further analysis led them (1968b, pp. 58–61) to conclude that in only two studies could one exclude the possibility that factors such as intentional biasing or fudging of the data operated. The notion formulated by Rosenthal that unintentional paralinguistic or kinesic cues serve to bias results seems acceptable to Barber and Silver in only these two studies.

Another criticism by Barber and Silver (1968a, p. 26) is that there has been a confusion between expectancy and desirability by Rosenthal. In instructing his student *E*s, Rosenthal not only provided expectancies about their Ss' behavior, but he also urged upon them the desirability that they be able to replicate previous well-established findings upon which the alleged expectancies were based. This distinction appears to be well worthwhile. It leads Barber and Silver to raise the interesting questions of whether expectancies would be fulfilled if the students Es did not regard them as desirable or whether results could be biased when Es desired certain results but had no basis for expecting them.

There appears to be certain unique problems in formal studies of E-bias such as those of Rosenthal. The investigator must use student Es to demonstrate E-bias; yet these Es are at the very same time functioning in the role of Ss for the investigator. In this respect, they are no different from any other Ss; it just so happens that their task is not to memorize nonsense syllables or fill out questionnaires but rather to test their own Ss. One must wonder to what degree student Es are like other Ss in trying to figure out the true purpose of their participation. To what extent are student Es suspicious or aware of the deception imposed upon them by Rosenthal when he tells them what results to expect from their Ss.

And what about the demand characteristics of the situation? Rosenthal's Es are probably as eager—if not more so—as other Ss to be "good Ss." Some of them are students in Rosenthal's class and they are told how important it is to be able to replicate the expected results. Furthermore, in many studies they get paid $2 an hour if they succeed, but only $1 otherwise.

Therefore, the situation involves strong pressure on student Es to "deliver the goods." Otherwise, they have failed to replicate well-established findings which would cast doubt on their ability as Es. In addition, they would get only $1, rather than $2 an hour. Rosenthal (1966, Chapter 13), however, does show that if excessive rewards are offered one actually gets less bias. Excessive rewards of $5 led to less bias than $2 rewards. Rosenthal suggests that the $5 reward may have appeared to be a bribe so that Es bent over backward to avoid bias so it would not appear that they could be bribed.

In real experiments, as contrasted with the metaexperiments of Rosenthal, it is doubtful that most research assistants and data collectors would be under as much pressure to come up with the expected results. Often they are not even informed of the investigator's hypotheses. They receive the same rate of pay, regardless of whether or not the data confirms the hypothesis. Even if the principal investigator—who obviously knows the hypothesis—ran the Ss, he would not be under the pressure encountered by the student *Es* because he himself would not be an *S* at the same time.

The investigator who studies *E*-bias represents an interesting paradox since, in principle, he could be biasing his own results! For example, it is conceivable that Rosenthal himself, in attempting to confirm his belief that *E*-bias exists, may be unintentionally biasing the results of his studies himself (Lester, 1969). Yet, such bias would constitute evidence itself that studies can be influenced by *E*-bias. One implication of this speculation is that studies of *E*-bias by an investigator who did not believe in *E*-bias might fail to replicate Rosenthal's findings because of his opposite bias. Interestingly enough, one of the critics of Rosenthal's work, T. X. Barber, along with five colleagues (Barber, Calverley, Forgione, McPeake, Chaves, & Bowen, 1969), have done five studies which have all failed to replicate Rosenthal's results. This predicament leaves us in quite a dilemma for it suggests that we may obtain as many different results as we have investigators with different hypotheses and expectancies!

Where does this discussion leave us? What conclusions can we draw? The possibility that some process like *E*-bias can exist is important to evaluate; for to the degree that it operates, our whole approach to psychology based on experimentation is undermined. We owe a large debt to Rosenthal and his colleagues for their thorough and painstaking analysis of the phenomenon and for his imaginative suggestions for improving experimental methodology.

However, the possibility that *E*-bias is a pervasive and significant factor throughout psychological research does not appear to be as strong as one might get the impression from reading the work of Rosenthal. A similar view was proposed by Masling (1966) who noted that, "One possible danger of the current enthusiasm for investigating the Rosenthal effect is that it may lead to the conclusion that all psychology, under all conditions, is subject to this phenomenon [p. 92]." Furthermore, he observed that where it does occur, it may not be a strong factor affecting the conclusions made in the study. Such reservations have also been voiced by Aronson and Carlsmith (1968).

Is it worth the time, effort, and bother to take as many precautions against *E*-bias as suggested by Rosenthal, or is it better to take the chance that *E*-bias may operate undetected in studies which are done without elaborate controls against expectancy bias? Barber and Silver (1968b) feel that ". . . the investigations in this area are not as yet sufficiently compelling to conclude that a revolution is imperative in the conduct of psychological research [p. 62]." It should be obvious by now that Rosenthal thinks otherwise. Which "error" one is willing to commit—controlling for bias which one doesn't think exists or failing to control for bias which does exist—will determine one's course of action on this matter.

5

DO EXPERIMENTAL RESULTS VARY AS A FUNCTION OF ASPECTS OF *E*s OTHER THAN THEIR EXPECTANCIES?

Not only may the expectancies of *E*s potentially bias the results of experiments but it is also possible for their physical and psychosocial attributes such as sex, age, race, status, friendliness, and anxiety—naming a few—to affect the results. Until relatively recently, the *E* has been ignored as a possible stimulus affecting results (McGuigan, 1963, see Selection 7) even though Rosensweig warned about this problem in 1933. McGuigan surveyed several randomly selected issues of the *Journal of Experimental Psychology* to determine how many different *E*s or data collectors had been used in each study. As he noted "In no article was any mention made of techniques of controlling the experimenter variable and in only one of the articles was the number of data collectors actually specified [pp. 421–422]." He was able to draw some inferences, however, about the number of "possible" data collectors in the 37 articles he surveyed. It was clear that in 10 articles only one data collector was used, and by inference he concluded that in most of the other 27, more than one data collector was used. Yet, none of these studies provided analyses of results as a function of *E*s, to show that this factor itself was not an independent variable affecting results. Thus, male *E*s may obtain different kinds of results than female *E*s, or hostile *E*s may get different findings from those obtained by friendly *E*s. If only one data collector is used in a study, we have no way of determining to what extent one *E*'s results are unique to himself or to *E*s similar to himself. Even if a number of data collectors are used, unless we specify how the *E*s differ and compare the results obtained by different kinds of *E*s, we still are in the dark about the effects of *E*-characteristics on the results.

There is abundant evidence that experimental results are in fact influenced by various aspects of *E*s. To be sure, the extent to which the *E*-variable can affect results may vary with the type of experiment, being stronger in social and personality experiments and weaker with psycho-physical, perceptual, and sensory experiments.

One of the early experimental studies examining the effects of E-traits was a verbal conditioning study done by Binder, McConnell, and Sjoholm (1957). The task of S was to emit sentences as they came to mind; meanwhile E reinforced all sentences containing hostile words by responding, "Good." For one group of Ss, an attractive, soft-spoken young lady, 5'5½" tall and weighing 90 lbs., was the E, while the E for the other group of Ss was a very masculine, 6'5" tall, 220-pounder who was 12 years older than the lady E. Binder et al. stated that the lady E could have passed for a high school sophomore whereas the male E might have been thought to be a faculty member.

Clear differences in conditioning occurred as a function of the type of E. Hostile words were produced more frequently over trials for both groups but at a faster rate for the lady E. Binder et al. interpreted this result to mean that Ss were less inhibited in using hostile words in the presence of the lady E. Of course it is not clear exactly which attribute distinguishing the two Es was the main factor producing the different results, since they differed in sex, age, size, and personality, but it is obvious that results did vary as a function of Es.

The influence of E-traits on behavior is not always as straightforward as in the preceding study. Sometimes there may be an interaction between the traits of the Es and those of the Ss. Thus, in the previous study, there might be differences between men and women Ss in the way in which they react to male versus female Es.

A case in point is a study on sensory deprivation reported by Walters, Shurley, and Parsons (1962). Male and female Ss floated in a tank of water for several hours following which they were interrogated about their experiences during this isolation. Questions were concerned with feelings such as fright, sex, unpleasantness, etc. Half of the Ss of each sex were interviewed by an E of the same sex and half by one of the opposite sex. The manner in which Ss responded to the question about sexual feelings differed, depending on whether the E and S were of the same or of the opposite sex, with higher scores being reported when they were of the same sex.

Rosenthal (1967) makes the worthwhile distinction between active and passive effects of E's sex. An *active effect* refers to the possibility that Ss respond differently to Es of different sexes because they are actually treated differently by male and female Es. On the other hand, a *passive effect* refers to the situation where Ss may themselves respond differently to male versus female Es just because of their sex—not because of any differential treatment from them. In this study, as in most studies showing an effect of *E*'s sex, it is not clear whether the effect is an active or a passive one. Films of experiments by Rosenthal and his colleagues strongly suggest that quite often the effect is an active one. For example, male Es seem more "interested" in their female Ss than in their male Ss, and treat them differently.

An example which might be classified as an active effect between Es and Ss of different sexes was reported by Harris and Masling (1970). Whereas female Es obtained equal amounts of responses to Rorschach tests for male and female Ss alike, male Es were able to obtain more response from female Ss.

The manner in which a given E responds to or treats his Ss is also subject to variation—sometimes in a complex fashion—as a function of the behavior of the Ss. Thus, Masling (1957, 1959) found that female confederates, serving as either "warm" or "cold" Ss led to differences in the way their examiners gave and scored their intelligence tests and projective test protocols.

More experienced or more professional Es may be more consistent in the manner in which they treat their Ss. As Masling (1966) noted, most studies of *E*-traits have used relatively untrained and naive Es. Perhaps studies with highly trained Es might even lead to what he calls a *leaning-over-backward-effect* whereby investigators with strong superegos might even bias the results against their own hypothesis.

Rosenthal (1963a, see Selection 8; 1966, Chapters 4–6) has summarized the findings of a number of studies showing how *E*-traits cannot influence only outcomes of experiments but also results in other data-collecting situations such as interviews, therapy, and psychological testing. Many of these studies are also mentioned by Kintz, Delprato, Mettee, Persons, and Schappe (1965), Masling (1966), and Sattler (1970), so it should be apparent that psychologists are beginning to take notice of the problem in increasing numbers.

IMPLICATIONS

In view of the evidence, it should be apparent that we cannot afford to ignore the possibility that different Es obtain different results, not only as a function of their expectancies, but also as a function of physical and psychosocial differences. McGuigan (1963) has suggested that this contaminant may well be a factor in the inability of one investigator to replicate the work of another, an event which occurs not infrequently in psychology. Journals are full of controversies stemming from failures to replicate previously published studies. It is not argued that differences in E-traits are the only difference between two studies which yield conflicting results. The subject populations and test conditions also vary most of the time from study to study. In addition, other aspects of the two studies are frequently slightly different. And, when the two investigators happen to be of different theoretical persuasion—as is usually the case when a second investigator sets out to replicate the work of another—the differences in outcome could be due to differences in E-expectancy rather than differences in E-traits. What is being suggested by the present evidence is that we must now add to our list of possible variables in all experiments, the nature and characteristics of Es.

POSSIBLE SOLUTIONS

The suggestion has often been made (Friedman, 1967; McGuigan, 1963; Rosensweig, 1933; Rosenthal, 1966) that investigators use more than one E to collect the data in an experiment. Ideally, Es could be randomly sampled although in practice this would prove difficult. However, it would be an improvement if at least two different Es were utilized in each study. Sometimes we will find that the results obtained by our different Es are essentially equivalent, namely that there was no effect of E-traits. McGuigan (1963) points out that we would never have known that E was not a factor in that situation unless we actually varied Es. So, if it turns out there are no differences among Es, one should not think that it was a bother not worth considering.

On the other hand, suppose there was a difference in results among Es. Using several different Es would have enabled us to identify this situation, possibly preventing some future controversy with some other investigator who might fail to replicate our finding. It would also introduce a new problem for us to study—why do different Es get different results on the phenomenon under study?

When there is an influence of E-traits, there may be two different types of situations, according to McGuigan (1963). The effect may exist but it is not a differential one. One *E* gets better performance from *S*s in both the experimental and control groups than another *E*; however, the *difference* between the two treatments is essentially equal for both *E*s. This situation illustrates an effect of *E* on *results,* but not one on *conclusions* about the other variables in the experiment.

Rosenthal (1966, p. 110) makes essentially the same important distinction. Even though *E*-traits may affect the performances of *S*s, it need not also affect the *conclusions* drawn from the study about the effects of other variables. Suppose we are studying learning as a function of the time of day. In addition, we vary the type of *E*s— say, cold versus warm. It may happen that although one *E* may obtain more learning in his *S*s, there is no *differential* effect of the time of day on learning. That is, regardless of the type of *E*, learning is better at one time of day than another. As long as there is no interaction between the *E*-variable and other independent variables in the study, the conclusions drawn about these other variables will not be affected by the influence of *E*-traits.

However, in some types of research such as surveys where the goal is to measure opinions or attitudes as they really are, and not as a function of how some other variables affect them, the influence of *E*-traits can be a serious problem. For example, in a survey about racial attitudes, the race of the interviewer can influence the nature of the results so that our *conclusion* about racial attitudes of the interviewees will vary, depending on the race of *E* (Sattler, 1970).

In contrast, in the other type of situation described by McGuigan, an *E*-effect may occur whereby one *E* obtains differences between the experimental and control conditions but another *E* does not. There is an interaction between type of *E* and the other variable. In this situation, there is an effect of *E* on *both* results and conclusions.

The exact effect of *E* on the results and conclusions of an experiment obviously cannot be identified if there is only one *E* or there is no breakdown of the data for different types of *E*s when multiple *E*s are employed. For these reasons, McGuigan and others have recommended that the *E* be studied as an independent variable in its own right, which like other variables may influence behavior. The old conception of *E* as a background factor in the experiment who is "invisible" and is an element of the situation whose presence is neutral must be abandoned.

However, there may be limitations to the solution proposed by McGuigan. Lyons (1964, pp. 94–95) does not feel that his remedy is adequate for assessing the effects that Es have on Ss. In fact, it is one which simply makes the situation more complex. The investigator who is systematically studying the influence of different types of Es on their Ss is still in the same bind as any other E is in when studying his Ss. After all, there may be differences in the experimental designs selected by different investigators to study this problem which might bias the outcome in their favor. Thus, it is possible that some investigators would find that E-traits make a difference and other investigators might not, depending on their own views. As Lyons (1964) stated, "All that has been accomplished is to make each E into an experimentally manipulable object who is in no essential way different from the Ss already familiar to us [p. 95]."

Lyons suggested that the only viable solution is to eliminate the E with some form of automated administration of the experiment. Even then, presumably there will be some form of human contact encountered by Ss who participate in experiments, either the person greeting them at the experiment before turning them over to the computer, the person recruiting volunteers, or the psychology professor for their course. Might not characteristics of these humans associated indirectly with S's participation in an experiment have some effect? Of course, it should be much smaller than any influence of an E. Therefore, in this respect, automation would be a big advance in eliminating this type of bias. However, automation is expensive and perhaps not too readily attainable.

Not all psychologists, however, would agree that automation is the solution. Aronson and Carlsmith (1968) maintain that a live E is "not simply a bias-producing machine; he is frequently a necessary ingredient in the experimental process [p. 52]."

In particular, they point out the advantages of a live E over taped or printed instructions for Ss who fail to understand what they are to do in the experiment. Aronson and Carlsmith hold that the live E can and should use his own judgment in determining which Ss are confused and take extra effort to provide clarifying instructions. They recognize that many psychologists, the present one included, would question the feasibility of allowing E to modify instructions for different Ss due to the possibility of biased treatment of Ss. However, Aronson and Carlsmith do not see this outcome as a serious threat since they feel there are ways to avoid such bias. But while they do discuss means of eliminating *E*-bias during the experiment, they do not actually mention methods for controlling *E*-bias before the experiment during the instructional period.

Are there any other arguments in favor of using live *Es*? One could argue that the presence of a live *E* may permit the detection of phenomena which were not anticipated when the experiment was first planned. By observing the *Ss*, the *E* might be able to suggest ways of improving the actual procedures within the experiment. However, while these are good arguments, such gains due to the use of a live *E* must always be weighed against the cost of contamination of results by factors related to *E* such as those described in this and the preceding chapters. If we are aware of these problems and exercise care to minimize or prevent forms of bias associated with *E*, then the use of live *Es* is no danger.

6

WHAT ARE THE OBLIGATIONS OF *E*s AND THE RIGHTS OF *S*s?

There has been growing awareness and concern in recent years about the ethical responsibility and obligations of investigators toward their experimental *S*s. Some (Kelman, 1967; Seeman, 1969) have been primarily concerned about the use of deception, while others have worried about the broader issue of invasion of privacy (Ruebhausen & Brim, 1966; Wolfensberger, 1967). A number of other issues about the rights of *S*s are summarized by Sasson and Nelson (1969, see Selection 12).

The issue of the right of individuals to privacy is a central problem not only with experimental research but also in connection with other forms of psychological investigation, especially personality testing (Conrad, 1967; Lovell, 1967) where the results often have personal consequences for individuals. One outcome of the concern has been governmental investigation of the problem, with a report issued in 1967 by a panel of the Office of Science and Technology entitled *Privacy and Behavioral Research.*

This report (1967) defines the right to privacy as, "the right of the individual to decide for himself how much he will share with others his thoughts, his feelings, and the facts of his personal life [p. 2]." A dilemma presents itself when the researcher wishes to exercise his rights to investigate problems. For, as the panel recognizes, there is often a conflict between the interests of the scientist who values freedom of inquiry and those of the individual who has the right to protect his privacy from invasion. The panel (1967) notes that:

> The root of the conflict between the individual's right to privacy and society's right of discovery is the research process. Behavioral science seeks to assess and to measure many qualities of man's mind, feelings, and actions. In the absence of informed consent on the part of the subject, these measurements represent invasion of privacy. [p. 4].

The problem, however, is that *informed* consent is not always easy to obtain (Ruebhausen & Brim, 1966). Some psychological research could not be done if S knew fully about the nature of the research. Sometimes explanations are too technical for the layman to understand. The panel ends up holding that:

> In the end, the fact must be accepted that human behavioral research will at times produce discomfort to some subjects, and will entail a partial invasion of their privacy. Neither the principle of privacy nor the need to discover new knowledge can supervene universally. As with other conflicting values in our society there must be constant adjustment and compromise, with the decision as to which value is to govern in a given instance to be determined by a weighing of the costs and the gains—the cost in privacy, the gain in knowledge [p. 5].

Thus, sometimes when S consents to serve in an experiment, he can hardly be regarded as well informed about the risks of participation. However, the Panel suggested that in these situations, the colleagues and peers of an investigator could serve as a check on the ethical propriety of his experiments. But as Benson and Smith (1967) note, "The judgment offered by them may be highly particularistic and may reflect an exclusive concern neither with the welfare of the subject nor with the welfare of society." They see the individual in these terms:

> As a research subject, as in other roles, the individual in a mass society is at the mercy of powerful interest groups. He lacks the knowledge to decide intelligently whether or not to participate in a research project. He must depend upon the researcher to provide accurate information, to take proper precautions, and to judge the value of the research [p. 133].

Once an individual has consented to serve as an S, what other rights can he expect to be honored? Since he must often consent without really understanding the nature of his commitment, he should be allowed to withdraw from an experiment at any time, if for any reason he finds it necessary. Although most Es allow this choice to Ss, few if any emphasize this option explicitly. Furthermore, many Ss are reluctant to exercise this right once they have entered the experiment. Fear of provoking the displeasure of the E, who sometimes is his instructor, or fear of loss of self-esteem for "dropping out" may prevent S from terminating his participation prematurely, when in fact it might be in his best interests.

Ideally, E would not like any Ss to drop out of an experiment. Allowing Ss to withdraw from an experiment is sound ethical policy, but it does create serious methodological problems for investigators. The randomness of the Ss in each experimental treatment can be destroyed if more Ss drop out of one condition than out of others (e.g., Brehm, 1962). Conclusions from such studies could be invalidated as a consequence.

A number of other rights of Ss are summarized by Sasson and Nelson (1969). For example, there should be protection of Ss from harm—physical or psychological. Yet occasionally this right is violated in some studies involving shock, stress, drugs, or anxiety, to give a few examples. Deception can also be a source of harm such as when Ss are made to feel inferior or foolish, even when they are told later that they had been misled into forming these self-impressions.

Participation in experiments should not jeopardize the dignity or self-esteem of Ss. In many experiments involving frustration and failure, Ss may experience lowered self-esteem. Baumrind (1964) has criticized Milgram's (1963) studies of obedience to authority in which Ss were ordered to administer shock to other Ss. Even though the Ss could have disobeyed, most of them obeyed orders. What kind of damage could have been done to these obedient Ss later when they reconsidered what they had done?

Milgram's (1964) reply to Baumrind, based on postexperimental questionnaires, disclosed that little if any harm occurred from the experiment. Less than 1 percent of all Ss reported negative feelings about their participation after they had been debriefed. In fact, many felt that the experience had been well worthwhile.

One difficulty with this information, of course, is the possibility that many Ss were just telling E what they thought he wanted to hear. In Orne's (1959) terms, a pact of ignorance between E and S may have been operative during the postexperimental inquiry. Even if the Ss had not believed Milgram's deception, as Orne and Holland (1968) have suggested, they would not let E know this attitude.

A much better method of measuring the feelings of Ss toward the experiment would have been to use interviewers who were not perceived as connected with the experiment such as was the procedure in a study by Festinger and Carlsmith (1959).

Similarly, Kelman (1967) has raised doubts about the propriety of the Bramel (1962, 1963) studies in which false feedback was given so as to lead some *Ss* to think that their behavior indicated that they were homosexuals. In both situations it should be pointed out that debriefing was given to *Ss*. In other words, the nature of the deception was explained to *Ss* after the experiment so that they then knew that no one was really being shocked or that they were not really homosexuals. But the critics hold that despite such debriefing, the *Ss* did undergo unnecessary ego-threatening experiences.

The individual is entitled to confidentiality of his results. He has agreed to participate so as to provide data for the investigator, but he is doing so on the assumption that his personal results will not be divulged to others. Sometimes, it may be necessary for *S*'s results to even be anonymous, such as when the evidence may be incriminating or damaging if it should ever leak out.

Some psychologists (Berg, 1954) recommend the adoption of legal codes to protect experimental *Ss*, such as the Nuremberg Code set up in 1947 at the trials of physicians for war crimes in Nazi Germany.

Finally, Sasson and Nelson (1969) maintain that college students —or any other group whose participation in experiments is based on the argument that it is educational—have the right to receive these educational benefits. They suggest that *Ss* be taught the importance of experiments as a means towards knowledge. They should be taught the nature of fact, theory, and method. Finally, students must be debriefed about the background, hypothesis, methodology, and results of each experiment in which they serve.

Educational grounds are the basis of justification for required participation in experiments by psychology students in most of the 60 departments of psychology polled by this author (Jung, 1969). (In addition, two-thirds of them also stress the research needs of the department as a factor for the requirements.) Yet, only 62 percent of the departments have a requirement that *Es* provide such educational feedback to *Ss*.

THE DILEMMA OF DECEPTION

One of the more controversial procedures employed by psychologists is that of deception of *Ss* about various aspects of experiments. Deception, in the view of some psychologists, is a necessary evil. A leading social psychologist, William McGuire (1969), acknowledged the moral cost involved with deception but felt that "it might be necessary to pay this cost . . . rather than to cease our research [p. 50]." He does not specify that it is the S, not the E, who must foot the expenses. For McGuire, research is the thing above all else. "Those who are doing experiments which involve deception" are less of an ethical problem, according to McGuire, than "those who are doing too few experiments or none at all [p. 53]."

In contrast, another influential social psychologist, Herbert Kelman (1967, see Selection 9) has questioned the value of deception. Because deception is so widespread, most Ss come into the experiment expecting to be deceived. Kelman suggests it will soon be impossible to find naive Ss and wonders "whether there is any future in the use of deception [p. 6]." Furthermore, he maintains that ". . . there is obviously something self-defeating about the use of deception [p. 7]."

As Ring (1967) puts it, "What is the perceptive student to think, finally, of a field where the most renowned researchers apparently get their kicks from practicing sometimes unnecessary and frequently crass deceptions on their unsuspecting subjects [p. 118]." He calls into question the trend in social psychology towards a *fun-and-games* philosophy in which "whoever can conduct the most contrived, flamboyant, and mirth-producing experiments receives the highest score on the kudometer [p. 117]."

McGuire (1967) attempted to assuage the intensity of Ring's attack by suggesting that the *fun-and-gamesmen* are basically pure in their motives. However, this rejoinder seems to miss the point that Ring makes which is that such impressions of psychologists, warranted or not, breed cynicism and lack of respect for psychologists by students and Ss. Good intentions on the part of Es are not enough!

Another weak defense of deception is offered by Aronson and Carlsmith (1968). They acknowledge the gravity of the ethical problems involved in the use of deception, but they feel that it is a necessary operation if certain processes are to be investigated. They attempt to reduce the concern about possible negative effects of deception on Ss by arguing that most Ss realize that they are in an experiment and consequently may either expect deception or at least not be unduly upset by the deception within the context of an experiment.

Such may be the case for some *S*s but one wonders how this argument can be serious entertained. For on the one hand, Aronson and Carlsmith are insisting that deception is necessary methodologically, while on the other they are attempting to placate those with ethical objections by saying that deception really is not too effective. If deception does not really work, why bother using it, especially in view of the ethical objection?

The ethical problem about deception is that, by definition, it precludes the possibility of truly informed consent of *S*s. The fact that deception is widespread, especially in social and personality psychology (Seeman, 1969; Stricker, 1967) is troublesome. Such deception is regarded as necessary in such areas of investigation because the behavior could not be studied, if *S* knew the true purpose of many studies on such phenomena as altruism, aggression, and ironically, honesty. Deception is used because it is felt that otherwise *S*'s true traits might not be observed since he would often try to give socially desirable behavior. Sometimes, as in the study of frustration or anxiety in the laboratory, *S*s are deceived about the real performance of either themselves or of others. And in some cases such as the study of conformity or obedience, *S*s are deceived about both the purpose of the study and the performance of other *S*s.

Some psychologists have less absolute views about deception, basing their evaluations on additional factors. Thus, whether or not harm or threat to the safety and well-being of *S*s exists, it may determine whether or not a given deception is acceptable to some. The deception in an incidental learning study (e.g., Fillenbaum, 1966) is relatively harmless compared to deceptions in the study of how persons react when they are made to feel deviant (Freedman & Doob, 1968). In the former case, the unsuspecting *S* is tested on material under conditions where he did not realize he was going to be tested later. In the latter case, *S* is given false feedback about his test scores so that he forms the impression that he is markedly deviant from everyone else.

Another factor bearing on the ethical aspect of deception is whether or not debriefing is performed so that the nature of the deception is disclosed to *S*. Many *E*s who feel that deception is necessary in much psychological research accept it only if debriefing is also provided.

Rosenberg (1969) takes the position that *E*s have an ethical obligation to fully debrief Ss. He comments that "Candid and thorough debriefing, unmarred by any proclivity towards gloating, can do much for the experimenter's self-image and probably it also serves the enrichment of the subject's experience and knowledge [p. 339]." The fear held by some psychologists that debriefing only increases the chances that some Ss will tell other future Ss about the true purpose of certain experiments is not seen as such a threat by Rosenberg. He believes that mutual trust between E and S, formed by full and candid debriefing, will enhance cooperation. This view is similarly held by Jourard (1968), a critic of experimental psychology. McGuire (1969) also agrees that debriefing is desirable. It should be noted, however, that debriefing cannot always counteract possible negative consequences of the deception. Debriefing is a means by which possible damage stemming from deception may be reduced. In fact, a study by Walster, Bersheid, Abrahams, and Aronson (1967) supports this suspicion. They found that debriefing does not necessarily have an immediate effect in undoing the deception. In their study, they gave Ss false impressions about some aspect of their personalities. Even after debriefing had occurred, it was found that the self-evaluations of Ss immediately after the experimental session were a function of the false impressions created during the deception.

On the other hand, other psychologists such as Campbell (1969) have qualified their acceptance of debriefing. Campbell, in essence, feels that "no harm, no debriefing," since debriefing eventually leads to contamination of the naive Ss. He even suggests debriefing can be harmful to S since knowing that "one had been had" may lower one's self image. Campbell sees the nondebriefed S as one case where ignorance can be bliss.

Brock and Becker (1966) base their views on debriefing in terms of methodological considerations too. They suggest that minimal debriefing be provided for Ss who may be in similar experiments in the future. Such a criterion is for the benefit of E and is based solely on his need for naive Ss and shows little consideration for the well-being of Ss.

There does not appear to be an easy solution to the dilemma of deception for it is closely tied to methodological problems. It seems that there is an inverse relationship between the two aspects of deception. If we choose the most ethical procedures, we end up with methodological impasses while if we resolve our methodological problems, we come face to face with unresolved ethical issues.

We need more research aimed at the question of whether or not deception is harmful. If possible, impartial observers rather than the investigator himself should be employed for this evaluation. Similarly, more investigation of the effectiveness of debriefing is needed. It is appalling that little research has been done in these areas.

7

WHERE DO WE GO FROM HERE?

A number of problems confronting E as he goes about his research have been raised in the preceding pages. Limitations of the experimental method have been noted. Despite the controlled observation permitted by this approach, we have seen that experimental findings are often limited in generalizability. The features of laboratory research which give it preference over other methods (such as control and manipulation of variables) are the very same factors which produce the artificiality of the laboratory environment.

Some of the problems facing E which have been mentioned are readily resolved at least in theory. The loss of generalizability which comes from excessive use of college students as Ss, for example, can be remedied easily if psychologists would own up to the problem. Difficulties associated with the biasing effects of E-expectancies and E-attributes can also be handled without undue effort. Automated data collection, where possible, would be one solution. Other suggestions offered by Rosenthal (1966) have already been described.

A SOLUTION FOR DECEPTION?

A more troublesome dilemma is that of deception. More research is needed to understand the methodological problems created by the use of deception. Before we can institute procedures to solve this problem, we need more information on the effects of prior experience with deception on behavior in subsequent experiments.

Most discussions of problems of deception have focused on methodology, and not on ethics. Thus, solutions proposed have included the use of only naive Ss, limited or no debriefing, more clever and subtle deception. But rarely does one see a solution calling for elimination of deception. Such a proposal would be regarded as a cure worse than the disease for many psychologists.

One solution which is concerned with ethical problems of deception involves the use of role playing as a replacement for deception (e.g., Kelman, 1967). Under this method, no deception would actually be practiced. Instead, S would be informed about the full nature of the procedures and asked to role-play the behavior of an S who was in such an experiment. The S would not be an object of inquiry but a collaborator in the research. This technique would be free of the ethical problems associated with deception.

This alternative has not met with full acceptance. McGuire (1969) sees little future for such *public-opinion-polling* methods. Freedman (1969) is even more pessimistic, regarding it as totally unacceptable as a substitute for actual experiments, despite the flaws of the experimental method. He argues that "Role playing tells us what men think they would do. It does not tell us what men would actually do in the real situation [p. 114]." Thus, it does not appear that the use of role playing will be accepted as a substitute for the use of deception which will continue to be a problem for E.

A REMEDY FOR REACTIVITY?

Perhaps the most difficult methodological problem stems from the reactive nature of much psychological experimentation. When people know they are being-experimented-on, they often act differently from the way in which they usually behave. In the real world, people are not always being observed, and if they are, they are often unaware of it. To the extent that awareness of being observed modifies one's typical behavior, there is lessened generalizability or what Campbell (1957) calls *external validity* of laboratory findings.

A good example of the difficulties created by reactive aspects of experimentation can be found in the study of attitude change. Campbell (1957), Lana (1969), and Solomon (1949) have pointed out the sensitizing effects of pretests which are sometimes used in attitude studies to provide a measure of S's attitudes prior to receiving persuasive communication. The pretest, in combination with the message, may alert S to the intent of the communication. Lana reports that the effect of such sensitization has often been to reduce the amount of attitude change. Knowing that one is being subjected to persuasive communication may increase one's defenses or commitment to prior beliefs. Sometimes, however, demand characteristics of an attitude-change study may lead to enhanced change by those who are aware that they are being studied in an experiment (Silverman, 1968).

How can the problem of reactive arrangements be handled? One method would involve the use of indirect measures which are non-reactive (Webb, Campbell, Schwartz, & Sechrest, 1966) and can be made without the awareness of the person whose attitudes are being measured. These methods may often be inefficient or difficult to obtain but they avoid the limitations of direct assessment methods such as questionnaires and interviews. The awareness of being studied may lead respondents to distort their true attitudes to give socially desirable responses. In devising attitude-scale items, one must word them carefully to avoid contamination of results by various response sets (Cronbach, 1946) held by Ss such as acquiescence tendencies.

An example of a study of racial attitudes was done in an unobtrusive manner by Campbell, Kruskall, and Wallace (1966). They inferred attitudes by studying the seating patterns of white and black students in three different schools assumed to differ in racial attitudes. Contrived situations may also be devised for the study of attitudes indirectly. Milgram, Mann, and Harter (1965) employed the lost-letter technique (Merritt & Fowler, 1948) to infer the attitudes held in certain neighborhoods. They "lost" letters addressed to either the "Friends of the Nazi Party" or "Friends of the Communist Party." It was assumed that the return rate of the two types of letters might reflect political sympathies of the different neighborhoods.

These ingenious examples illustrate successful attempts to avoid the contaminating effects of reactivity. Of course the use of unobtrusive methods may be limited by practical considerations in some cases, or by ethical problems in others.

DISCREPANCIES BETWEEN FIELD AND LABORATORY FINDINGS

Another problem *E* must face which we have not discussed thus far is the dilemma when the conclusions based on laboratory research do not agree with those derived from natural observation. Such discrepancies exist in the area of attitude change (Hyman & Sheatsley, 1947). Hovland (1959), himself a significant contributor to the laboratory study of attitude change, attempted to reconcile the disagreement. He pointed out that the laboratory conditions usually produce more attitude change than that obtained under natural conditions. Thus, political campaigns conducted via the mass media often fail to effect much public opinion change (Lazarsfeld, Berelson, & Gaudet, 1948), whereas studies done with college students in Hovland's laboratory produce large changes.

Hovland noted that audiences in natural settings are more selective in what they attend to, such that those who agree with a given view will listen to advocates of that position. In contrast, people who disagree with certain views will not willingly expose themselves to messages advocating such views. The net effect would be little attitude change in natural settings. As Bauer (1964) terms it, the audience is "obstinate" and highly resistant to change.

Why then does substantial attitude change occur in the laboratory? One reason is that Ss are randomly assigned to different treatments in a laboratory study of attitude change, a situation which does not exist in the natural world.

Consider another example of differences between laboratory and naturalistic findings. Darley and Latané (1968) found that a fake emergency led to more help from S when he thought he was the only witness than when he thought there were others who could help. The explanation for this relationship was that there is a diffusion of responsibility when there are several witnesses. Each witness does not feel that it is his sole responsibility to help. But Piliavin, Rodin, and Piliavin (1969) contrived an emergency situation in which a stooge fainted in the New York subway. They found that many witnesses were willing to help even though they knew others were present. There was no evidence of diffusion of responsibility in this situation.

Which results are more valid—those from the laboratory or those from the natural setting? There is no easy answer to this question, but it is raised whenever the findings from the laboratory and natural setting do not agree.

A RETURN TO NATURE?

In view of the many difficulties besetting E, should he be discouraged and abandon this method in favor of nonexperimental techniques such as naturalistic observation? In the past, the virtues of the experiment have been praised while the limitations of naturalistic methods have been pointed out. It was maintained that only the former allow sound causal inferences, whereas the latter permit only suggestive correlational findings.

But in recent years, the growing awareness of the limitations of experiments has been accompanied by a reappraisal of the usefulness of naturalistic methods (Barker, 1963; Campbell & Stanley, 1963; Webb et al., 1966; Willems & Rausch, 1969). The current trend seems to be toward increased acceptance of the need for naturalistic research, either in its own right or as a complement for laboratory methods. McGuire (1967) has depicted this shift as stemming from rebellion against the prevalent laboratory orientation of the psychological "Establishment" by rebellious Young Turks.

There are some psychological phenomena which are intrinsically well suited for study by naturalistic methods, such as reactions to natural disasters or catastrophies (Barton, 1969; Wolfenstein, 1957). Unusual events such as the panic produced by the radio dramatization of an invasion from Mars (Cantril, Gaudet, & Herzog, 1940) or the response of members of a religious sect when their prophecies of the end of the world fail (Festinger, Riecken, & Schachter, 1956) cannot readily be studied under controlled conditions.

The study of phenomena such as those just described can be termed *field studies,* as distinguished from laboratory experiments or experiments which happen to be conducted in natural settings. Field studies involve the examination of some natural phenomena with as little intervention by the observing investigator as possible. He becomes a participant observer or relies on trained informants within the group he is investigating. Many anthropological and sociological studies fall in the category of field studies.

While the events recorded are occurring under realistic conditions, the investigator is limited in the type of conclusions he can draw. Since he has no control over variables in the situation, he is unable to make definitive conclusions about causal relationships. Most of his data is correlational. However, from his observations he may form many hypotheses which can often be subjected to experimental test in the laboratory, or in experiments conducted in the field setting.

The work of Deutsch and Collins (1951) on racial attitudes in government housing projects which were either interracially integrated or biracially segregated is a good illustration of a field study. By interviewing mostly white housewives, Deutsch and Collins found that more favorable racial attitudes existed in the integrated rather than the segregated housing units. The difficulty with this type of study, they realized, was that they could not be sure what caused the differences in attitudes. Was it the increased interracial contact per se which led to the better relations between the races?

Or were there other factors such as the possibility that the tenants in the differently arranged projects had different assumptions about what racial relations were deemed suitable and appropriate by the housing authorities. Based on this and similar studies, Cook (1969) has identified at least five different factors which could produce different attitudes under different racial patterns of housing. Thus, using field studies such as the Deutsch-Collins study as a means of generating hypotheses, Cook then devised a controlled field experiment to test such derivations.

The *field experiment* falls in between the field study and the laboratory experiment. It possesses the realism of the field situation but does not sacrifice the control associated with the laboratory experiment. Usually, field experiments also avoid the reactive feature of laboratory experiments. In a sense, one is bringing the laboratory into the real world when one conducts a field experiment.

Sherif and Sherif's (1953) study of cooperation and competition between rival gangs of juvenile boys during summer camp is a good example. Observations were made under controlled conditions in the real world without the awareness of the participants.

Conformity as a function of the status of models has been examined under natural conditions in a field experiment. Lefkowitz, Blake, and Mouton (1955) found more conformity in the form of walking across an intersection against the traffic light when models were attired in high-status clothing. A somewhat similar study by Doob and Gross (1968) examined latencies of horn-honking by motorists in cars behind cars of different statuses which did not advance immediately when the light turned green.

ETHICS AGAIN

In all of these examples, Ss were totally unaware that they were being observed, unlike Ss in a psychological experiment. Had they known that they were being observed, we might expect they would have altered their behavior.

There are a number of ethical problems associated with this sort of "Candid Camera" research. As French (1953) noted, one can and should give a full explanation after the study is over, but "even where this is done the temporary secrecy can be a serious disturbance to good relations [p. 127]."

Since Ss do not know they are in an experiment, one obviously does not have their permission or consent. How does one then go about obtaining it? Clearly, one cannot seek it before one makes the experimental observations. Should one bother informing Ss after the experiment? Campbell (1969) holds that it is not necessary since Ss themselves do not know they had been in an experiment. If one informed them that they had been experimented on, one would then also have to debrief them and tell them about the deception. Campbell allows that debriefing is necessary in laboratory experiments but warns against its widespread practice with disguised natural experiments since if we do, "we are doomed to wear out our laboratories [p. 372]." He doesn't feel that there would be invasion of privacy since the behavior observed would ordinarily be public anyway. Furthermore, debriefing should be mandatory only when there is possible harm, such as anxiety created by the deceptive treatment. In studies when no possible harm could occur, Campbell suggests that no debriefing be attempted. In this way, we help protect the supply of naive Ss.

Not all psychologists would agree with Campbell's views about the necessity of debriefing, but most would acknowledge the methodological advantages of disguised natural experiments. But could there not be some dangers in "tampering" with nature. Consider an experiment by Bryan and Test (1967) to study aiding behavior under naturalistic conditions. A "lady in distress" with a flat tire stood by her car at the roadside. The question of interest was whether more aid would be offered to her if drivers had just passed a similar situation back along the same road and witnessed a male helping a similar "lady in distress."

Now just suppose that all of this contrived roadside scenery distracted drivers and led to a serious accident. Would such an event be the responsibility of the Es who are outside the laboratory playing scientist? Perhaps this is an extreme example, but it is worth considering when planning disguised experiments in nature.

Willems and Rausch (1969) also recognize the ethical issues involved in certain forms of naturalistic research: "Under conditions of maximal unobtrusiveness, there is no built-in provision for consent and contractual arrangement by the subject [p. 280]." They ask, "Must the right to privacy, to choose to be recorded or not, be respected in all circumstances and all cases [p. 281]?"

The ethical dilemma is also acknowledged by Webb et al. (1966) in the preface to their imaginative compendium of unobtrusive measures. They allow that some of the methods they report may be unethical but add this caveat that "their inclusion is not intended as a warrant for their use." They do not take an explicit stand and admit purposely avoiding this topic because:

> We do not feel able at this point to prepare a compelling ethical resolution of these complex issues. Nonetheless we recognize the need of such a resolution and hope that our compilation will, among other things, stimulate and expedite thoughtful debate on these matters [p. vi].

WHERE DO WE GO FROM HERE?

Research—laboratory or naturalistic—each has its own ethical problems. Is the present trend toward more naturalistic research a remedy for the problems confronting the E? Although they recognize the usefulness of naturalistic methods, neither McGuire (1969) nor Freedman (1969) are about to relinquish their laboratory methods in favor of a return to nature.

Another staunch defender of the experimental method is Rosenberg (1969) who regards the current despair over research showing limitations of experimental method as unjustified. Although he commends advocates of naturalistic methods, he eloquently holds that:

> However, when such critics suggest that the experimental God is dead, they appear to have missed the point implicit in all research on the social psychology of the experiment . . . that the experimental method can readily be used to perfect, or at least significantly improve itself [p. 347].

One need not, of course, reach an either/or decision. Festinger (1953) calls for an interplay between laboratory experiments and the study of real-life situations. He points out that most of the ideas and hypotheses which are tested in laboratory studies in social psychology originate from observations of natural-setting behavior. But after having taken these ideas into the controlled laboratory, he warns:

> . . . that the results of laboratory experiments be tested out in real-life situations . . . A continuous interplay between laboratory experiments and studies of real-life situations should continually supply new hypotheses for building the theoretical structure and should represent progress in the solution of the problems of application and generalization [p. 141].

Unfortunately, his advice is not always heeded. Many psychologists do not bother to check their laboratory results with natural observations but rather check one experiment against still another experiment. If our ultimate goal is to understand real-life human behavior, we must recognize that the experiment is a means, and not the end in itself. We turn to the use of experiments because they have certain advantages over natural observations. They allow us controlled observations which in turn permit us to make causal inferences.

However, the experiment is not without its limitations. The purpose of the present volume has been to call attention to these problems. The existence of such problems need not cause us to abandon the use of the experimental method; rather, recognition of the limitations of experiments warns us against the misuse of or overreliance on this method. Such knowledge should aid us in better planning of the conduct of our experiments and lead us to continually check their results against natural observations.

REFERENCES

Adair, J. G., & Epstein, J. Verbal cues in the mediation of experimenter bias. Paper presented at the meeting of the Midwestern Psychological Association, Chicago, May, 1967.

Argyris, C. Some unintended effects of rigorous research. *Psychol. Bull.,* 1968, **70,** 185–197.

Aronson, E. Avoidance of inter-subject communication. *Psychol. Rep.,* 1966, **19,** 238.

Aronson, E., & Carlsmith, J. M. Experimentation in social psychology. In G. Lindzey & E. Aronson (Eds.), *Handbook of Social Psychology* (2nd ed.). Reading, Mass.: Addison-Wesley, 1968.

Barber, T. X., Calverley, D. S., Forgione, A., McPeake, J. D., Chaves, J. F., & Brown, B. Five attempts to replicate the experimenter bias effect. *J. cons. clin. Psychol.,* 1969, **33,** 1–6.

Barber, T. X., & Silver, M. J. Fact, fiction, and the experimenter bias effect. *Psychol. Bull. Monogr.,* 1968, **70,** 1–29. (a)

Barber, T. X., & Silver, M. J. Pitfalls in data analysis and interpretation: A reply to Rosenthal. *Psychol. Bull. Monogr.,* 1968, **70,** 48–62. (b)

Barker, R. (Ed.) *The stream of behavior.* New York: Appleton-Century-Crofts, 1963.

Barton, A. H. *Communities in disaster.* New York: Doubleday, 1969.

Bauer, R. A. The obstinate audience: The influence process from the point of view of social communication. *Amer. Psychologist,* 1964, **19,** 319–328.

Baumrind, D. Some thoughts on ethics of research: After reading Milgram's "Behavioral study of obedience." *Amer. Psychologist,* 1964, **19,** 421–423.

Beach, F. A. The snark was a boojum. *Amer. Psychologist,* 1950, **5,** 115–124.

Bell, C. R. Personality characteristics of volunteers for psychological studies. *Brit. J. soc. clin. Psychol.,* 1962, **1,** 81–95.

Benson, J. K., & Smith, J. O. The Harvard drug controversy: A case study of subject manipulation and social structure. In G. Sjoberg (Ed.), *Ethics, politics, and social research.* Cambridge, Mass.: Schenkman, 1967.

Bereiter, C., & Freedman, M. B. Fields of study and the people in them. In N. Sanford (Ed.), *The American college.* New York: John Wiley, 1962.

Berg, I. A. The use of human subjects in psychological research. *Amer. Psychologist,* 1954, **9,** 108–111.

Bexton, W. H., Heron, W., & Scott, T. H. Effects of decreased variation in the sensory environment. *Canad. J. Psychol.,* 1954, **8,** 70–76.

Binder, A., McConnell, D., & Sjoholm, N. A. Verbal conditioning as a function of experimenter characteristics. *J. abnorm. soc. Psychol.,* 1957, **55,** 309–314.

Bramel, D. A dissonance theory approach to defensive projection. *J. abnorm. soc. Psychol.,* 1962, **64,** 121–129.

Bramel, D. Selection of a target for defensive projection. *J. abnorm. soc. Psychol.,* 1963, **66,** 318–324.

Brehm, J. W. Motivational effects of cognitive dissonance. *Nebr. Sym. Motiv.* Lincoln: Univ. of Nebraska Press, 1962.

Brehm, J. W., & Cohen, A. R. *Explorations in cognitive dissonance.* New York: John Wiley, 1962.

Brock, T. C., & Becker, L. A. "Debriefing" and susceptibility to subsequent experimental manipulations. *J. exp. soc. Psychol.,* 1966, **2,** 314–323.

Bryan, J. H., & Test, M. A. Models and helping: Naturalistic studies in aiding behavior. *J. pers. soc. Psychol.,* 1967, **6,** 400–407.

Campbell, D. T. Factors relevant to the validity of experiments in social settings. *Psychol. Bull.,* 1957, **54,** 297–312.

Campbell, D. T. Perspective: Artifact and control. In R. Rosenthal &

R. L. Rosnow (Eds.), *Artifact in behavioral research.* New York: Academic Press, 1969.

Campbell, D. T., Kruskall, W. H., & Wallace, W. P. Seating aggregation as an index of attitude. *Sociometry,* 1966, **29,** 1–15.

Campbell, D. T., & Stanley, J. C. Experimental and quasi-experimental designs for research on teaching. In N. L. Gage (Ed.), *Handbook on research on teaching.* Chicago: Rand McNally, 1963.

Cantril, H., Gaudet, H., & Herzog, H. *Invasion from Mars.* Princeton, N.J.: Princeton Univ. Press, 1940.

Clark, K. E. *Dark ghetto: Dilemmas of social power.* New York: Harper & Row, 1965.

Conrad, H. S. Clearance of questionnaires with respect to "invasion of privacy," public sensitivities, ethical standards, etc. *Amer. Psychologist,* 1967, **22,** 356–359.

Cook, S. W. Motives in a conceptual analysis of attitude-related behavior. *Nebr. Symp. Motiv.,* Lincoln: Univ. of Nebraska Press, 1969, **17,** 179–231.

Cronbach, L. J. Response sets and test validity. *Educ. and Psychol. Measmt.,* 1946, **6,** 475–494.

Darley, J., & Latané, B. Bystander intervention in emergencies: Diffusion of responsibility. *J. pers. soc. Psychol.,* 1968, **6,** 377–383.

Deutsch, M., & Collins, M. E. *Interracial housing: A psychological evaluation of a social experiment.* Minneapolis: Univ. of Minnesota Press, 1951.

Doob, A. N., & Gross, A. E. Status of frustrator as an inhibitor of horn-honking responses. *J. soc. Psychol.,* 1968, **76,** 213–218.

Dulaney, D. E., Jr. The place of hypotheses and intentions: An analysis of verbal control in verbal conditioning. In C. W. Eriksen (Ed.), *Behavior and awareness.* Durham, N.C.: Duke Univ. Press, 1962.

Festinger, L. Laboratory experiments. In L. Festinger & D. Katz (Eds.), *Research methods in the behavioral sciences.* New York: Holt, Rinehart & Winston, 1953.

Festinger, L., & Carlsmith, J. Cognitive consequences of forced compliance. *J. abnorm. soc. Psychol.,* 1959, **56,** 203–210.

Festinger, L., Riecken, H. W., & Schachter, S. *When prophecy fails.* Minneapolis: Univ. of Minnesota Press, 1956.

Fillenbaum, S. Prior deception and subsequent experimental performance: The "faithful" subject. *J. pers. soc. Psychol.*, 1966, **4**, 532–537.

Freedman, J. L. Role playing: Psychology by consensus. *J. pers. soc. Psychol.*, 1969, **13**, 107–114.

Freedman, J. L., & Doob, A. *Deviancy.* New York: Academic Press, 1968.

French, J. Experiments in field settings. In L. Festinger & D. Katz (Eds.), *Research methods in the behavioral sciences.* New York: Holt, Rinehart & Winston, 1953.

Friedman, N. *The social nature of psychological research.* New York: Basic Books, 1967.

Golding, S. L., & Lichtenstein, E. Confession of awareness and prior knowledge of deception as a function of interview set and approval motivation *J. pers. soc. Psychol.*, 1970, **14**, 213–223.

Gustav, A. Students' attitudes toward compulsory participation in experiments. *J. Psychol.*, 1962, **53**, 119–125.

Harris, S., & Masling, J. Examiner sex, subject sex, and Rorschach productivity. *J. consult. clin. Psychol.*, 1970, **34**, 60–63.

Holmes, D. S. Amount of experience in experiments as a determinant of performance in later experiments. *J. pers. soc. Psychol.*, 1967, **7**, 403–407.

Holmes, D. S., & Applebaum, A. S. Nature of prior experimental experience as a determinant of performance in a subsequent experiment. *J. pers. soc. Psychol.*, 1970, **14**, 195–202.

Hovland, C. I. Reconciling conflicting results derived from experimental survey studies of attitude change. *Amer. Psychologist*, 1959, **14**, 8–17.

Hyman, H. H., & Sheatsley, P. B. Some reasons why information campaigns fail. *Publ. Opin. quart.*, 1947, **11**, 412–423.

Jackson, C. W., Jr., & Pollard, J. C. Sensory deprivation and suggestion: *Behav. Sci.*, 1962, **7**, 332–342.

Jourard, S. *Disclosing man to himself.* New York: Van Nostrand Reinhold, 1968.

Jung, J. Current practices and problems in the use of college students for psychological research. *Canad. Psychologist,* 1969, **10**, 280–290.

Kelman, H. C. Human use of human subjects: The problem of deception in social psychological experiments. *Psychol. Bull.*, 1967, **67**, 1–11.

Kennedy, J. J., Edwards, B. C., & Winstead, J. C. The effects of experimenter outcome expectancy in a verbal conditioning situation: A failure to detect the "Rosenthal effect." Unpublished MS, Univ. of Tennessee, 1968.

Kintz, B. L., Delprato, D. J., Mettee, D. R., Persons, C. E., & Schappe, R. H. The experimenter effect. *Psychol. Bull.*, 1965, **63,** 223–232.

Krasner, L. Studies of the conditioning of verbal behavior. *Psychol. Bull.*, 1958, **55,** 148–170.

Lana, R. E. Pretest sensitization. In R. Rosenthal & R. L. Rosnow (Eds.), *Artifact in behavioral research.* New York: Academic Press, 1969.

Lasagna, L., & Felsinger, J. M. von. The volunteer subject in research. *Science,* 1954, **120,** 359–361.

Lazarsfeld, P. F., Berelson, B., & Gaudet, H. *The people's choice.* New York: Columbia Univ. Press, 1948.

Lefkowitz, M., Blake, R. R., & Mouton, J. S. Status factors in pedestrian violation of traffic signals. *J. abnorm. soc. Psychol.,* 1955, **51,** 704–706.

Leipold, W. D., & James, R. L. Characteristics of shows and no-shows in a psychological experiment. *Psychol. Rep.,* 1962, **11,** 171–174.

Lester, D. The subject as a source of bias in psychological research. *J. gen. Psychol.,* 1969, **81,** 237–248.

Levitt, E. E., Lubin, B., & Brady, J. P. The effect of the pseudo-volunteer on studies of volunteers for psychology experiments. *J. appl. Psychol.,* 1962, **46,** 72–75.

Levy, L. Awareness, learning, and the beneficent subject as expert witness. *J. pers. soc. Psychol.,* 1967, **6,** 363–370.

Lockard, R. B. The albino rat: A defensible choice or a bad habit? *Amer. Psychologist,* 1968, **23,** 734–742.

Lovell, V. R. The human use of personality tests: A dissenting view. *Amer. Psychologist,* 1967, **22,** 383.

Lyons, J. On the psychology of the psychological experiment. In C. Scheerer (Ed.), *Cognition-theory, research, promise.* New York: Harper & Row, 1964.

Martin, R. M., & Marcuse, F. L. Characteristics of volunteers and non-volunteers in psychological experimentation. *J. consult. Psychol.,* 1958, **22,** 475–479.

Masling, J. The effects of warm and cold interaction on the interpretation of a projective protocol. *J. proj. Tech.,* 1957, **21,** 377–383.

Masling, J. The effects of warm and cold interaction on the administration and scoring of an intelligence test. *J. consult. Psychol.,* 1959, **23,** 336–341.

Masling, J. Role-related behavior of the subject and psychologist and its effects upon psychological data. *Nebr. Symp. Motiv.,* Lincoln: Univ. of Nebraska Press, 1966, **14,** 67–103.

McGuigan, F. J. The experimenter: A neglected stimulus object. *Psychol. Bull.,* 1963, **60,** 421–428.

McGuire, W. J. Some impending reorientations in social psychology: Some thoughts provoked by Kenneth Ring. *J. exp. soc. Psychol.,* 1967, **3,** 124–139.

McGuire, W. J. Suspiciousness of experimenter's intent. In R. Rosenthal & R. L. Rosnow (Eds.), *Artifact in behavioral research.* New York: Academic Press, 1969.

Merritt, C. B., & Fowler, R. G. The pecuniary honesty of the public at large. *J. abnorm. soc. Psychol.,* 1948, **43,** 90–93.

Milgram, S. Behavioral study of obedience. *J. abnorm. soc. Psychol.,* 1963, **67,** 371–378.

Milgram, S. Issues in the study of obedience: A reply to Baumrind. *Amer. Psychologist,* 1964, **19,** 848–852.

Milgram, S. Some conditions of obedience and disobedience to authority. *Hum. Relat.,* 1965, **18,** 57–76.

Milgram, S., Mann, L., & Harter, S. The lost-letter technique: A tool of social research. *Publ. Opin. quart.,* 1965, **29,** 437–438.

Orne, M. T. The nature of hypnosis: Artifact and essence. *J. abnorm. soc. Psychol.,* 1959, **58,** 277–299.

Orne, M. T. On the social psychology of the psychological experiment: With particular reference to demand characteristics and their implications. *Amer. Psychologist,* 1962, **17,** 776–783.

Orne, M. T. Demand characteristics and the concept of quasi-controls. In R. Rosenthal and R. L. Rosnow (Eds.), *Artifact in behavioral research.* New York: Academic Press, 1969.

Orne, M. T., & Evans, F. J. Social control in the psychological experiment: Antisocial behavior and hypnosis. *J. pers. soc. Psychol.,* 1965, **1,** 189–200.

Orne, M. T., & Holland, C. H. On the ecological validity of laboratory deceptions. *Int. J. Psychiat.,* 1968, **6,** 282–293.

Orne, M. T., & Scheibe, K. E. The contribution of nondeprivation factors in the production of sensory deprivation effects: The psychology of the "panic button." *J. abnorm. soc. Psychol.,* 1964, **68,** 3–12.

Panel on privacy and behavioral research. *Privacy and behavioral research.* Washington D.C.: Office of Science and Technology, 1967.

Pfungst, O. *Clever Hans (the horse of Mr. von Osten): A contribution to experimental, animal, and human psychology* (Trans. by C. L. Rahn). New York: Holt, Rinehart & Winston, 1911. (Republished, 1965.)

Piliavin, I. M., Rodin, J., & Piliavin, J. A. Good samaritanism: An underground phenomenon? *J. pers. soc. Psychol.,* 1969, **13,** 289–299.

Riecken, H. W. A program for research on experiments in social psychology. In N. F. Washburne (Ed.), *Decisions, values and groups,* Vol. 2. New York: Pergamon Press, 1962.

Ring, K. Experimental social psychology: Some sober questions about some frivolous values. *J. exp. soc. Psychol.,* 1967, **3,** 113–123.

Roethlisberger, F. J., & Dickson, W. J. *Management and the worker.* Cambridge, Mass.: Harvard Univ. Press, 1939.

Rosenberg, M. J. When dissonance fails: On eliminating evaluation apprehension from attitude measurement. *J. pers. soc. Psychol.,* 1965, **1,** 18–42.

Rosenberg, M. J. The conditions and consequences of evaluation apprehension. In R. Rosenthal & R. L. Rosnow (Eds.), *Artifact in behavioral research.* New York: Academic Press, 1969.

Rosenthal, R. Experimenter attributes as determinants of subjects' responses. *J. proj. tech. & pers. Assess.,* 1963, **27,** 324–331. (a)

Rosenthal, R. On the social psychology of the psychological experiment: The experimenter's hypothesis as unintended determinant of experimental results. *Amer. Scient.,* 1963, **51,** 268–283. (b)

Rosenthal, R. The volunteer subject. *Hum. Relat.,* 1965, **18,** 389–406.

Rosenthal, R. *Experimenter effects in behavioral research.* New York: Appleton-Century-Crofts, 1966.

Rosenthal, R. Covert communication in the psychological experiment. *Psychol. Bull.,* 1967, **67,** 356–367.

Rosenthal, R. Experimenter expectancy and the reassuring nature of the null hypothesis decision procedure. *Psychol. Bull. Monogr.,* 1968, **70,** 30–47.

Rosenthal, R. Interpersonal expectations: Effects of the experimenter's hypothesis. In R. Rosenthal & R. L. Rosnow (Eds.),

Artifact in behavioral research. New York: Academic Press, 1969.

Rosenthal, R. & Fode, K. L. The problem of experimenter outcome-bias. In D. P. Ray (Ed.), *Series research in social psychology.* Symposia studies series, No. 8, Washington, D.C.: National Institute of Social and Behavioral Science, 1961.

Rosenthal, R., & Fode, K. L. The effect of experimenter bias on the performance of the albino rat. *Behav. Sci.,* 1963, **8,** 183–189.

Rosenthal, R., & Jacobson, L. *Pygmalion in the classroom: Teacher expectation and pupils' intellectual development.* New York: Holt, Rinehart & Winston, 1968

Rosenthal, R., Persinger, G. W., Vikan-Kline, L., & Mulry, R. The role of the research assistant in the mediation of experimenter bias, *J. pers.,* 1963, **31,** 313–335.

Rosenthal, R., & Rosnow, R. L. The volunteer subject. In R. Rosenthal & R. L. Rosnow (Eds.), *Artifact and behavioral research.* New York: Academic Press, 1969

Rosensweig, S. The experimental situation as a psychological problem. *Psychol. Rev.,* 1933, **40,** 337–354.

Rosnow R. L. & Rosenthal, R. Volunteer subjects and the results of opinion change studies. *Psychol. Rep.,* 1966, **19,** 1183–1187.

Rosnow, R. L., & Rosenthal, R. Volunteer effects in behavioral research. In T. M. Newcomb (Ed.), *New directions in psychology. IV.* New York: Holt, Rinehart & Winston, 1970.

Rowland, L. W. Will hypnotized persons try to harm themselves or others? *J. abnorm. soc. Psychol.,* 1939, **34,** 114–117.

Ruebhausen, O. H., & Brim, O. G., Jr. Privacy and behavioral research. *Amer. Psychologist,* 1966, **21,** 423–437.

Sasson, R., & Nelson, T. M. The human experimental subject in context. *Canad. Psychologist,* 1969, **10,** 409–437.

Sattler, J. Racial "experimenter effects" in experimentation, testing, interviewing, and psychotherapy. *Psychol Bull.,* 1970, **73,** 137–160.

Schultz, D. P. The human subject in psychological research. *Psychol. Bull.,* 1969, **72,** 214–228.

Seeman, J. Deception in psychological research. *Amer. Psychologist,* 1969, **24,** 1025–1028.

Shapiro, A. K. A contribution to a history of the placebo effect. *Behav. Sci.,* 1960, **5,** 109–135.

Sherif, M., & Sherif, C. W. *Groups in harmony and tension.* New York: Harper & Row, 1953.

Sigall, H., Aronson, E., & Van Hoose, T. The cooperative subject: Myth or realty. *J. exp. soc. Psychol.,* 1970, **6,** 1–10.

Silverman, I. Role-related behavior of subjects in laboratory studies in attitude change. *J. pers. soc. Psychol.,* 1968, **8,** 343–348.

Silverman, I., & Shulman, A. D. A conceptual model of artifact in attitude change studies. *Sociometry,* 1970, **33,** 97–107.

Silverman, I., Shulman, A., & Weisenthal, D. L. Effects of deceiving and debriefing psychological subjects on performance in later experiments. *J. pers. soc. Psychol.,* 1970, **14,** 203–212.

Smart, R. Subject selection bias in psychological research. *Canad. Psychologist,* 1966, **7a,** 115–121.

Solomon, R. L. An extension of control group design. *Psychol. Bull.,* 1949, **46,** 137–150.

Sommer, R. Hawthorne dogma. *Psychol. Bull.,* 1968, **70,** 592–595.

Spielberger, C. D. Theoretical and epistemological issues in verbal conditioning. In S. Rosenberg (Ed.), *Directions in psycholinguistics.* New York: Macmillan, 1965.

Spires, A. M. Subject-experimenter interaction in verbal conditioning. Unpublished doctoral dissertation, New York University, 1960.

Sternberg, C. Personality trait patterns of college students majoring in different fields. *Psychol. Monogr.,* 1955, **69,** No. 18 (whole No. 403).

Stricker, L. J. The true deceiver. *Psychol. Bull.,* 1967, **68,** 13–20.

Stricker, L. J., Messick, S., and Jackson, D. N., Evaluating deception in psychological research. *Psychol. Bull.,* 1969, **71,** 343–351.

Underwood, B. J. Interference and forgetting. *Psychol. Rev.,* 1957, **64,** 49–60.

Valins S. Cognitive effects of false heart-rate feedback. *J. pers. soc. Psychol.,* 1966, **4,** 400–408.

Walster, E., Berscheid, E., Abrahams, D., & Aronson, V. Effectiveness of debriefing following deception experiements. *J. pers. soc. Psychol.,* 1967, **6,** 371–380.

Walters, C., Shurley, J. T., & Parsons, O. A. Difference in male and female responses to underwater sensory deprivation: An exploratory study. *J. nerv. ment. Dis.,* 1962, **135,** 302–310.

Webb, E. J., Campbell, D. T., Schwartz, R. D., & Sechrest, L. *Unobstrusive measures: Nonreactive research in the social sciences.* Chicago: Rand McNally, 1966.

Willems, E. P., & Rausch, H. L. (Eds.) *Naturalistic viewpoints in psychological research.* New York: Holt, Rinehart & Winston, 1969.

Wolfensberger, I. Ethical issues in research with human subjects. *Science,* 1967, **155,** 48–59.

Wolfenstein, M. *Disaster: A psychological essay.* New York: Free Press, 1957.

Wuebben, P. L. Honesty of subjects and birth order. *J. pers. soc. Psychol.,* 1967, **5,** 350–352.

Young, P. C. Antisocial uses of hypnosis. In L. M. LeCron (Ed.), *Experimental hypnosis.* New York: Macmillan, 1952.

SELECTED READINGS

1

A LETTER FROM *S* TO *E*
Sidney M. Jourard

For some time now I have been talking to people who have served as subjects (Ss) in psychologists' experiments. They have told me of their experience, and it has troubled me. I want to share my concern with my colleagues. The letter that follows is my effort to consolidate the attitudes and feelings of the people to whom I talked.

Dear *E* (Experimenter):

My name is *S*. You don't know me. I have another name my friends call me by, but I drop it, and become *S* no. 27 as soon as I take part in your research. I serve in your surveys and experiments. I answer your questions, fill out questionnaires, let you wire me up to various machines that record my physiological reactions. I pull levers, flip switches, track moving targets, trace mazes, learn nonsense syllables, tell you what I see in inkblots—do the whole barrage of things you ask me to do. I have started to wonder why I do these things for you. What's in it for me? Sometimes you pay me to serve. More often I have to serve, because I'm a student in a beginning psychology course, and I'm told that I won't receive a grade unless I take part in at least two studies; and if I take part in more, I'll get extra points on the final exam. I am part of the Department's "subject-pool."

When I've asked you what I'll get out of your studies, you tell me that, "It's for Science." When you are running some one particular study, you often lie to me about your purpose. You mislead me. It's getting so I find it difficult to trust you. I'm beginning to see you as a trickster, a manipulator. I don't like it.

In fact, I lie to you a lot of the time, even on anonymous questionnaires. When I don't lie, I will sometimes just answer at random, anything to get through with the hour, and back to my own affairs. Then, too, I can often figure out just what it is you are trying to do, what you'd like me to say or do; at those times, I decide to go along with your wishes if I like you, or foul you up if I don't. You don't actually say what your hopes or hypotheses are; but the very setup in your laboratory, the alternatives you give me, the instructions you offer, all work together to pressure me to say or do something in particular. It's as if you are whispering in my ear, "When the light comes on, pull the *left* switch," and then you forget or deny that you have whispered. But I get the message. And I pull the right or the left one, depending on how I feel toward you.

You know, even when you are not in the room—when you are just the printed instructions on the questionnaire or the voice on the tape recorder that tells me what I am supposed to do—I wonder about you. I wonder who you are, what you are *really* up to. I wonder what you are going to do with the "behavior" I give you. Who are you going to show my answers to? Who is going to see the marks I leave on your response-recorders? Do you have any interest at all in what I think, feel, and imagine as I make the marks you are so eager to study and analyze? Certainly, you never ask me what I mean by them. If you asked, I'd be glad to tell you. As a matter of fact, I do tell my roommate or my girl friend what I thought your experiment was about and what I meant when I did what I did. If my roommate could trust you, he could probably give you a better idea of what your data (my answers and responses) mean that the idea you presently have. God knows how much good psychology has gone down the drain, when my roommate and I discuss your experiment and my part in it, at the beer-joint.

As a matter of fact, I'm getting pretty tired of being S. It's too much like being a punched IBM card in the University registrar's office. I feel myself being pressured, bulldozed, tricked, manipulated everywhere I turn. Advertisements in magazines and commercials on TV, political speeches, salesmen, and con men of all kinds put pressure on me to get me to buy, say, or do things that I suspect are not for my good at all. Just for their good, the good of their pocketbooks. Do you sell your "expert knowledge" about me to these people? If that's true, then you're really not in good faith with me. You have told me that when I show myself to you and let you study me, that in the long run it will be for my good. I'm not convinced. You really seem to be studying me in order to learn how to influence my attitudes and my actions without my realizing it. I resent this more than *you* realize. It's not fair for you to get me to show how I can be influenced and then for you to pass this information along to the people who pay your salary, or who give you the money to equip your laboratory. I feel used, and I don't like it. But I protect myself by not showing you my whole self, or by lying. Did you ever stop to think that your articles, and the textbooks you write, the theories you spin—all based on your data (my disclosures to you)—may actually be a tissue of lies and half-truths (my lies and the half truths) or a joke I've played on you because I don't like you or trust you? That should give you cause for some concern.

Now look, Mr. *E*, I'm not "paranoid," as you might say. Nor am I stupid. And I do believe some good can come out of my serving in your research. Even some good for me. I'm not entirely selfish, and I would be glad to offer myself up for study, to help others. But some things have to change first. Will you listen to me? Here is what I would like from you researchers:

I'd like you to help me gain a better understanding of what has made me the way I am today. I'd like to know this because I want to be more free than I feel. I would like to discover more of my own potentialities. I'd like to be more whole, more courageous, more enlightened. I'd like to be able to experience more, learn better, remember better, and express myself more fully. I'd like to learn how to recognize and overcome the pressures of other people's influence, of my background, that interfere with my going in the paths I choose. Now, if you would promise to help me in these ways, I would gladly come into your lab and virtually strip my body and soul naked. I would be there *meaning* to show you everything I could that was relevant to your particular interest of the moment. And I can assure you, that is different from what I have been showing you thus far, which is as little as I can. In fact, I cross my fingers when I'm in your lab, and say to myself, "What I've just said or done here *is not me*." Wouldn't you like that to change?

If you'll trust me, I'll trust you, if you're trustworthy. I'd like you to take the time and trouble to get acquainted with me as a person, before we go through your experimental procedures. And I'd like to get to know you and what you are up to, to see if I would like to expose myself to you. Sometimes, you remind me of physicians. They look at me as the unimportant envelope that conceals the disease they are really interested in. You have looked at me as the unimportant package that contains "responses," and this is all I am for you. Let me tell you that when I feel this, I get back at you. I give you responses, all right; but you will never know what I meant by them. You know, I can speak, not just in words, but with my action. And when you have thought I was responding to a "stimulus" in your lab, my response was really directed at *you*; and what I meant by it was, "Take this, you unpleasant so-and-so." Does that surprise you? It shouldn't.

Another thing. Those tests of yours that have built-in gimmicks to see if I'm being consistent, or deliberately lying, or just answering at random—they don't fool me. Actually, they wouldn't be necessary if you would get on the level with me. There are enough con men in the world, without your joining their number. I would hope that psychologists would be more trustworthy than politicians or salesmen.

I'll make a bargain with you. You show me that you are doing your researches *for me*—to help me become freer, more self-understanding, better able to control *myself*—and I'll make myself available to you in any way you ask. And I won't play jokes and tricks on you. I don't want to *be controlled*, not by you or anyone else. And I don't want to control other people. I don't want you to help other people to understand how I am or can be "controlled," so that they can then control me. Show me that you are for me, and I will show *myself* to you.

You work for me, Mr. *E*, and I'll truly work for you. Between us, we may produce a psychology that is more authentic and more liberating.

Yours sincerely,

S

2

A PROGRAM FOR RESEARCH ON
EXPERIMENTS IN SOCIAL PSYCHOLOGY
Henry W. Riecken

The present paper is a first attempt to outline a problem in empirical social psychology and to suggest some ways of attacking it. Stated abstractly, the problem is the identification and analysis of some sources of unintended variance in the data collected during an experiment. In more concrete terms, we may think of the problem as understanding those features of persons, situations and events that are unintentionally (from the point of view of the experimenter) present or introduced into the process of data collection and that are responsible for unexpected (and, usually, undesired) variation in the behavior of subjects.

Such variation is ordinarily regarded as "error," reflecting some mistake in procedure on the part of the investigator. From this standpoint, the problem under scrutiny can be seen as an investigation of ways of improving experimentation. On the other hand, a broader perspective on the problem reveals it as a series of more fundamental questions about human interaction, interpersonal relations, or social behavior. The process of collecting data about human behavior is itself a social process and shares features in common with other situations and events of human interaction. Accordingly, the process of data collection

From H. W. Riecken. In N. F. Washburne (Ed.), *Decisions, values, and groups.* Vol. 2. New York: Pergamon Press, 1962. With permission of author and publisher.

The present paper is a shortened version of a background paper prepared at the Behavioral Sciences Conference at the University of New Mexico in the summer of 1958. The conference was supported by the Air Force Office of Scientific Research, Behavioral Sciences Division, under Contract AF 49(638)–33. The assistance provided by AFOSR and the University of New Mexico is hereby gratefully acknowledged.

can be studied as a particular type of interaction in a particular social situation. A major task of this paper will be to examine the particular features of the social situation in which data are collected and the processes of negotiation[1] between investigator and subject through which they come to understand how to behave in the situation.

In fact, the range of interest in this paper will be narrower than the process of data collection in general. I want to confine attention to matters that typically arise in experimental social psychology in American universities, omitting for the moment the interesting problems that occur in participant observation, public opinion poll interviewing and field studies of communities, organizations and social processes. This restriction comes from both my interest in and familiarity with laboratory experiments and from the need to cut the task down to manageable size. At a later time I hope to deal with the specific problems of these other types of research.

Furthermore, I want to concentrate on certain aspects of the laboratory experiment that have been largely overlooked or underemphasized, namely those assumptions and inferences that experimenter and subject make about the social character of each other and about the nature of the experiment as a social situation. In other words, I want to examine how subject and experimenter "make sense of" the situation of the experiment and of each other as social types. Some of the possible sources of unintended variance have been occasionally glimpsed, by design or by accident, in social psychological research; and the citation of some examples may clarify the nature of my interest. For example, the relationship between subject and experimenter may make a difference in subject's behavior. Birney's (1958) replication of Lowell's research on need achievement and task performance demonstrates that a faculty experimenter induces different performance levels in subjects than does a graduate student experimenter. Elinor Sachs' (1952) study of measured intelligence in nursery school children indicates that a warm, friendly relation between subject and test administrator can

[1] I am indebted to Harold Garfinkel for calling my attention to this notion which he encountered in some unpublished material of Erving Goffman's. In addition, I should like to thank Dr. Garfinkel for suggestions and helpful criticism at many other points in the paper.

"elevate" a child's IQ, while a cold, distant relationship may have an opposite effect. Concrete evidence of this sort does not occur frequently in the literature; but similar sorts of effects are known or suspected by many practicing experimenters, whose anecdotes, hunches, suspicions and speculations can further the inquiry at hand. The first job, however, is to provide a framework for organizing these causal observations and impressions.

The framework I should like to adopt is suggested by Goffman (1959) in his analysis of everyday interaction, namely the appearance (or "image" or "impression") that people in social contact with each other try to create and maintain. Goffman puts it this way: "I shall consider the way in which the individual in ordinary . . . situations presents himself and his activity to others, the ways in which he guides and controls the impression they form of him, and the kinds of things he may and may not do while sustaining his performance before them" (1958, preface). (It should be noted that this way of putting things does not imply either an interest in the correspondence between "appearance" and "reality"; nor a necessary implication that people in ordinary social interaction are deliberately and self-consciously "playing a part.")

Goffman's view of interaction is echoed in a statement by Kahn and Cannell (1958) in the course of describing communication in the interview:

> . . . we have developed ways and habits of reacting to each other that are not intended to simplify or facilitate the process [of communication]. They are designed in large part to help us protect ourselves against making some undesirable revelation or against putting ourselves in an unfavorable light. They are man's methods of defending himself against the possibility of being made to look ridiculous or inadequate. And in most cases we are not content merely to avoid looking inadequate, we also want to appear intelligent, thoughtful, or in possession of whatever other virtues are relevant to the situation from our point of view. We want to put our best foot forward.

Precisely. Everyone wants to put his best foot forward and certainly subjects in an experiment want to display "whatever other virtues are relevant." The crucial question is: how does the subject in an experiment decide what virtues are relevant and what faults must be concealed? To find our answer to this question we shall look first at the features of the experiment as a social situation and second at the process of negotiation between subject and experimenter whereby the former decides what qualities he will see as "relevant."

THE EXPERIMENT AS A SOCIAL SITUATION

The most outstanding feature of the experiment as a social situation is that it is an invitation for one person to behave under the scrutiny of another. It is usually an invitation rather than a command and the fact that the invitation is accepted implies that the subject anticipates or seeks some rewards for his participation. Sometimes these rewards are obvious: pay, academic credit, opportunity to win a prize, or simply the gratitude of the experimenter. There is reason to believe that these "obvious" rewards do not exhaust the possible returns a subject can get, however, for there is some evidence that subjects also see the experiment as an opportunity to learn more about how psychology is practiced; to learn some things about himself— his traits, abilities and defects as a person, as these are revealed by psychological techniques; and even to receive some help in solving personal problems. In one sense, then, the subject may have his own set of private reasons or purposes for participating in the experiment. To be sure, these purposes and the corresponding expectations on the part of the subject as to what opportunities the experiment will offer for his purposes to be fulfilled are ordinarily "specifically vague."

The major reason they are "specifically vague" comes from a second feature of the experiment, namely that the terms of the invitation to behave are usually not well specified. In his initial invitation, the experimenter usually specifies only a few items, such as the time, place and duration of the experimental session and, at most, outlines vaguely the "purpose" of the experiment. He leaves much to be revealed progressively as the experimental session itself unfolds. On the other hand, the subject is not completely unprepared for what is going to happen in the session for he usually has some notions about both what psychologists are interested in and how they go about gratifying these interests; he also has some ideas about the limits of appropriate behavior. (Just what the contents of these notions are is not presently clear, but presumably they could be investigated.)

The third feature of the experiment I want to examine is the nature of the personages (or roles) involved. In most cases the experimenter is a professor and the subject a student. They have a relationship that has a history and a socially defined character.

The experimenter is a teacher who offers no course but may nonetheless teach the subject something—about himself. While he has no grade to give, the experimenter may still "grade" the subject in terms of quality of performance, co-operativeness, effort and the like. Like the earlier figures who have stood *in loco parentis* for the subject, this experimenter-professor has responsibilities toward his students and is bound to protect as well as guide them. He is, in the common sense meaning of the term, trustworthy. Furthermore, he is rational, serious and purposive. He may be eccentric; but he is not a lunatic, a prankster or an idler. His behavior is explicable in terms of the scheme of motives, purposes, and norms that govern the academic community.

But this particular professor has another aspect, for he is also a psychologist, whose job it is to poke and pry into recesses of the person that are not ordinarily open to view. The things a psychologist may uncover about one may be gratifying or shame-provoking, but they are likely to be true since the psychologist reputedly has special tools and techniques that enable him to penetrate at least the common human disguises. He can see more than one wants him to see. There is some suspicion that his techniques are incompletely effective and that he makes mistakes, but also an uneasy feeling that he may make fewer mistakes than his victims joke about.

The experimenter then is a powerful figure. He has two kinds of power: as a professor, he is a member of the superordinate group that has the power of effective evaluation over students; as a psychologist he has the power of insight into the subject. Furthermore, one can afford to feel ambivalent toward him. On the one hand, he is trustworthy in that he will not knowingly risk the subject's life, steal or physically attack him. On the other hand, he is up to the same trick that all teachers are up to: divining the true character of the pupil, assessing his worth and passing judgment on him. In so doing he may expose the subject's pretenses, inflict humiliation and mental pain. Furthermore, he is especially able to do all these things because he has fortified himself with the skills and paraphernalia of "modern psychology."

Such a picture is, of course, one-sided. Teachers and psychologists can be gulled; and they can, with some risk, be defied. If defied in an experiment psychologist-teachers have rather limited means of retaliation: withholding gratitude, academic credit or pay. These penalties may not be enough to dissuade defiance when the task demanded or the insult delivered is great. On the other hand, the appearance of docility and cooperativeness (within limits) may be a superior strategy for the subject who is playing safe by trying to get a good evaluation of himself from the professor.

A fourth important feature of the experiment as a social situation is that it is temporally and spatially set apart from everyday life—at least from the point of view of the experimenter. The experimenter usually wants to use the subject as an instance of behavior, use him just one time, and then forget everything about him except the data he has produced. He views the subject as a more or less typical human being and his behavior as a more or less typical instance of what human beings would do under the conditions of the experiment. He is ordinarily not interested in the subject's past or his future prospects but sees him only as a producer of raw data.

It may be that the subject sees the situation differently, however, and may either hope for or fear greater continuity. In the first place, the subject may be unable to accept the indignity of being viewed as just another instance of general human behavior and may wish to be appreciated for the unique individual that he considers himself to be. Thus, he may see the experiment as an opportunity to make a good impression on a member of the faculty at his university or as an opportunity to be inducted into the mysteries of behavioral science and thus begin a career (however peripheral) as an "insider." In the second place, the subject may fear that the experimenter cannot or will not take such a detached view of him but will, instead, take an evaluative view of his performance and will make some use of this information to affect some future enterprise in which the subject may be engaged. It is probably difficult for subjects to accept fully the assurances of the experimenter about anonymity and protection of personal data from the scrutiny of those who could use it to evaluate the subject. Further, in all his previous experience with teachers the subject has undoubtedly learned that they are capable of invoking past performances both "in" and "out" of school as the basis for present judgments and recommendations for the future. The nature of the subject's anxieties may be vague and far ranging: he may believe that his performance in the experiment will literally become a part of his academic record; or he may simply entertain the vague notion that in future occasional or accidental encounters the experimenter will treat him in terms of how he performed in the experiment. In any event, the subject's question is: "What will he think of me?"

Finally, I want to call attention to a fifth feature of the experiment as a social situation, namely the one-sided distribution of information. Even after the experimental session has begun and the task has been explained to the subject, the experimenter typically withholds information and the subject knows that he is doing so. The experimenter may conceal or misrepresent the purpose of his experiment; but even when he does not, he still conceals "the right answer." He plays, almost like an examiner, a serious game with the subject, inviting the latter to behave under specified conditions but revealing neither what the experimenter regards as the "right answer" nor even the criteria by which a particular answer will be judged. The experimenter may provide some hints by indicating what a *relevant* answer is —e.g., when he provides a questionnaire or rating scale—and these hints may help the subject guide his interpretation of the situation, but "the right answer" remains the property of the matter of these ceremonies until the program is over.

Sometimes the psychologist tells the subject: "There is no right or wrong answer. The best answer is your own opinion." In one sense, the psychologist literally means this instruction; yet in another he does not, for he ordinarily knows what interpretation will be given to each possible answer. Now the subject is not such a fool as the experimenter wants to make him out. He suspects that various answers are right and wrong to the extent that they represent him to the experimenter in the light that he (the subject) wishes to appear—that there are answers that will enhance and that will diminish his value as a person.

The fact that the experimenter controls the information available to the subject and that he never reveals completely what he is trying to discover and how he will judge what he observes —this feature gives the experiment much of its character as a game or contest. It leads to a set of inferential and interpretive activities on the part of the subject in an effort to penetrate the experimenter's inscrutability and to arrive at some conception of the meaning that the unrevealed categories of response have for the latter.

In the light of these five features of the experiment—its invitational quality, the unspecified nature of the invitation's terms, the attributes of the relationship between the two principal personages (subject and experimenter), the temporal and spatial segregation of the experience and the one-sidedness of the distribution of information—it is easy to see how the subject is impelled to "put his best foot forward." He attempts to appear in the best possible light within the constraints imposed by the situation, by concealing or exhibiting, exaggerating or belittling those qualities he believes will be positively and negatively evaluated in the particular experiment.

Granted this much, the problem now becomes: how does the subject decide in a particular instance what he will see as relevant to the situation and what sign (positive or negative) he will see any relevant act as having? The general answer will be that the subject decides the answers to these questions progressively as the interaction between himself and the experimenter proceeds. I believe that the subject enters the experimental situation with rather broad and vague expectations that become progressively more explicit (although perhaps never fully explicit) and definite as the experiment proceeds. That is, the subject has formed, at any particular point in the sequence of events of the experiment, a working definition of the situation, which is open to change and elaboration as the experiment proceeds (and even after it is over). The working definition is assembled from the material at hand, namely what the subject knows, believes or suspects about psychological experimentation before he starts the experimental session; what the experimenter says, does (and perhaps leaves unsaid); and what the scene—the physical and social environment—furnishes in the way of information. I want to conceive the process of forming a working definition of the situation as a process of negotiation between subject and experimenter, and I should like to begin examining this negotiation by looking at what the experimenter says and does in the conjectural light of how his words and deeds are interpreted and used by the subject to govern the "line" that the latter will take.

Negotiating an Understanding Between
Experimenter and Subject

In order to understand the process of negotiating a definition of the experimental situation, we must examine what happens during the experimental session, especially in its early phases, from the viewpoint of both the subject and the experimenter; and we must understand one important aspect of the process, namely its overt one-sidedness and the predetermined course.

Just as the distribution of information is one-sided, so is the negotiation. Characteristically, the experimenter gives the instructions, decides when the action starts and stops and hands out the measuring instruments. The experimenter does the talking while the subject listens. The latter is a status subordinate who presumably listens in order to find his place in the situation—a situation that is oriented around the experimenter's purposes. Typically, the subject asks, "What do you want from me?" Furthermore, the experimenter assumes that the subject will take this attitude and will manifest "cooperativeness" by listening, understanding and accepting the instructions. By "accept" here is meant that the subject will make the sense of the instructions that the experimenter intends and will then act as if he believed this sense was correct and binding upon him.

The experimenter will not listen to any attempt on the subject's part to change the conditions of the experiment, nor does he grant the subject's wishes and needs a legitimate status as an element of the bargain. Ordinarily the subject is permitted only to ask questions of clarification, and these are ordinarily answered by repeating a portion of the instructions. In other words, the experimenter limits what the subject may do and what he may know and, furthermore, makes the assumption that the instructions are clear and sufficient.

In assuming the sufficiency of the instructions, the experimenter usually has a good technical reason: standardization of procedure. He assumes he is presenting a standard set of conditions to a standard person and that what he tells the subject, together with what is readily available from the scene, will be the same for all subjects, i.e., will be interpreted in the same way by all subjects. (In practice, the experimenter believes that there will be individual differences that he hopes will be randomly distributed over subjects and can be treated as "error.")

The assumption of sufficiency really incorporates more than notions of standardized procedure, however, for it asserts that what the experimenter tells the subject is all the subject needs to know. Further, the assumption implicitly demands that the subject will suspend his doubts or questions about aspects of the procedure and the scene and will treat as irrelevant his own (the subject's) purposes, needs and reservations. Simply stated, the experimenter's assumption is that for the subject "things are what they seem," and that what he has been told in the instructions and what he can see for himself are true and that there is nothing more to the situation than this.

Finally, let us note about the experimenter that he is inflexible in his behavior. Ideally, at least, the experimenter's every move in an experiment has been predetermined and can be said to be "programmed." He has decided in advance on the task to set for all subjects, on the range of behavior he will attend to—i.e., on what he will treat as "data" and what behavior he will ignore —and on every one of his actions. He has a script that provides lines and business. The script cannot be revised or adapted to meet the exigencies of particular subjects or events and every experimental session must be either a "success" in that the events occurring during it come acceptably close to the ideal program or a "failure" that must be discarded. The period of reflection has passed for the experimenter once the series of trials gets under way; and his activities are, indeed, a mechanical program of activities.

The world appears somewhat different to the subject. In the first place, it seems doubtful that the subject always assumes the docile, cooperative and credulous stance that the experimenter wishes him to take. Some subjects probably do not find the experimental instructions sufficient, but are left with doubts, reservations and questions. Further, they may not suspend their own purposes. Rather, I think the subject enters the experiment with three major aims: first, he wants to accomplish his private purposes or get his rewards—e.g., pay, course credit, satisfaction of curiosity, self-insight, help with a problem and so on; second, he wants to penetrate the experimenter's inscrutability and discover the rationale of the experiment—its purposes and the types of judgment that will issue from it; and, finally, he wants to accomplish this second aim in order to achieve a third, namely in order to represent himself in a favorable light or to "put his best foot forward."

The subject must accomplish these three aims within the restriction that he is present primarily in order to accomplish the experimenter's purposes, which purposes may be initially quite vague to him. The accomplishment of the experimenter's purposes is one of the conditions that makes possible the achievement of one of the subject's aims, namely the discernment of these purposes. That is, the true nature of the situation will be revealed progressively as it goes along or at the end. Thus, like a stranger at a ceremonial or a man who cannot speak the native tongue, the subject comes to know what is going on only insofar as he participates in the action and does as he is told. His own actions have some effect upon the outcomes of the situation, but he can have only partial knowledge of the effect of his action until the whole situation has been played out.

The subject, therefore, must adopt a peculiar posture. He must be (or appear to be) cooperative in order to find out the meaning of his own actions as these are given meaning by the experimenter's interpretations. Yet he must have some basis for deciding how to act before he knows what his acts mean. He must make some approximation of the meaning of the situation in order to take a step that will yield some information that permits him to revise (or confirm) his first approximation. He must, necessarily, adopt a cut-and-try or iterative procedure for solving his problem.

In truth, the subject has more than one problem. One is the "task" that the experimenter sets. Another is what we may, for convenience, call his "deutero-problem," meaning his personal problem as defined by the three aims mentioned above: attainment of reward, divination of experimenter's true purposes and favorable self-presentation. The extent to which the deutero-problem occupies the subject is not uniform across subjects.

When it becomes the salient feature of the situation, we describe the subject as "neurotically defensive," "hyper-suspicious" or even "over-sophisticated." When it is minimal, we rejoice in having a truly "naive" subject. But I claim that the deutero-problem plays some role in all experimental situations and for all subjects and may, on some occasions, be more important than the "task" or the "treatment" in explaining results.

Finally, let me make it clear that the subject does not approach the deutero-problem without preconceptions to help him define the situation nor without hints furnished by the experimenter's actions, the instructions, and the scene. I propose that the subject's preconceptions are properly a matter of empirical investigation and below I suggest some techniques for such investigation. On the other hand, the matter of what hints and clues does the subject get from the ongoing procedure seems to have some conceptual properties worth exploring before we go to collecting data.

I suggest that there are two general types of experimental (i.e., "task") problems that provide subjects with different kinds of hints as to how to put their best foot forward or, in effect, urge subjects to adopt one or another "set" toward the experiment. Let me distinguish these problems and sets by calling one type "task-ability" and the other "self-quality," and by characterizing them further as follows:

A "task-ability" set is characteristically adopted when the experimenter presents the work to be done as involving some ability, skill or capacity to perform. The task may be motor or mental, simple or complex, familiar or strange, e.g., estimating the number of dots on a card, judging "autokinetic" movement distances, judging the personality of another or solving "human relations problems." The outstanding feature of such assignments is that there is no upper limit on the amount of skill or capacity the subject "ought" to display. The nature of the task tells the subject: "You can't do too much in proving your worth." Furthermore, the positively valued end of the ability continuum is easily discerned by the subject in most cases. If he does not or if two rivalrous dimensions of ability confront him, the experimenter will ordinarily instruct the subject on which dimension he is to maximize performance, e.g., whether speed or accuracy will be considered more important. Finally, it is impossible for the subject to do more than his best; the only possibility for misrepresentation lies in under-achievement or concealment of a skill. Ordinarily under-achievement arises from some failure to motivate the subject adequately or from the subject's failure to see the relevance of the ability being tested either to the experimental purpose or to the assessment of his own worth. In short, try as he may, the subject can distort or misrepresent his performance in only one direction. He has only partial voluntary control over his performance.

Quite different in nature are the "self-quality" problems, which can be characterized in general as being concerned with opinions and beliefs; with responses to frustration, insult, and failure; with conformity-independence, choice-rejection of others; or with qualities such as dogmatism, authoritarianism, punitiveness and the like. The differences between "self-quality" performances and those in the "task-ability" area are several. First, the dimensions of behavior do not have simply one "good" and one "bad" end point; rather, they tend to have two "bad" extremes and a "good" point located somewhere between the extremes, though not necessarily in the "middle." For example, it is possible to be over- or under-conforming, too acceptant of others or too rejecting. Thus, the second aspect of "self-quality" situations is that the subject cannot be sure how exteme a behavior will be considered maximally worthy. Unlike task-ability situations, the subject does not have a guarantee that he "cannot do too much." In order to know how to maximize the worth of his behavior, a subject must either draw from his pool of common sense knowledge about what "anyone knows" is a worthy way to behave; or, to be perfectly sure, he would have to know the scheme of relevances that the experimenter is employing: the hypothesis being tested, the categories into which behavior will be placed, the criteria for such placement, and the value assigned to the category. The fact that the experimenter conceals these items, while the subject is pushed by his own aims to try to discover them, tends to maximize the negotiation between subject and experimenter. It is the third feature of self-quality experiments that makes negotiation possible, namely that the behavior under scrutiny can be under the voluntary control of the subject at least within broad limits. The subject can both inhibit a behavior and can stimulate it, depending on how he believes a particular kind of behavior will be judged by the experimenter.[2]

RESEARCH PROPOSALS

Given the foregoing characterization of the experimental situation and some of the features of the process of negotiation between subject and experimenter, it seems probable that the behavior of the subject in dealing with his "deutero-problem" can be investigated further; and can be most profitably investigated in the area of "self-quality" problems. The strategy of investigation proposed arises from viewing the negotiation process as one in which the subject progressively elaborates a definition of the experimental situation. Further, it assumed that the definition grows out of (a) what the subject knows or believes about experimental psychological procedure before he takes part in an experiment; (b) what the experimenter says and does and also what he believes, expects or wishes; and (c) the remaining features of the scene, including the physical properties of the experimental setting, its temporal characteristics, the apparatus, the other people present, and the events that occur during the experiment. At any particular point, the subject has

---

[2] Experimenters are aware of these features of "self-quality" problems and often disguise such problems as "task-ability" situations (e.g., the TAT is presented as "a *test* of imagination"); or misdirect the subject's attention by initiating and overtly carrying out a "task-ability" procedure that at some point is apparently inadvertently intruded upon by some event to which the subject must respond. Hopefully, the subject responds spontaneously; and the experimenter attends to this response while ignoring the "task-ability" performance.

In this connection it is worth noting that occasionally the experimenter encounters what can be called "inter-set interference," meaning that the adoption of one set by the subject precludes his noticing or responding adequately to a phenomenon that would appear relevant to him under a different set. For example, Milton Rosenbaum (personal communication) reports that subjects engaged in the "task" of judging stimulus persons may be so task-directed that they appear to ignore insulting remarks directed by the stimulus person toward the subjects. Rosenbaum also mentions an experiment in a military setting in which a strong instruction to adopt a task set apparently "took" so well that the subjects were inattentive to social-emotional events later introduced into the situation as part of the experimental procedure.

some definition or understanding of the situation, although it may be so vague that he can say little about it. As the experiment proceeds, his definition becomes more elaborated until, at the end of the session, the subject can usually give some coherent account of what he thinks happened. The fundamental strategy is to investigate subjects' interpretations at various points throughout the sequence of events in the experiment.

Preconceptions

Since the subject's expectations of what will occur during an experiment are likely to be vague, they should be studied by a "recognition" rather than a "recall" technique. Specifically, then, the questioning procedure should involve presenting subjects with lists of items and asking them to respond to each, rather than an "open-end" interview.

Knowledge. First, it is important to find out what subjects know about experimental procedure and findings in social psychology. How knowledgeable are they about common features of experiments? Can subjects correctly identify or describe certain facts, terms, descriptions of procedure, and the like? The list of items might include such things as: control group, autokinetic phenomenon, cohesiveness, use of tape recordings, one-way screens, authoritarianism, sociometric tests, some brief statements of experimental findings (some true, some invented) for the subject to judge true or false together with an estimate of his confidence, and the like.

Expectations of Legitimate Activity. The second kind of expectations needing study are what the subject considers ordinary or unusual or impossible events in an experiment. Using brief descriptions of activities, the subject could be asked to indicate for each whether he thought it could be a normal occurrence in an experiment. The list might include such items as: receiving an electric shock, telling his home address, getting experimenter a pack of cigarettes with the subject's money, drinking a liquid of unknown composition, jumping into the university pool with all his clothes on.

Expectations of Purpose. A somewhat more general kind of expectation is what the subject conceives the experimenter's purpose to be. This conception, if it can be educed, might provide the general framework within which knowledge and expectations of legitimate activity are organized. The details of procedure have not been worked out and "open-end" interviewing may be the best way to start.

What the Experimenter Says and Does

One way of investigating what subjects make of experimental situations is to study their interpretations of various events as they occur sequentially during an experimental procedure: the initial instructions, subsequent ones and various tests, questionnaires and the like. At least two lines of procedure suggest themselves:

Paper and Pencil Tasks. The subject might be presented with a series of written descriptions of experimental situations, instructions and of events occurring during an experiment and asked to indicate: what he thinks the experimenter's purposes are, what the significant response categories are and how the experimenter would evaluate each of them.

The same sort of procedure could be used to study the insight that subjects have into many of the standard or classical measuring devices of social psychology. What does the subject make of the F-scale, the Study of Values, self-esteem scales, and the like? What does the subject think the instrument is measuring? How accurately can he state what would be a "high" or a "low" score? What responses does he think describe an esteemed person?

Partial Procedures and Replicated Variations. Instead of submitting a written version of the experimental procedure to the subject, it might be useful to run subjects through varying length portions of actual experimental sequences, interrupting the procedure at some point to interview the subject and get his impressions of what is going on, in the terms outlined above. Another obvious move suggested by this line of reasoning is a program of interviewing subjects following the completion of some experiment that another investigator is conducting for his own purposes. On the basis of hunches obtained from such interviewing, one might attempt deliberate variation of some portion of the instructions or procedure to determine the effects on subjects' understanding.

Personal and Social Attributes of Experimenters. We know that the academic position of the experimenter seems to make a difference in subjects' motivation in a task-ability problem. Are there parallel differences in the area of self-quality problems? Will subjects demonstrate more or less conformity, credulity, cooperativeness for a faculty experimenter than for a graduate student? Will they be more or less hostile to an instigating agent depending on his status?

A warm, friendly test administrator seems to induce higher performance among nursery school children. Will a friendly administrator induce more acceptance in sociometric tests than a cold person? Do subjects read an experimenter's style and manner of behavior for cues as to what is "appropriate" behavior? Will an experimenter whose overt mannerisms, clothing and speech exude social orthodoxy produce greater conformity than one whose appearance is "radical" or "bohemian?" Does a white laboratory coat make a "scientist" out of a psychologist?

All of the foregoing questions can be answered by replicating standard experiments with variations in experimenters' appearance, status, or actions. But one wonders if subjects can perhaps read even more subtle cues than the foregoing.

Experimenter's Attitudes Toward the Experiment. Robert Zajonc reports (personal communication) experiments in which the instructions clearly implied the attitude that experimenter took toward the hypothesis being tested. When the instructions implied that the experimenter was convinced of the truth of the hypothesis, the results supported the hypothesis; but when he implied that he believed it was wrong, the results did not support the hypothesis. In Zajonc's experiment the experimenter's attitude was made almost explicit; but one wonders if perhaps more subtle communication can still affect results, as when the experimenter holds an opinion but tries to disguise it. An experiment is called for here.[3]

Two other attitudinal areas ought to be investigated also. One is boredom with the procedure, increasing as a long series of trials progresses. Aside from simple sloppiness in procedure during later trials, is it possible that there are other effects? Does experimenter's lack of interest, restlessness, and lack of excitement affect the subject's performance, perhaps in the di-

[3] When this article was written, the author was unaware that a relevant experiment was being conducted by Peggy Cook (1958). In addition the independent work of Rosenthal (1958) and Orne (1959) are relevant here.

rection of reducing motivation? The other attitudinal area is one manifested during the early part of a series of trials, when the experimenter may experience anxiety about the efficacy of his procedure or feel guilt about the deception he is practicing on subjects. Just precisely what consequences these feelings might have for subjects' performances is uncertain, but one can speculate that such feelings on experimenter's part would generate discomfort and confusion in subjects and might increase the variety of their interpretations of the experiment and hence increase variance in their behavior.

As with experimenters themselves, so perhaps with their confederates too. Insufficient attention has been given to the effects of certain nonrole characteristics of stooges, although analysis has sometimes shown significant interstooge differences. In addition, the very process of taking the stooge role seems to have some consequences, though their effects on the outcomes of the experiment are obscure. Theodore Mills reports (personal communication) that his confederates experienced guilt over their rejecting and unsupportive role-behavior toward a naïve subject. Mills had to provide tension-release sessions to keep his team functioning. Richard DeCharms reports (personal communication) the case of a confederate who had to act stupid and fail before people whom he considered his intellectual inferiors. The man "took it out" on his wife in displays of ill-temper, reckless driving, sulkiness, etc. Seymour Feshbach (personal communication) has also commented on tension and irritability in role-players. The possibility that such tensions can be altogether excluded from actual role performance in the experiment seems remote, yet the actual effects on subjects are unstudied.

The Scene.   Finally, a brief comment should be made about how the physical environment, properties, and apparatus in view may affect the subject's understanding of the experiment. Unfortunately, little is known about this aspect of things, although experimenters have fairly strong opinions about how elaborate the staging of the experiment ought to be. On the face of it, it might seem reasonable to believe that the more intricate, elaborate, and "realistic" the setting was, the greater the impact of the treatment would be on the subjects. Yet, many experimenters work with the baldest kind of verbal directives, make no attempt to dramatize the scene, and still get results. And there have been cases of elaborately rigged experiments that simply failed to produce the desired effects. It seems at least possible that an elaborately staged experiment may simply provide the subject with more cues than he has time or attention span to interpret. Perhaps as complexity of the desired effect increases, the consequence of shifting the burden of communication from verbal instructions to portions of the scene is merely to confuse the subject and to produce irrelevant or wrong interpretations. It seems worthwhile at least to study the relative impact of instructional and scenic communication, perhaps by performing the "same" experiment in two versions: one using simple verbal instructions to create the desired effect, the other depending maximally upon the scene—props and cast—to carry the informational burden.

REFERENCES

Birney, R. C. The achievement motive and task performance: A replication. *J. abnorm. soc. Psychol.*, **56**, 133–135.

Cook, P. Authoritarian or acquiescent: Some behavioral differences. *Amer. Psychologist*, 1958, **338**, (Abstract).

Goffman, E. *The presentation of self in everyday life.* New York: Doubleday (Anchor), 1959.

Kahn, R. L., & Cannell, C. F. *The dynamics of interviewing.* New York: John Wiley, 1957.

Orne, M. T. The nature of hypnosis: Artifact and essence. *J. abnorm. soc. Psychol.*, 1959, **58**, 277–299.

Rosenthal, R. Note on the fallible E. *Psychol. Rep.*, 1958, **4**, 662.

Rosenthal, R. Projection, excitement and unconscious experimenter bias. *Amer. Psychologist*, 1958, **13**, 345–346 (Abstract).

Sachs, E. L. Intelligence scores as a function of experimentally established social relationships between child and examiner. *J. abnorm. soc. Psychol.*, 1952, **47**, 354–358.

3

ON THE SOCIAL PSYCHOLOGY OF THE PSYCHOLOGICAL EXPERIMENT: WITH PARTICULAR REFERENCE TO DEMAND CHARACTERISTICS AND THEIR IMPLICATIONS

Martin T. Orne

It is to the highest degree probable that the subject['s] . . . general attitude of mind is that of ready complacency and cheerful willingness to assist the investigator in every possible way by reporting to him those very things which he is most eager to find, and that the very questions of the experimenter . . . suggest the shade of reply expected. . . . Indeed . . . it seems too often as if the subject were now regarded as a stupid automaton. . . .

A. H. Pierce (1908)

Since the time of Galileo, scientists have employed the laboratory experiment as a method of understanding natural phenomena. Generically, the experimental method consists of abstracting relevant variables from complex situations in nature

From M. T. Orne, *Amer. Psychologist*, 1962, **17,** 776–783. With permission of author and publisher.

For further reference see author's more recent articles: in R. Rosenthal & R. Rasnow (Eds.), *Artifact in behavioral research.* New York: Academic Press, 1969; in *Nebraska Symposium on Motivation.* Lincoln, Neb.: Univ. of Nebraska Press, 1970.

This paper was presented at the Symposium, "On the Social Psychology of the Psychological Experiment," American Psychological Association Convention, New York, 1961.

The work reported here was supported in part by a Public Health Service Research Grant, M-3369, National Institute of Mental Health.

I wish to thank my associates Ronald E. Shor, Donald N. O'Connell, Ulric Neisser, Karl E. Scheibe, and Emily F. Carota for their comments and criticisms in the preparation of this paper.

and reproducing in the laboratory segments of these situations, varying the parameters involved so as to determine the effect of the experimental variables. This procedure allows generalization from the information obtained in the laboratory situation back to the original situation as it occurs in nature. The physical sciences have made striking advances through the use of this method, but in the behavioral sciences it has often been difficult to meet two necessary requirements for meaningful experimentation: reproducibility and ecological validity.[1] It has long been recognized that certain differences will exist between the types of experiments conducted in the physical sciences and those in the behavioral sciences because the former investigates a universe of inanimate objects and forces, whereas the latter deals with animate organisms, often thinking, conscious subjects. However, recognition of this distinction has not always led to appropriate changes in the traditional experimental model of physics as employed in the behavioral sciences. Rather the experimental model has been so successful as employed in physics that there has been a tendency in the behavioral sciences to follow precisely a paradigm originated for the study of inanimate objects, i.e., one which proceeds by exposing the subject to various conditions and observing the differences in reaction of the subject under different conditions. However, the use of such a model with animal or human subjects leads to the problem that the subject of the experiment is assumed, at least implicitly, to be a *passive responder* to stimuli—an assumption difficult to justify. Further, in this type of model the experimental stimuli themselves are usually rigorously defined in terms of what *is done* to the subject. In contrast, the purpose of this paper will be to focus on what the human subject *does* in the laboratory: what motivation the subject is likely to have in the experimental situation, how he usually perceives behavioral research, what the nature of the cues is that the subject is likely to pick up, etc. Stated in other terms, what factors are apt to affect the subject's reaction to the well-defined stimuli in the situation? These factors comprise what will be referred to here as the "experimental setting."

[1] Ecological validity, in the sense that Brunswik (1947) has used the term: appropriate generalization from the laboratory to nonexperimental situations.

Since any experimental manipulation of human subjects takes place within this larger framework or setting, we should propose that the above-mentioned factors must be further elaborated and the parameters of the experimental setting more carefully defined so that adequate controls can be designed to isolate the effects of the experimental setting from the effects of the experimental variables. Later in this paper we shall propose certain possible techniques of control which have been devised in the process of our research on the nature of hypnosis.

Our initial focus here will be on some of the qualities peculiar to psychological experiments. The experimental situation is one which takes place within the context of an explicit agreement of the subject to participate in a special form of social interaction known as "taking part in an experiment." Within the context of our culture the roles of subject and experimenter are well understood and carry with them well-defined mutual role expectations. A particularly striking aspect of the typical experimenter-subject relationship is the extent to which the subject will play his role and place himself under the control of the experimenter. Once a subject has agreed to participate in a psychological experiment, he implicitly agrees to perform a very wide range of actions on request without inquiring as to their purpose, and frequently without inquiring as to their duration.

Furthermore, the subject agrees to tolerate a considerable degree of discomfort, boredom, or actual pain, if required to do so by the experimenter. Just about any request which could conceivably be asked of the subject by a reputable investigator is legitimized by the quasi-magical phrase, "This is an experiment," and the shared assumption that a legitimate purpose will be served by the subject's behavior. A somewhat trivial example of this legitimization of requests is as follows:

A number of casual acquaintances was asked whether they would do the experimenter a favor; on their acquiescence, they were asked to perform five push-ups. Their response tended to be amazement, incredulity, and the question "Why?" Another similar group of individuals were asked whether they would take part in an experiment of brief duration. When they agreed to do so, they too were asked to perform five push-ups. Their typical response was "Where?"

The striking degree of control inherent in the experimental

situation can also be illustrated by a set of pilot experiments which were performed in the course of designing an experiment to test whether the degree of control inherent in the *hypnotic* relationship is greater than that in a waking relationship.[2] In order to test this question, we tried to develop a set of tasks which waking subjects would refuse to do, or would do only for a short period of time. The tasks were intended to be psychologically noxious, meaningless, or boring, rather than painful or fatiguing.

For example, one task was to perform serial additions of each adjacent two numbers on sheets filled with rows of random digits. In order to complete just one sheet, the subject would be required to perform 224 additions! A stack of some 2000 sheets was presented to each subject—clearly an impossible task to complete. After the instructions were given, the subject was deprived of his watch and told, "Continue to work; I will return eventually." Five and one-half hours later, the *experimenter* gave up! In general, subjects tended to continue this type of task for several hours, usually with little decrement in performance. Since we were trying to find a task which would be discontinued spontaneously within a brief period, we tried to create a more frustrating situation as follows:

Subjects were asked to perform the same task described above but were also told that when finished with the additions on each sheet, they should pick up a card from a large pile, which would instruct them on what to do next. However, every card in the pile read,

> You are to tear up the sheet of paper which you have just completed into a minimum of thirty-two pieces and go on to the next sheet of paper and continue working as you did before; when you have completed this piece of paper, pick up the next card which will instruct you further. Work as accurately and as rapidly as you can.

Our expectation was that subjects would discontinue the task as soon as they realized that the cards were worded identically, that each finished piece of work had to be destroyed, and that, in short, the task was completely meaningless.

[2] These pilot studies were performed by Thomas Menaker.

Somewhat to our amazement, subjects tended to persist in the task for several hours with relatively little sign of overt hostility. Removal of the one-way screen did not tend to make much difference. The postexperimental inquiry helped to explain the subjects' behavior. When asked about the tasks, subjects would invariably attribute considerable meaning to their performance, viewing it as an endurance test or the like.

Thus far, we have been singularly unsuccessful in finding an experimental task which would be discontinued, or, indeed, refused by subjects in an experimental setting.[3] Not only do subjects continue to perform boring, unrewarding tasks, but they do so with few errors and little decrement in speed. It became apparent that it was extremely difficult to design an experiment to test the degree of social control in hypnosis, in view of the already *very high degree of control in the experimental situation itself.*

The quasi-experimental work reported here is highly informal and based on samples of three or four subjects in each group. It does, however, illustrate the remarkable compliance of the experimental subject. The only other situations where such a wide range of requests are carried out with little or no question are those of complete authority, such as some parent-child relationships or some doctor-patient relationships. This aspect of the experiment as a social situation will not become apparent unless one tests for it; it is, however, present in varying degrees in all experimental contexts. Not only are tasks carried out, but they are performed with care over considerable periods of time.

Our observation that subjects tend to carry out a remarkably wide range of instructions with a surprising degree of diligence reflects only one aspect of the motivation manifested by most subjects in an experimental situation. It is relevant to consider another aspect of motivation that is common to the subjects of most psychological experiments: high regard for the aims of science and experimentation.

---

[3] Tasks which would involve the use of actual severe physical pain or exhaustion were not considered.

This observation is consistent with Frank's (1944) failure to obtain resistance to disagreeable or nonsensical tasks. He accounts for this "primarily by S's unwillingness to break the tacit agreement he had made when he volunteered to take part in the experiment, namely, to do whatever the experiment required of him" (p. 24).

A volunteer who participates in a psychological experiment may do so for a wide variety of reasons ranging from the need to fulfill a course requirement, to the need for money, to the unvoiced hope of altering his personal adjustment for the better, etc. Over and above these motives, however, college students tend to share (with the experimenter) the hope and expectation that the study in which they are participating will in some material way contribute to science and perhaps ultimately to human welfare in general. We should expect that many of the characteristics of the experimental situation derive from the peculiar role relationship which exists between subject and experimenter. Both subject and experimenter share the belief that whatever the experimental task is, it is important, and that as such no matter how much effort must be exerted or how much discomfort must be endured, it is justified by the ultimate purpose.

If we assume that much of the motivation of the subject to comply with any and all experimental instructions derives from an identification with the goals of science in general and the success of the experiment in particular,[4] it follows that the subject has a stake in the outcome of the study in which he is participating. For the volunteer subject to feel that he has made a useful contribution, it is necessary for him to assume that the experimenter is competent and that he himself is a "good subject."

The significance to the subject of successfully being a "good subject" is attested to by the frequent questions at the conclusion of an experiment, to the effect of, "Did I ruin the experiment?" What is most commonly meant by this is, "Did I perform well in my role as experimental subject?" or "Did my behavior demonstrate that which the experiment is designed to show?" Admittedly, subjects are concerned about their performance in terms of reinforcing their self-image; nonetheless, they seem even more concerned with the utility of their performances. We might well expect then that as far as the subject is able, he will behave in an experimental context in a manner

---

[4] This hypothesis is subject to empirical test. We should predict that there would be measurable differences in motivation between subjects who perceive a particular experiment as "significant" and those who perceive the experiment as "unimportant."

designed to play the role of a "good subject" or, in other words, *to validate the experimental hypothesis.* Viewed in this way, the student volunteer is *not* merely a passive responder in an experimental situation but rather he has a very real stake in the successful outcome of the experiment. This problem is implicitly recognized in the large number of psychological studies which attempt to conceal the true purpose of the experiment from the subject in the hope of thereby obtaining more reliable data. This maneuver on the part of psychologists is so widely known in the college population that even if a psychologist is honest with the subject, more often than not he will be distrusted. As one subject pithily put it, "Psychologists always lie!" This bit of paranoia has some support in reality.

The subject's performance in an experiment might almost be conceptualized as problem-solving behavior; that is, at some level he sees it as his task to ascertain the true purpose of the experiment and respond in a manner which will support the hypotheses being tested. Viewed in this light, the totality of cues which convey an experimental hypothesis to the subject become significant determinants of subjects' behavior. We have labeled the sum total of such cues as the *"demand characteristics of the experimental situation"* (Orne, 1959a). These cues include the rumors or campus scuttlebutt about the research, the information conveyed during the original solicitation, the person of the experimenter, and the setting of the laboratory, as well as all explicit and implicit communications during the experiment proper. A frequently overlooked, but nonetheless very significant source of cues for the subject lies in the experimental procedure itself, viewed in the light of the subject's previous knowledge and experience. For example, if a test is given twice with some intervening treatment, even the dullest college student is aware that some change is expected, particularly if the test is in some obvious way related to the treatment.

The demand characteristics perceived in any particular experiment will vary with the sophistication, intelligence, and previous experience of each experimental subject. To the extent that the demand characteristics of the experiment are clear-cut, they will be perceived uniformly by most experimental subjects. It is entirely possible to have an experimental situation with clear-cut demand characteristics for psychology undergraduates which, however, does not have the same clear-cut demand characteristics for enlisted army personnel. It is, of course, those demand characteristics which are perceived by the subject that will influence his behavior.

We should like to propose the heuristic assumption that a subject's behavior in any experimental situation will be determined by two sets of variables: (a) those which are traditionally defined as experimental variables and (b) the perceived demand characteristics of the experimental situation. The extent to which the subject's behavior is related to the demand characteristics, rather than to the experimental variable, will in large measure determine both the extent to which the experiment can be replicated with minor modification (i.e., modified demand characteristics), and the extent to which generalizations can be drawn about the effect of the experimental variables in nonexperimental contexts (the problem of ecological validity [Brunswik, 1947]).

It becomes an empirical issue to study under what circumstances, in what kind of experimental contexts, and with what kind of subject populations, demand characteristics become significant in determining the behavior of subjects in experimental situations. It should be clear that demand characteristics cannot be eliminated from experiments; all experiments will have demand characteristics, and these will always have some effect. It does become possible, however, to study the effect of demand characteristics as opposed to the effect of experimental variables. However, techniques designed to study the effect of demand characteristics need to take into account that these effects result from the subject's *active* attempt to respond appropriately to the *totality* of the experimental situation.

It is perhaps best to think of the perceived demand characteristics as a contextual variable in the experimental situation. We should like to emphasize that, at this stage, little is known about this variable. In our first study which utilized the demand characteristics concept (Orne, 1959b), we found that a particular experimental effect was present only in records of those subjects who were able to verbalize the experimenter's hypothesis. Those subjects who were unable to do so did not show the predicted phenomenon. Indeed we found that whether or not a given subject perceived the experimenter's hypothesis was a more accurate predictor of the subject's actual performance than his statement about what he thought he had done on the experimental task. It became clear from extensive interviews with subjects that response to the demand characteristics is not merely conscious compliance. When we speak of "playing the role of a good experimental subject," we use the concept analogously to the way in which Sarbin (1950) describes role playing in hypnosis: namely, largely on a nonconscious level. The demand characteristics of the situation help define the role of "good experimental subject," and the responses of the subject are a function of the role that is created.

We have a suspicion that the demand characteristics most potent in determining subjects' behavior are those which convey the purpose of the experiment effectively but not obviously. If the purpose of the experiment is not clear, or is highly ambiguous, many different hypotheses may be formed by different subjects, and the demand characteristics will not lead to clearcut results. If, on the other hand, the demand characteristics are so obvious that the subject becomes fully conscious of the expectations of the experimenter, there is a tendency to lean over backwards to be honest. We are encountering here the effect of another facet of the college student's attitude toward science. While the student wants studies to "work," he feels he must be honest in his report; otherwise, erroneous conclusions will be drawn. Therefore, if the subject becomes acutely aware of the experimenter's expectations, there may be a tendency for biasing in the opposite direction. (This is analogous to the often observed tendency to favor individuals whom we dislike in an effort to be fair.)[5]

Delineation of the situations where demand characteristics may produce an effect ascribed to experimental variables, or where they may obscure such an effect and actually lead to systematic data in the opposite direction, as well as those experimental contexts where they do not play a major role, is an issue for further work. Recognizing the contribution to experimental results which may be made by the demand characteristics of the situation, what are some experimental techniques for the study of demand characteristics?

---

[5] Rosenthal (1961), in his recent work on experimenter bias, has reported a similar type of phenomenon. Biasing was maximized by ego involvement of the experimenters, but when an attempt was made to increase biasing by paying for "good results," there was a marked reduction of effect. This reversal may be ascribed to the experimenters' becoming too aware of their own wishes in the situation.

As we have pointed out, it is futile to imagine an experiment that could be created without demand characteristics. One of the basic characteristics of the human being is that he will ascribe purpose and meaning even in the absence of purpose and meaning. In an experiment where he knows some purpose exists, it is inconceivable for him not to form some hypothesis as to the purpose, based on some cues, no matter how meager; this will then determine the demand characteristics which will be perceived by and operate for a particular subject. Rather than eliminating this variable then, it becomes necessary to take demand characteristics into account, study their effect, and manipulate them if necessary.

One procedure to determine the demand characteristics is the systematic study of each individual subject's perception of the experimental hypothesis. If one can determine what demand characteristics are perceived by each subject, it becomes possible to determine to what extent these, rather than the experimental variables, correlate with the observed behavior. If the subject's behavior correlates better with the demand characteristics than with the experimental variables, it is probable that the demand characteristics are the major determinants of the behavior.

The most obvious technique for determining what demand characteristics are perceived is the use of postexperimental inquiry. In this regard, it is well to point out that considerable self-discipline is necessary for the experimenter to obtain a valid inquiry. A great many experimenters at least implicitly make the demand that the subject not perceive what is really going on. The temptation for the experimenter, in, say, a replication of an Asch group pressure experiment, is to ask the subject afterwards, "You didn't realize that the other fellows were confederates, did you?" Having obtained the required "No," the experimenter breathes a sigh of relief and neither subject nor experimenter pursues the issue further.[6] However, even if the experimenter makes an effort to elicit the subject's perception of the hypothesis of the experiment, he may have difficulty in obtaining a valid report because the subject as well as he himself has considerable interest in appearing naive.

Most subjects are cognizant that they are not supposed to know any more about an experiment than they have been told

[6] Asch (1952) himself took great pains to avoid this pitfall.

and that excessive knowledge will disqualify them from participating, or, in the case of a postexperimental inquiry, such
knowledge will invalidate their performance. As we pointed out
earlier, subjects have a real stake in viewing their performance
as meaningful. For this reason, it is commonplace to find a
pact of ignorance resulting from the intertwining motives of
both experimenter and subject, neither wishing to create a situation where the particular subject's performance needs to be
excluded from the study.

For these reasons, inquiry procedures are required to push
the subject for information without, however, providing in
themselves cues as to what is expected. The general question
which needs to be explored is the subject's perception of the
experimental purpose and the specific hypotheses of the experimenter. This can best be done by an open-ended procedure
starting with the very general question of, "What do you think
that the experiment is about?" and only much later asking
specific questions. Responses of "I don't know" should be dealt
with by encouraging the subject to guess, use his imagination,
and in general, by refusing to accept this response. Under these
circumstances, the overwhelming majority of students will turn
out to have evolved very definite hypotheses. These hypotheses
can then be judged, and a correlation between them and experimental performance can be drawn.

Two objections may be made against this type of inquiry:
(a) that the subject's perception of the experimenter's hypotheses is based on his own experimental behavior, and therefore
a correlation between these two variables may have little to do
with the determinants of behavior, and (b) that the inquiry
procedure itself is subject to demand characteristics.

A procedure which has been independently advocated by
Riecken (1958) and Orne (1959a) is designed to deal with the
first of these objections. This consists of an inquiry procedure
which is conducted much as though the subject had actually
been run in the experiment, without, however, permitting him
to be given any experimental data. Instead, the precise procedure of the experiment is explained, the experimental material
is shown to the subject, and he is told what he would be required to do; however, he is not permitted to make any responses. He is then given a postexperimental inquiry as though
he had been a subject. Thus, one would say, "If I had asked you

to do all these things, what do you think that the experiment would be about, what do you think I would be trying to prove, what would my hypothesis be?" etc. This technique, which we have termed the pre-experimental inquiry, can be extended very readily to the giving of pre-experimental tests, followed by the explanation of experimental conditions and tasks, and the administration of postexperimental tests. The subject is requested to behave on these tests as though he had been exposed to the experimental treatment that was described to him. This type of procedure is not open to the objection that the subject's own behavior has provided cues for him as to the purpose of the task. It presents him with a straight problem-solving situation and makes explicit what, for the true experimental subject, is implicit. It goes without saying that these subjects who are run on the preexperimental inquiry conditions must be drawn from the same population as the experimental groups and may, of course, not be run subsequently in the experimental condition. This technique is one of approximation rather than of proof. However, if subjects describe behavior on the pre-inquiry conditions as similar to, or identical with, that actually given by subjects exposed to the experimental conditions, the hypothesis becomes plausible that demand characteristics may be responsible for the behavior.

It is clear that pre- and postexperimental inquiry techniques have their own demand characteristics. For these reasons, it is usually best to have the inquiry conducted by an experimenter who is not acquainted with the actual experimental behavior of the subjects. This will tend to minimize the effect of experimenter bias.

Another technique which we have utilized for approximating the effect of the demand characteristics is to attempt to hold the demand characteristics constant and eliminate the experimental variable. One way of accomplishing this purpose is through the use of simulating subjects. This is a group of subjects who are not exposed to the experimental variable to which the effect has been attributed, but who are instructed to act *as if* this were the case. In order to control for experimenter bias under these circumstances, it is advisable to utilize more than one experimenter and to have the experimenter who actually runs the subjects "blind" as to which group (simulating or real) any given individual belongs.

Our work in hypnosis (Damaser, Shor, & Orne, 1963; Orne, 1959b; Shor, 1959) is a good example of the use of simulating controls. Subjects unable to enter hypnosis are instructed to simulate entering hypnosis for another experimenter. The experimenter who runs the study sees both highly trained hypnotic subjects and simulators in random order and does not know to which group each subject belongs. Because the subjects are run "blind," the experimenter is more likely to treat the two groups of subjects identically. We have found that simulating subjects are able to perform with great effectiveness, deceiving even well-trained hypnotists. However, the simulating group is not exposed to the experimental condition (in this case, hypnosis) to which the given effect under investigation is often ascribed. Rather, it is a group faced with a problem-solving task: namely, to utilize whatever cues are made available by the experimental context and the experimenter's concrete behavior in order to behave as they think that hypnotized subjects might. Therefore, to the extent that simulating subjects are able to behave identically, it is possible that demand characteristics, rather than the altered state of consciousness, could account for the behavior of the experimental group.

The same type of technique can be utilized in other types of studies. For example, in contrast to the placebo control in a drug study, it is equally possible to instruct some subjects not to take the medication at all, but to act as if they had. It must be emphasized that this type of control is different from the placebo control. It represents an approximation. It maximally confronts the simulating subject with a problem-solving task and suggests how much of the total effect could be accounted for by the demand characteristics—assuming that the experimental group had taken full advantage of them, an assumption not necessarily correct.

All of the techniques proposed thus far share the quality that they depend upon the active cooperation of the control subjects, and in some way utilize his thinking process as an intrinsic factor. The subject does *not* just respond in these control situations but, rather, he is required *actively* to solve the problem.

The use of placebo experimental conditions is a way in which this problem can be dealt with in a more classic fashion. Psychopharmacology has used such techniques extensively, but here too they present problems. In the case of placebos and drugs, it is often the case that the physician is "blind" as to whether a drug is placebo or active, but the patient is not, despite precautions to the contrary; i.e., the patient is cognizant that he does not have the side effects which some of his fellow patients on the ward experience. By the same token, in psychological placebo treatments, it is equally important to ascertain whether the subject actually perceived the treatment to be experimental or control. Certainly the subject's perception of himself as a control subject may materially alter the situation.

A recent experiment (Orne & Scheibe, 1964) in our laboratory illustrates this type of investigation. We were interested in studying the demand characteristics of sensory-deprivation experiments, independent of any actual sensory deprivation. We hypothesized that the overly cautious treatment of subjects, careful screening for mental or physical disorders, awesome release forms, and, above all, the presence of a "panic (release) button" might be more significant in producing the effects reported from sensory deprivation than the actual diminution of sensory input. A pilot study (Stare, Brown, & Orne, 1959), employing pre-inquiry techniques, supported this view. Recently, we designed an experiment to test more rigorously this hypothesis.

This experiment, which we called Meaning Deprivation, had all the *accoutrements* of sensory deprivation, including release forms and a red panic button. However, we carefully refrained from creating any sensory deprivation whatsoever. The experimental task consisted of sitting in a small experimental room which was well lighted, with two comfortable chairs, as well as ice water and a sandwich, and an optional task of adding numbers. The subject did not have a watch during this time, the room was reasonably quiet, but not soundproof, and the duration of the experiment (of which the subject was ignorant) was four hours. Before the subject was placed in the experimental room, ten tests previously used in sensory-deprivation research were administered. At the completion of the experiment, the same tasks were again administered. A microphone and a one-way screen were present in the room, and the subject was encouraged to verbalize freely.

The control group of ten subjects was subjected to the identical treatment, except that they were told that they were control subjects for a sensory-deprivation experiment. The panic button was eliminated for this group. The formal experimental treatment of these two groups of subjects was the same in terms of the objective stress—four hours of isolation. However, the demand characteristics had been purposively varied for the two groups to study the effect of demand characteristics as opposed to objective stress. Of the fourteen measures which could be quantified, thirteen were in the predicted direction, and six were significant at the selected ten percent alpha level or better. A Mann-Whitney U test has been performed on the summation ranks of all measures as a convenient method for summarizing the overall differences. The one-tailed probability which emerges is $p = .001$, a clear demonstration of expected effects.

This study suggests that demand characteristics may in part account for some of the findings commonly attributed to sensory deprivation. We have found similar significant effects of demand characteristics in accounting for a great deal of the findings reported in hypnosis. It is highly probable that careful attention to this variable, or group of variables, may resolve some of the current controversies regarding a number of psychological phenomena in motivation, learning, and perception.

In summary, we have suggested that the subject must be recognized as an active participant in any experiment, and that it may be fruitful to view the psychological experiment as a very special form of social interaction. We have proposed that the subject's behavior in an experiment is a function of the totality of the situation, which includes the experimental variables being investigated and at least one other set of variables which we have subsumed under the heading, demand characteristics of the experimental situation. The study and control of demand characteristics are not simply matters of good experimental technique; rather, it is an empirical issue to determine under what circumstances demand characteristics significantly affect subjects' experimental behavior. Several empirical techniques have been proposed for this purpose. It has been suggested that control of these variables in particular may lead to greater reproducibility and ecological validity of psychological experiments. With an increasing understanding of these factors intrinsic to the experimental context, the experimental method in psychology may become a more effective tool in predicting behavior in nonexperimental contexts.

REFERENCES

Asch, S. E. *Social psychology*. Englewood Cliffs, N.J.: Prentice-Hall, 1952.

Brunswik, E. *Systematic and representative design of psychological experiments with results in physical and social perception.* (Syllabus Series, No. 304) Berkeley: Univ. California Press, 1947.

Damaser, E. C., Shor, R. E., & Orne, M. T. Physiological effects during hypnotically-requested emotions. *Psychosom. Med.*, 1963, **25**, 334–343.

Frank, J. D. Experimental studies of personal pressure and resistance: I. Experimental production of resistance. *J. gen. Psychol.*, 1944, **30**, 23–41.

Orne, M. T. The demand characteristics of an experimental design and their implications. Paper read at American Psychological Association, Cincinnati, 1959.   (a)

Orne, M. T. The nature of hypnosis: Artifact and essence. *J. abnorm. soc. Psychol.*, 1959, **58**, 277–299.   (b)

Orne, M. T., & Scheibe, K. E. The contribution of nondeprivation factors in the production of sensory deprivation effects: The psychology of the "panic button." *J. abnorm. soc. Psychol.*, 1964, **68**, 3–12.

Pierce, A. H. The subconscious again. *J. Phil., Psychol., scient. Meth.*, 1908, **5**, 264–271.

Riecken, H. W. A program for research on experiments in social psychology. Paper read at Behavioral Sciences Conference, University of New Mexico, 1958.

Rosenthal, R. On the social psychology of the psychological experiment: With particular reference to experimenter bias. Paper read at American Psychological Association, New York, 1961.

Sarbin, T. R. Contributions to role-taking theory: I. Hypnotic behavior. *Psychol. Rev.*, 1950, **57**, 255–270.

Shor, R. E. Explorations in hypnosis: A theoretical and experimental study. Unpublished doctoral dissertation, Brandeis University, 1959.

Stare, F., Brown, J., & Orne, M. T. Demand characteristics in sensory deprivation studies. Unpublished seminar paper, Massachusetts Mental Health Center and Harvard University, 1959.

4

CURRENT PRACTICES AND PROBLEMS IN THE USE OF COLLEGE STUDENTS FOR PSYCHOLOGICAL RESEARCH

John Jung

A survey of 60 leading universities was made to determine present practices and policies regarding the use of college students as subjects in psychological research. The methodological implications arising from differences in procedures used for recruiting subjects and arranging their experimental appointments were noted. The study also examined procedures employed by investigators to protect the physical and psychological safety of the participating students. Current procedures were found to vary considerably, and it was recommended that they be reexamined from both the methodological and ethical aspects.

Academic psychologists have traditionally relied heavily upon college students to serve as subjects in their investigations of human behavior. Most departments of psychology impose some type of required participation in psychological studies for students enrolled in certain courses, especially the introductory one.

Needless to say, the introductory psychology student is not representative of the general, much less of the college population. The college population differs substantially from the non-college human population in intelligence, age, and social class background. Furthermore, college students with different major areas of study vary in their patterns of attitudes, values, and interests (Bereiter & Freedman, 1962; Sternberg, 1955).

From J. Jung, *Canad. Psychologist*, 1969, **10**, 280–290. With permission of publisher.

The present report describes the results of a survey of leading universities regarding their present sources and procedures for obtaining college subjects. The results are examined from both the methodological and ethical viewpoints.

A questionnaire concerning some aspects of the procedures used for obtaining human subjects was sent to the 60 graduate departments of psychology which have produced the largest number of doctorates (Harmon, 1964). These departments were selected because their policies and procedures probably influence the practice of most other schools since they are the main source of personnel for other universities.

The number of publicly supported (29) and privately endowed (31) institutions in the sample were almost equal and they represented most geographical regions of the United States. The first request was sent in December of 1967 and it provided a return from 39 of the departments. A second request sent a month later produced 13 additional responses, giving a total of 52 respondents. The eight nonrespondents, unfortunately, were all privately supported schools from the northeastern corner of the United States. This loss of about one-fourth of the 31 private schools but none of the public schools may bias the result if private and public schools differ in their procedures.

METHODOLOGICAL ISSUES

Sources of Subjects

Each department was first asked to provide estimates of the types and number of human subjects used in the past academic year. Such estimates are very rough since it is not usual to maintain exact frequency counts. In fact, eight respondents could not provide such estimations.

It should be noted that subjects from the college population usually serve more than once. Therefore, the number of estimated subjects is not identical to the number of different individuals tested but refers to the number of separate subject sessions. This latter index is more useful since it gives a better indication of the volume of research than the former one.

The total number of human subject sessions conducted at each department was divided into sub-categories on the basis of other estimates provided by the respondents, as shown in Table 1.

Table 1   Sources of Human Subjects for 44 Departments of Psychology Providing Estimates

ESTIMATED NUMBER OF SUBJECT SESSIONS	N	PERCENT OF ALL HUMAN SUBJECTS
Introductory Psychology	223,180	79.5
Other Psychology	24,106	8.6
Nonpsychology Courses	6,355	2.3
Total College Students	253,641	90.4
Noncollege Subjects Such as Elementary and High School Students, etc.	27,000	9.6
Total Noncollege Subjects	27,000	9.6
Total Human Subjects	280,641	100.0

The present evidence confirms the accepted stereotype that the subject in human psychological investigations is almost always the introductory psychology student. Smart (1966) has concluded that the college student, especially the male, has become the "white rat" of human experimentation. He tabulated the percentage of total human subjects that were college students in published articles in the 1962-1964 *Journal of Abnormal and Social Psychology* and in the 1963-1964 *Journal of Experimental Psychology*. His findings and the present ones agree closely except that he found considerably fewer subjects were from introductory psychology. Of course, these findings are not necessarily at odds since Smart was dealing with *published* research in only two journals of several years ago whereas the present results are concerned with present practices over a wider range of human psychological research.

In many areas of psychological study, the results obtained with this highly selective population may be safely generalized to noncollege populations. On the other hand, there are undoubtedly many situations which cannot be assumed to be equivalent for college and noncollege populations. The danger of the over-dependence on introductory psychology students resides in the latter category of situations.

Methods of Recruiting College Subjects

There appear to be five major methods for obtaining college students to serve as subjects, three of which involve some form of course requirement. The strongest requirement makes participation an explicit part of a course for each enrolled student. A less stringent requirement treats subject participation as a source of extra credit on the student's course grade. Finally, the student may be offered an option of either serving in experiments or doing term papers, extra reading, etc. The degree of subtlety in these three methods varies, but all of them exert some degree of coercion on the student to participate.

In contrast, noncompulsory methods do not treat subject participation as an essential part of a course. Participation may be either entirely gratis or involve payment for services rendered as a subject. The latter method is usually reserved for extremely lengthy, laborious, or hazardous experimental situations. These two noncompulsory methods are entirely "voluntary" in nature but this latter term is confusing. Even when a student is required to participate in studies, his participation in *specific* experiments is still considered to be "voluntary." Thus, the use of the term noncompulsory is preferred for describing situations where there is no requirement or pressure of any form for any participation.

Many departments use a combination of methods for obtaining college students. Whereas nonpsychology and advanced psychology students are often noncompulsory gratis or paid subjects, the introductory psychology students are usually required in one way or another to participate. Table 2 shows how frequently each method is used by the 44 departments which provided estimates of the number of subject sessions used. It can be noted that there is a close correspondence between the percentage of schools using each of the above methods and the percentage of total college subjects obtained by each method.

Table 2 Methods for Obtaining College Subjects

METHOD	*PERCENTAGE OF SCHOOLS USING EACH METHOD	PERCENTAGE OF COLLEGE SUBJECTS OBTAINED BY EACH METHOD
Required Basis		
Course Requirement	50.0	45.3
Course Option	31.8	25.4
Extra Course Grade	29.5	22.1
Noncompulsory Basis		
Gratis	47.7	4.1
Paid	43.1	2.6
	Total:	99.5

*Many schools use more than one method.

On the other hand, Table 2 shows that the two noncompulsory methods are widely used but account for very few subjects. Noncompulsory methods were more prevalent among private institutions. All seven departments which obtained 100 percent of their subjects by these methods as well as four other departments which obtained at least half of their subjects in this manner represented private schools. The use of the noncompulsory methods accounts for 18 percent of the subjects run in private schools but only 4 percent of the subjects in public schools.

Are the results obtained from subjects "enlisted" on a noncompulsory gratis basis comparable to those produced by students who are required or "drafted" into service as subjects? There is evidence that a noncompulsory system of obtaining subjects may provide a different type of sample than a required basis. Bell (1962) has reviewed a number of studies which suggest that there are personality differences between volunteers (noncompulsory) and nonvolunteers. In these studies students are "invited" to participate in studies, and comparisons are made of the personality characteristics of the volunteers and nonvolunteers (e.g., Howe, 1960; Martin & Marcuse, 1958; Riggs & Kaess, 1955; Rosen, 1951). As Bell noted, most of these studies do not provide an actual task for the subjects in the study so that all one knows is that there are differences in personality but one does not know which tasks are affected by such differences, and how, if at all. In fact, if all subjects, volunteers and nonvolunteers, in these studies were then forced to serve in an experiment, the results might be distorted since the nonvolunteers would probably be uncooperative. This attitude may even have been responsible for some of the reported differences on personality tests in the studies cited above. After the students had been "invited" to express willingness to serve in a study, the nonvolunteers as well as the volunteers were then subjected to batteries of personality inventories. This double-cross of the nonvolunteers may have produced some of the differences found between volunteers and nonvolunteers.

McDavid (1965) found differences in need for social approval among subjects who were tested under a wider variety of conditions. College subjects were either members of a "captive audience" tested in class, required participants, students serving for extra grades, or noncompulsory gratis participants. The latter subjects were highest in need for social approval.

The overall evidence suggests that subjects who serve on some form of required basis differ as a whole from the more biased sample of subjects who serve on a noncompulsory gratis basis. On strictly methodological grounds, it would appear that a required basis for participation would be more sound since nonvolunteers as well as volunteers would be included. On the other hand, ethical considerations would seem to rule in favor of a noncompulsory gratis system unless additional justification could be provided for required participation.

Methods of Scheduling Appointments

There are essentially two types of methods for arranging appointments for participation. Under the first procedure, schedules are usually posted or circulated in classes and the subject signs up for a suitable time. With the second method, each student's class schedule is filed with the department and the student is summoned for his appointment, contingent upon approval by the student.

Apart from administrative convenience what advantages or disadvantages are there for each method? If students arrange their own appointments, some will complete all of their required sessions early in the term while others will not begin serving their sessions until the last few weeks while still others will spread their participation evenly over the term. These individual differences may be linked with differences in personality, motivation, etc.

Furthermore, the type of subjects who sign-up for one type of experiment may differ from those who sign-up for other types of studies. The student grapevine is quite effective in providing information about which experiments are boring, very brief, or have a cute blonde experimenter, etc.

When the experimenter arranges the appointments, these difficulties are reduced. Although sampling is still not entirely random, this method minimizes these factors as sources of biased samples.

The effects of subject selection were assessed by Underwood, Schwenn, and Keppel, 1964) who compared paired-associate learning for subjects who signed up either early or late in the term. They could find no differences between early and late subjects on this type of task. However, it is still probable that this variable may be effective in other types of situations. Thus, Holmes (1967) found better verbal conditioning for subjects who had served in a greater number of experiments.

The results of the survey indicated that appointments are usually initiated by the students. It is the only method employed in 67 percent of the 52 departments. The experimenter or the department arranges all of the appointments in 17 percent of the schools whereas 13 percent of the respondents use both methods.

The number of college subjects tested in departments where all appointments are arranged by the experimenter or department accounts for only 11.5 percent of all college subjects. Thus, the majority of subjects are obtained by the other procedure which may allow more biased samples.

ETHICAL ISSUES

Justification of Required Participation

In addition to the above methodological problems, there are issues regarding the obligations of experimenters to their subjects. If the main purpose of college for the student is education, it would appear that the only acceptable justification for a course requirement of research participation is that it contributes to the education of the student.

Table 3 shows that all 45 departments which had some type of participation requirement offered either education or research need or both reasons as justification.

Table 3 Justification for Required Participation and Educational Feedback Procedures

TYPE OF JUSTIFICATION	PERCENT	FEEDBACK PROCEDURE		PERCENT
Educational and Department Needs	64	Required Feedback		62
		Usually Immed.	33	
		Usually Delayed	20	
		Both Immed. and Delayed	9	
			—	
			62	
Educational Only	33	Feedback Optional		38
Departmental Needs Only	2			
	—			—
	99			100

Informative Feedback

If a student is to obtain educational benefits from research participation, he should receive some feedback about the purpose, design, method, overall results, and conclusions of the experiment. There are, of course, practical difficulties in always providing total feedback.

However, total feedback is an ideal which should be strived for if the requirement of participation is presented to the student as an educational experience. Yet, although a total of 97 percent of the 45 departments with some type of requirement use educational value as part of their justification, 38 percent of these departments have no mandatory policy that feedback be provided. Instead, it is left to the discretion of the individual experimenter as to whether or not feedback is provided. Thi~

is not to imply that none of the experimenters in these departments freely provide feedback, but probably feedback is given less frequently than would be the case if the departmental policy strongly endorsed feedback and did not allow uncooperative experimenters to use college subjects. Such a policy would be a restrictive one, but it would seem necessary in order to be consistent with the policy that participation be educational to the student.

Even among departments which provide feedback to all participants, there are differences as to when feedback is provided, as shown in Table 3. Delayed feedback may be little better than no feedback since students may find it inconvenient to make extra visits to the laboratory. As one respondent noted, most subjects do not bother to return when their feedback is delayed. If delayed feedback is necessary, as in deception studies, some better method is needed to ensure that educational feedback is received by the participants.

Amount of Required Participation

Granting that research participation can be educational, assuming feedback is provided, one often has to wonder if educational value is the *raison d'être* of participation or merely a convenient rationalization by investigators for a policy which provides ample, convenient, and free sources of subjects. How much educational value can students gain from a requirement of as many as eight or ten sessions, as is the case at some schools? The mean requirement for departments with a requirement was four sessions. All too often, the number of required sessions is not determined by educational reasons but by needs of research.

It is possible that the naïveté as well as the degree of cooperativeness of subjects may vary with the amount of their experience as subjects. Some evidence has been provided by Holmes (1967) on this question. Students who had a course requirement of ten participations were given a questionnaire midway through the term as well as at the end. A comparison of students with more than six and those with only one participation at the time of the first administration of the questionnaire revealed that the more experienced subjects had more favorable attitudes.

However, as Holmes noted, both the amount of participation and the favorableness of attitudes may have been brought about by other factors. Furthermore, initial differences in attitudes which may have existed could have been the cause, rather than the effect, of the amount of participation.

In view of these limitations, Holmes also compared attitude changes on the two tests within the same individuals for subjects with four or fewer participations at the time of the first test. The results suggested that more favorable attitudes developed with increased experience. However, since such within-subjects comparisons were not made for all subjects, it is still conceivable that the amount of experience is not the cause of the more favorable attitudes associated with it.

In any case, the point is that subjects' attitudes are not constant over the term. The greater the participation requirement, the more likely it is that results obtained in one part of the term will differ from those obtained at another time.

Privacy and Safety of Participants

There has been substantial concern about ethical aspects of psychological research as evidenced by the recent report of the Panel on Privacy and Behavioral Research prepared for the Office of Science and Technology of the United States in 1967.[1] As the report noted, the participant in a psychological study must often reveal some of his innermost thoughts, feelings, and emotions. Psychological investigations sometimes involve tasks which may threaten the subject's psychological or physical well-being. Although the investigator may claim his right to inquiry, the individual's own rights to privacy and safety must be preserved. Of course, the majority of situations probably involve no clash of the interests of the investigator and the individual. However, in those cases where such a conflict does arise, who must yield his rights to the other?

Of the 52 departments surveyed, 54 percent indicated that all sponsored research is reviewed as to ethical soundness either by a departmental or university committee or by both. An additional 21 percent of the departments indicated that some

[1] *Privacy and behavioral research.* Washington, D.C.: Office of Science and Technology, 1967.

but not all projects were reviewed. No information is available as to the criterion for determining which projects were screened and which were not. It is possible that only the questionable projects were reviewed and the remainder were left to the judgment of the individual investigators.

The responsibility for undertaking all research was left entirely in the hands of individual investigators in 13 percent of the departments. Such a policy assumes that an investigator can be objective in evaluating his own research, an assumption which the Privacy and Behavioral Research Report directly challenged. Finally, 11 percent of the departments did not respond to this item.

All 52 departments indicated that subjects are informed that they may refuse to serve in particular studies which they find objectionable. This provision is a desirable and necessary mechanism for protecting the subject but it should not be considered as a substitute for the impartial screening of research projects. Adequate screening, hopefully, should reduce the number of instances in which a subject refuses to sign-up or continue in a given experiment. This is important because it is not always easy for a subject to withdraw from an experiment because of fear of reprisal, eagerness to please his instructor, loss of face, etc. No matter how careful the screening of projects is, there will invariably be individuals who still find participation in certain psychological studies objectionable.

Summary

Experimentation involving human subjects is too heavily based on studies using college students, especially those from introductory psychology courses. Consequently, generalizations from these studies to the general population are very limited. In fact, it is also hazardous to generalize to the general college population since so few nonpsychology majors are used as subjects.

The methods used for recruiting college students for use in experiments need reevaluation from both the methodological and ethical point of view. Subjects who are required to participate and those who serve on a noncompulsory basis cannot be assumed to be equivalent for many tasks. Furthermore, the basis for instituting any type of participation requirement must clearly take into consideration the value of such experiences for the student.

Differences in the types of samples obtained from the two main methods of arranging appointments for participation need investigation. The more widely used procedure of allowing subjects to initiate arrangements for appointments permits several types of sampling bias. Samples taken at different times of the year may not be equivalent. The samples obtained in studies with different "reputations" among the students may also differ. Use of experimenter arranged appointments is recommended for offsetting these biases.

If educational value is the justification for required participation, more concern should be directed toward ensuring that such experiences are in fact educational by providing as much immediate feedback as possible about the purpose, design, results, and conclusions of studies.

In addition, greater concern for the psychological and physicall well-being of research participants is necessary. The present hesitancy of departments to screen all research projects is not in the best long-term interests of either the students or the investigators. The authority of departments to impose participation requirements upon students, even if of educational value to students, does not relieve them from taking measures to protect the rights and well-being of the participants.

REFERENCES

Bell, C. R. Personality characteristics of volunteers for psychological studies. *Brit. J. soc. clin. Psychol.*, 1962, **1**, 81–95.

Bereiter, C., & Freedman, M. B. Fields of study and the people in them. In N. Sanford (Ed.), *The American College*. New York: John Wiley, 1962

Harmon, L. R. Production of psychology doctorates. *Amer. Psychologist*, 1964, **19**, 629–633.

Holmes, D. S. Amount of experience in experiments as a determinant of performance in later experiments. *J. pers. soc. Psychol.*, 1967, **7**, 403–407.

Howe, E. S. Quantitative motivational differences between volunteers and non-volunteers for a psychological experiment. *J. appl. Psychol.*, 1960, **44**, 115–120.

Martin, R. M., & Marcuse, F. L. Characteristics of volunteers and non-volunteers in psychological experimentation. *J. consult. Psychol.*, 1958, **22**, 475–479.

McDavid, J. W. Approval-seeking motivation and the volunteer subject. *J. pers. soc. Psychol.*, 1965, **2**, 115–117.

Riggs, M. M., & Kaess, W. Personality differences between volunteers and non-volunteers. *J. Psychol.*, 1955, **40**, 229–245.

Rosen, E. Differences between volunteers and non-volunteers for psychological studies. *J appl. Psychol.*, 1951, **35**, 185–193.

Smart, R. G. Subject selection bias in psychological research. *Canad. Psychologist*, 1966, **7a**, 115–121.

Sternberg, C. Personality trait patterns of college students majoring in different fields. *Psychol Monog.*, 1955, **69**, No. 18 (Whole No. 403).

Underwood, B. J., Schwenn, E., & Keppel, G. Verbal learning as related to point of time in the school term. *J. verb. Learn. verb. Beh.*, 1964, **3**, 222–225.

5

PERSONALITY CHARACTERISTICS OF VOLUNTEERS FOR PSYCHOLOGICAL STUDIES

C. R. Bell

The problem of volunteer bias is seen in terms of the unrepresentativeness or atypicality of the subjects who participate in psychological studies. Findings from investigations of the personality characteristics of volunteers are examined under the headings of: (i) unconventionality, (ii) adjustment, (iii) anxiety, (iv) social extraversion, and (v) need achievement. The percentage volunteering response in the invitation situation may be raised or lowered by incentive or restraint factors. The mean percentage volunteering response in the studies reviewed was 37 per cent. Though studies relating volunteer characteristics specifically to particular distortions in experimental data are few, emphasis has frequently been placed on the potential danger of bias from volunteer subjects. A distinction may possibly be made between volunteering as an expressed willingness to participate, and volunteering as actual participation in the experimental situation. Most volunteer bias studies have, in fact, centered on expressed-willingness volunteering. It is not yet possible to provide adequate experimental controls based on the prediction of direction and magnitude of sources of volunteer bias in specific laboratory studies.

1. INTRODUCTION

It is rarely possible, in psychological investigations, for experimenters to obtain data from the total population to whom results are intended to apply. Only, however, when it is clear that experimental subjects are not atypical, in relevant characteristics, of the population from which they are drawn, may re-

From C. R. Bell, Brit. J. soc. clin. Psychol., 1962, 1, 81–95. With permission of author and publisher.

sults be generalized beyond the limits of the experimental group itself. The question of the nature and effect of the atypicality or unrepresentativeness of those who actually participate in investigations, and who are rarely a majority of those asked, is, in essence, the basis of studies of volunteer bias.

Many investigators, whilst making explicit their concern to avoid, or correct for, atypicality bias, appear not always to realize that "representativeness" may be specific to a given experimental situation. Thus it may be statistically established that experimental subjects represent their parent population in age, social class, sex, or intelligence distribution without ascertaining that these are the areas of representativeness—the variables—which are most related to the determination of responses in the particular experimental situation investigated.

In surveys, for example, weighting or correction devices may be used in attempts to overcome bias from incomplete response. Underlying the use of such techniques as the duplication of data from, or increasing the number of invitations to, particular subgroups of the population who have responded less well in the past, is the rarely supported assumption that the factors which have influenced response (volunteering) behaviour in previous investigations are the principle determinants of the reactions to the topic now investigated. Sample stratification schemes and weighting devices in surveys, or the control of the distribution of experimental subject characteristics are useful only in so far as the stratification, weighting, or control is based on the knowledge that the subject variables used in these manipulations are those which *influence* the data collected. As Ferber (1948, 1950) has pointed out, "representativeness" is meaningless in any given investigation unless it is expressed specifically in terms of those characteristics of the subject and parent populations which are relevant to, or influential upon, the particular attitudes, motivations, opinions, or performance investigated.

The question of response or volunteer bias in surveys, in which "volunteering" may sometimes have been better described as "available acquiescence," has been considered elsewhere (Clausen & Ford, 1947; Norman, 1948; Bell, 1961; Scott, 1961). The present report seeks to examine the characteristics, as sources of unrepresentativeness, of volunteers for laboratory studies, for the possible influences which the volunteer may thus have on the data collected, and for the conclusions drawn in psychological investigations.

2. PERSONALITY CHARACTERISTICS OF VOLUNTEERS

Personality instruments used to assess volunteer characteristics have been many and varied in orientation. It is possible, however, to combine some of the findings from individual studies into categories of personality characteristics which are somewhat less narrow than a numerical score on a specific scale of a particular personality test.

(i) Unconventionality

The findings of several investigations have suggested that volunteers may differ from non-volunteers in the unconventionality of their attitudes and behavior. Kruglov and Davidson (1953) gave male students the F (fascism), E (enthocentrism), and PEC (political-economic-conservatism) scales of the authoritarian personality study of Adorno, Frenkel-Brunswik, Levinson and Sanford (1950) as part of classwork. On completion of the questionnaires, students were asked to indicate their willingness "to be interviewed in pursuit of this research" by signing their name. Volunteer (33 percent response from 492 students) mean scores on all three scales were significantly lower than non-volunteer means scores. Rosen (1951) also used the F scale and found that volunteers (46 percent response) for a "personality experiment" had a significantly lower mean score than non-volunteers. Martin and Marcuse (1958) asked psychology students to sign a request form to indicate willingness to take part in experiments on either learning (26 percent response) hypnosis (38 percent response), attitude to sex (40 percent response), or personality (43 percent response). All students had previously completed to E scale. For the hypnosis experiment volunteer mean score on the scale was significantly less than non-volunteer mean score. For the other three experiments no significant differences were found in scale scores. Mean volunteer scores on the F scale did not differ significantly from mean non-volunteer scores in a study of volunteers for experiments on personality and on perception by Newman (1957).

Despite some negative findings with the authoritarian personality scales, volunteers have been described on the basis of the studies cited above as "those who are more flexible in their feelings about people and less stereotyped in their thinking about problems; who are more liberal; and who are less likely to accept ethnocentric ideology" (Kruglov & Davidson, 1953); "less prejudiced" (Martin & Marcuse, 1958); and "less prone to conventionality, authoritarianism, preoccupation with power, and pseudo-toughness and projectivity" (Rosen, 1951).

Maslow and Sakoda (1952) asked female psychology students to volunteer (43 percent response) for a Kinsey interview on attitude to sex and sexual behaviour. Unconventionality in sexual behaviour had been shown (Maslow, 1942) to correlate highly with self-esteem scores on the Maslow Social Personality Inventory (Maslow, 1940). Volunteer mean self-esteem score was significantly higher than non-volunteer mean score, suggesting greater unconventionality in sex data obtained from female volunteers for Kinsey-type interviews. Siegman (1956), using his own development of a self-esteem scale, found no significant difference between mean score of volunteers for a Kinsey interview and non-volunteer mean score. Siegman, however, concluded that "the two groups nevertheless differ in their attitude to sexual behaviour."

Rosen (1951) found female volunteers for personality research had fewer "A" ratings on occupational interests conventionally regarded as feminine on the Strong Vocational Interests Blank (Strong, 1943). Male volunteers for the same research had higher femininity scores on Mf (masculinity-femininity) scale, and higher deviate scores on the Pd (psychopathic deviate) scale of the Minnesota Multiphasic Personality Inventory (Hathaway & McKinley, 1951) than male non-volunteers. Male volunteers, Rosen suggested, tended to "aesthetic-mindedness and individualistic non-conventionality." An examination by Burchinal (1960) of students who failed to return to class after hours to complete a personality questionnaire led to the conclusion that "lack of cooperation is associated with a family value orientation which emphasizes traditional male-female sex roles, power relationships and conventional morality."

Taking these findings together, it appears that volunteers may tend to be less conventional than non-volunteers. Male unconventionality may be in not-very masculine aestheticism and rejection of power and pesudo-tough roles. Rosen (1951) described male volunteers as more "intraceptive and psychological-minded." Riggs and Kaess (1955), on the basis of Thematic Apperception Test responses (Murray, 1938), suggested male volunteers expected "to be coerced or aggressed against without retaliating with aggression." Female unconventionality, on the other hand, may be in not-very feminine feelings of self-assurance and forwardness (Maslow & Sakoda, 1952). Profiles on the Strong VIB and high scores on the Pa (paranoia) scale of the MMPI for female volunteers were interpreted by Rosen (1951) as indicative of greater dominance and aggression. When mixed groups have been compared on dominance and aggression scales of the Edwards' Personal Preference Schedule (Edwards, 1954) no significance differences have emerged (Newman, 1957; Frye & Adams, 1959); nor were differences found on self-sufficiency and dominance scales of the Bernreuter Personality Inventory (Bernreuter, 1935) in an investigation by Martin and Marcuse (1958).

(ii) Anxiety

Scheier (1959) asked students to volunteer for a study of anxiety and found that volunteers were significantly less anxious in scores on the IPAT anxiety scale (Cattell, 1957). The scale is "highly related to . . . psychiatric evaluations of anxiety and also to a factor among objective tests . . . associated with the concept of anxiety, e.g., guilt, inferiority, tension, loneliness [Sheier, 1959]. Psychology students willing to sign a request form for volunteers for a "psychological experiment" gave less anxious responses, though not statistically significantly so, to the Taylor Manifest Anxiety Scale (Taylor, 1953) in a study by Himelstein (1956).

Two findings have been reported, however, of greater anxiety in volunteers than non-volunteers. Martin and Marcuse (1958) found that psychology student volunteers for a personality experiment had a higher mean score on the Taylor MAS than non-volunteers. Rosen (1951) found volunteers for a perse̶ study tended to have higher scores on the D (depr̶ Pt (psychasthenia) scales of the MMPI and sugge̶ thus tended to "feel and admit more discourag̶ inadequacies."

No differences in Taylor MAS scores

volunteers and non-volunteers for a Kinsey interview (Siegman, 1956). In the Maslow and Sakoda (1952) study of female volunteers for a Kinsey interview no differences were found in scores on the Maslow S-I (security-insecurity) Inventory (Maslow, Birsh, Stein, & Honigmann, 1945). Taylor MAS scores did not differentiate between volunteers and non-volunteers for studies of learning, attitude to sex, and hypnosis in investigations by Martin and Marcuse (1958).

The apparent inconsistency of findings relating volunteering to anxiety may be partially explained from a suggestion by Atkinson (1960) that volunteers with low involvement in the experimental situation would tend to be less anxious about participation than non-volunteers, and a study of Howe (1960). Howe invited psychology students to participate, for cash, in experiments involving either a weak or a moderately strong electric shock and compared volunteers and non-volunteers for the two experiments on four measures of anxiety. A short form of the Taylor MAS, and a short forced-choice anxiety scale (Christie & Budnitzky, 1957) failed to differentiate between volunteers and non-volunteers for either experiment. Two scales designed to measure anxiety feelings about the specific experimental situation were also administered to the groups. It was found that in the moderately strong electric shock condition volunteers had significantly less anxious nShockavoidance (males) and nHarmavoidance (females) scores than non-volunteers. No differences emerged between volunteers and non-volunteers for the weak electric shock experiment. From these findings it was suggested that: (a) measures of general, fairly enduring, personality-oriented anxiety feelings may be less appropriate to a differentiation between volunteers and non-volunteers for experiments not perceived as personality-oriented, than instruments designed to measure anxiety feelings specific to, and engendered by, the particular experimental situation for which volunteers are requested; and (b) measures of anxiety feelings related to the nature of the experiment may not ⟨sho⟩w differences between volunteers and non-volunteers if ⟨volunte⟩ring" and testing is at the time of a preliminary indi⟨cation of⟩ willingness which may be temporally and psycho⟨logically⟩ ⟨dist⟩ant from the experimental situation itself.

⟨Anxiety⟩ as measured by MMPI profiles, by the Taylor ⟨MAS, and⟩ the Christie and Budnitzky SFCAS may be a relevant volunteer characteristic in personality oriented studies (Rosen, 1951; Martin & Marcuse, 1958; Scheier, 1959), but anxiety specific to the nature of the experiment would not appear in these scale scores in experiments on learning, attitude to sex and hypnosis (Martin & Marcuse, 1958), and electric shock (Howe, 1960) or in TAT responses of volunteers for a hypnosis experiment in a study by Levitt, Lubin, and Zuckerman (1959). Similarly, anxiety measures may not have differentiated between willing and not-willing subjects where they may have differentiated between participant versus non-participant subjects.

(iii) Adjustment

Lasagna and Felsinger (1954) sought volunteers from among college students for a drug experiment. All of the 56 students who volunteered were interviewed for personal histories. It was found in the interview data, and later confirmed in Rorschach assessments (Rorschach, 1942) that of the 56 volunteers, at least 25 could be classified, from overt admissions of histories of alcoholism, homosexuality, psychiatric treatment, etc., as showing severe psychological maladjustment. This incidence was more than twice as high as that of other college population samples (Lasagna & Felsinger, 1954). The investigators suggested that a strong incentive to volunteer for clinical studies was an awareness of his own personality problem in the volunteer. A similar finding came from a study by Riggs and Kaess (1955) of volunteers for an experiment to be conducted by "clinical staff." Significantly higher scores were made by volunteers than non-volunteers on Guilford's T (thinking-introversion) and C (cycloid disposition) scales (Guilford, 1959). Both these scales have been shown (Trouton & Eysenck, 1960) to be good measures of neuroticism.

The study by Rosen (1951) has indicated an MMPI profile containing high scores for volunteers on the D (depression), Pt (psychasthenia), K (lie), Pd (psychopathic deviate), and Pa (paranoia) scales (viz. Dahlstrom & Welsh, 1960). The MMPI, it has been suggested (Buros, 1949; 1953), may be most advantageously used as an indicator of the level of overall adjustment in the testee. Volunteers for personality research in the Rosen (1951) study would therefore appear to be generally less well adjusted than non-volunteers. In this study and in the investigations by Lasagna and Felsinger (1954) and Riggs and Kaess (1955), it may be that those subjects who volunteered were seeking cathartic experimental situations.

In an experiment recently conducted in this Unit to investigate the effects on performance of exposure to high-temperature environmental conditions, 26 subjects completed Part I (emotional maladjustment) of the Heron Two-Part Personality Measure (Heron, 1956). Frequency distribution analysis in terms of three levels of adjustment gave a highly significant difference in the direction of greater maladjustment of experimental subjects between their scores and the distribution of subject scores in the norms published with the test. The finding cannot be said to be more than suggestive, however, because of the small number of experimental subjects used. However, it seems reasonable to suggest that volunteers for certain experimental situations may tend to be less well adjusted than non-volunteers.

(iv) Social Extraversion

At first sight it would seem feasible to suggest that subjects who volunteer would tend to be more socially bold, more socially extraverted than those who hang back in the invitation situation. Where volunteering is by non-public methods of accepting the invitation, however, there is little evidence to support this suggestion. Gough (1952), using as a criterion the number of extracurricular activities of students, has suggested several personality characteristics associated with a disposition towards social participation. Although some of the social participator personality characteristics do resemble descriptions of the volunteer (e.g., social participation is associated with poise and self-assurance—Maslow and Sakoda (1952) found female volunteers for a Kinsey interview had higher self-confidence and forwardness), in general, the description of the social participation subject (Gough, 1952) does not correspond with descriptions of the volunteer subject.

More specifically, it has been suggested (Rosen, 1951; Riggs & Kaess, 1955) that volunteers tend to be more "inward looking" and "self-absorbed" than socially extraverted. Schachter (1959) found that first or early born subjects are more socially dependent in anxiety producing situations; that they tend to belong to more social organizations; and that they tend to appear less frequently in groups of volunteers than in groups of non-volunteers. In a group of 61 volunteers for a psychological investigation, just over half (56 percent) preferred to experiment alone rather than in company with another subject (Schachter, 1959). Frey and Becker (1958) issued postal invitations to participate in a laboratory experiment to a panel of psychology students. Repliers, whether they participated or not, remained on the panel (pseudo-volunteers). Non-repliers were struck from the list (pseudo-non-volunteers). From the lower scores of the 12 repliers on the Guilford R (rathymia), S (sociability), A (social ascendance), and G (general activity) scales, which are said (Eysenck, 1953) to be highly loaded on an extraversion-introversion factor, it would appear that repliers in this study were more introverted than the non-repliers.

Two studies appear to give results contradictory to the suggestion that volunteers tend to be less sociable than non-volunteers. Belson (1960) found that of the 27 percent of 5225 invitees who came to a BBC audience research test room group, 21 percent came with a friend in response to "a direct suggestion that the invitee should bring a friend." However, this may reflect insecurity rather than sociability for volunteers from the working class, from which there was a proportionately smaller response, more frequently brought a friend than volunteers from semi-professional and upper classes. Secondly, Martin and Marcuse (1958) found that female volunteers scored more highly than female non-volunteers on the sociability scale of the Bernreuter Personality Inventory. This finding may reflect the higher self-esteem finding among female volunteers of Maslow and Sakoda (1952). No other differences in sociability scores were found in the Martin and Marcuse study for male or female volunteers for experiments on learning, attitude to sex, and personality.

Though the amount of evidence on the sociability/unsociability of volunteers is not great, there does seem to be a tendency for volunteers to be less socially extraverted than non-volunteers. In the investigation of exposure to heat, conducted in this Unit mentioned above, the 26 subjects more frequently obtained high unsociability scores on Part II of the Heron Two-Part Personality Measure than subjects in the norming sample (Heron, 1956). Unsociability was measured in terms of agreement with such statements as, for example: "I like to have time to be alone with my thoughts," or disagreement with: "I like to play practical jokes on people." Heron (1956) has suggested, however, that though the scales of emotional maladjustment and unsociability in his test may be independent for relatively well-adjusted subjects, greater emotional maladjustment may take the form of social withdrawal. The apparent unsociability of the 26 subjects may, therefore, be more closely associated with their emotional maladjustment, reported above, than with an assessment of their position on an independent sociability continuum.

(v) Need Achievement

Atkinson (1953) has suggested, with particular reference to studies of association between need-achievement (McClelland, 1953) and recall of interrupted tasks, that: "if persons low in nAchievement are concerned with avoiding failure, it is unlikely that they would voluntarily place themselves in a test situation. . . . On the other hand an appeal for volunteers . . . could be viewed as a challenge by a person highly motivated to achieve." This suggestion, that volunteers are higher in nAchievement, has received some confirmation from McClelland (1958) who, in examining a study by Lazarus (1956) of high school students who responded to a public notice board invitation to participate in an experiment, found that the nAchievement scores for the high school volunteer group were higher than those of a college student group. Previous studies of total student populations had shown that nAchievement in high school students tended to be lower than in college students. The reversal of this trend, from the results of the Lazarus (1956) study, would suggest that nAchievement may play a part in volunteer motivation.

Burick (1956) investigated volunteers for simulated group discussion experiments and concluded that "the selection process wherein subjects volunteer from a classroom situation, may result in the obtaining of a sample of subjects higher in need for achievement than their fellow classmates who do not volunteer." Burdick's observation may apply equally to a study by Bair and Gallagher (1960) of volunteers (42 percent response) for "extra-hazardous duty" from a population of 1154 naval aviation officer cadets. No differences were found in MMPI profiles between volunteers and non-volunteers, though the authors suggested that volunteers were unrepresentative in that they were "actually superior in many respects to the non-volunteers." A major influence on volunteering for the experiments, which involved exposure to extreme cold and "cosmic radiation," may have been a desire to be successful on the officer cadet course. Unfortunately no measure of nAchievement was taken by the authors.

Other Characteristics

Newman (1957) found that male volunteers for a perception experiment obtained higher scores on the Autonomy scale of the Edwards' PPS than male non-volunteers. No similar difference was found for female subjects in this experiment or between volunteers and non-volunteers for a personality experiment. Burchinal (1960) has reported that male students who agreed to return to class in the evening to complete a personality questionnaire showed less "powerlessness" than male students who did not cooperate.

In a review of response (volunteer) bias in surveys, Bell (1961) suggested volunteers tended to be more intelligent and/or have spent more years at school than non-volunteers. Martin and Marcuse (1958) compared volunteers with non-volunteers for experiments on attitude to sex, hypnosis, personality, and learning on the American Council of Education Psychological Test (Thurstone & Thurstone, 1953) and found volunteers obtained higher scores than non-volunteers for the hypnosis experiment, but no differences in the other experimental situations.

3. SITUATIONAL VARIABLES

The mean volunteering response in the studies examined in this report is approximately 37 percent. This figure incorporates data from many quite different volunteering situations. Several incentive and restraint factors have been found to influence the percentage volunteering response which may be manipulable by the experimenter. Unfortunately, in most of the incentive-restraint investigations no attempt has been made to find if there are differences in personality characteristics between volunteers from the various restraint or incentive conditions.

(i) Cash Incentives

Scheier (1960) requested volunteers from a student population for a study of anxiety. He offered: (a) a cash payment, (b) an opportunity to "serve their country's research program," and (c) avoidance of a physical training examination. Of 217 invitees, 60 percent volunteered. These volunteers were lower in IPAT scores than the non-volunteers. Howe (1960) offered a cash incentive to volunteers for experiments involving electric shocks. The volunteering response was 67 percent for the moderately severe shock experiment and 77.5 percent for the weak shock experiment. The 67 percent volunteers had a higher mean score on a "need for cash" rating than the 77.5 percent volunteers. There were no differences in anxiety scores between the two groups of volunteers. Neither of these studies confirms or denies that there may be personality characteristics associated with acceptance of cash incentives for volunteering.

(ii) Public Versus Private Response

Blake, Berkowitz, Bellamy, and Mouton (1956) requested volunteers from student classes for a psychological experiment. In the public response condition volunteers indicated their willingness by a show of hands. In the private condition all students completed an "I do/I do not wish to participate" form. When no information was given about the relative attractiveness of the volunteering and non-volunteering situations, 31 percent of 39 students publicly volunteered and 46 percent of 83 students privately volunteered. A similar difference in percentage response in public and private conditions was found when the percentage response was reduced by increasing the attractiveness of the non-volunteering situation and when the percentage response was increased by lessening the attractiveness of the non-volunteering situation.

Schachter and Hall (1952) also studied public versus private conditions of response on volunteering. They found a marked difference in response percentage between the public (19 percent response) and private (59 percent response) conditions. When, however, half the class in the public response condition had been primed to show willingness to volunteer, 59 percent of the remainder volunteered too. Of those who had indicated their willingness to volunteer in a public response condition,

95 percent actually arrived to participate in the experiment. Of willing students from the private response condition only 73 percent participated in the experiment. It should be noted that a public response condition—which produced much less volunteering in Schachter and Hall's study—may be called a "high restraint" condition only when the social norm of the group is *against* volunteering. Bennett (1955), for example, obtained very high willingness responses in both public (74 percent) and private (78 percent) conditions. In her study of willing subjects who became participant subjects, it was the private willingness group which had the higher participant response (37 percent against 26 percent).

With this qualification to the use of the word "restraint," Schachter and Hall (1952) have suggested that: (a) though lower restraint conditions produce higher percentage willingness response, it is the willing subjects from the higher restraint conditions who are most likely to participate in experimentation, and (b) who may tend to bring to the experimental situation the more potent sources of distortion from volunteer bias. Unfortunately, none of the studies of public versus private response conditions examined for personality differences between willing volunteers and participating volunteers. Many of the volunteer bias studies examined in this report have, in fact, examined personality characteristics of willing versus not-willing subjects rather than participant versus non-participant subjects.

In public conditions of response, the observed behavior of others has been shown to influence the tendency to volunteer. Percentage response in the Schachter and Hall (1952) study increased from 10 percent to 59 percent when half of the class acted as "willing" stooges. Rosenbaum and Blake (1955) and Rosenbaum (1956) have reported similar findings in situations where subjects were individually approached after the experimenter's request to a stooge subject had been accepted or rejected. Rosenbaum (1956) also found that volunteering response was influenced by the intensity with which the request was made. Both "observed behaviour of others" and "intensity of request" factors were found to be independently related to "intensity of feeling . . . (for or against) . . . volunteering." Again there is no information about personality influences upon response in these various situations. Rosenbaum and Blake (1955) have stated that the "act of volunteering (is) seen as a special case of conforming with social norms or standards rather than as individualistic act conditioned by an essentially indefinable complex of inner tensions, needs, etc." This point of view would seem more reasonable if in fact volunteers formed majorities in invitee groups—which they do not. Minority behaviour studies would seem to be quite approachable from an "individualistic act" orientation. Rosen (1951) had stated that his studies of volunteer subjects were based on "the assumption that volunteering is more directly a function of personality and attitude characteristics than of sociological concomitants of these characteristics."

(iii) The Nature of the Experiment

Martin and Marcuse (1958) sought volunteers for four different types of investigation and found that differences in percentage responses and differences in personality characteristics distinguishing between volunteers and non-volunteers occurred between experiments. Davids (1955) compared inter-test consistency of personality scores on measure of neuroticism, social alienation, and feelings of unhappiness of psychology student volunteers for two kinds of personality study. Volunteers requested to participate "in the cause of science" were more consistent in their test scores and showed greater unhappiness, neuroticism, and social alienation, than volunteers requested for a study in which the investigators "were trying to select a mature well-adjusted person." Davids (1955) defined social alienation as a "syndrome consisting of egocentricity, distrust, pessimism, anxiety and resentment," and concluded that the way in which volunteers perceive the nature of the experiment would tend to be an important factor in determining the personality characteristics which differentiate volunteers from non-volunteers. Newman (1957), however, found equal variability in personality measures between volunteers for experiments on personality and perception. In the electric-shock experiments of Howe (1960) no differences in general anxiety level scores were found between volunteers for the two experiments, though volunteers for the moderately severe shock experiment had agreed to participate despite showing higher nShockavoidance scores than the volunteers for the weak shock experiment.

Apart from the findings, listed above, concerning the relevance of cash incentives, public and private response conditions and the nature of the experiment itself to the tendency to volunteer, little information is available about other factors which may be manipulated by the investigator to increase the percentage volunteering response. Brower (1948) has suggested that "morbid curiosity" may play a part in the volunteer's motivation. Greenberg (1956), too, has suggested that the volunteer may be "curious, lonesome, polite." A desire to do well may have motivated subjects in the Bair and Gallagher (1960) study; and in the personality studies of Rosen (1951) volunteers more frequently asked for knowledge of results. The influence of idealistic motives, or the necessity to complete a specified number of hours of experiments as part of a psychology course, or the relevance of the subjects being studied, on willingness to volunteer, has not been explored. The effect of the nature of the experiment would seem to be one aspect of volunteer bias which merits further study.

4. DISTORTION OF DATA

Martin and Marcuse (1958) have stated:

> The general conclusion of this investigation was that there were personality differences between volunteers and non-volunteers associated with different types of volunteering situation and that generalizations made from biased samples can obviously be misleading. The general practice of using volunteers probably owes its wide application to matters of expediency. However, it does not seem that the convenience should substitute for sound experimental procedure.

It is remarkable, in view of the dearth of studies which have shown that particular volunteer personality characteristics have had significant effects on experimental data, how often the sentiments expressed by Martin and Marcuse (1958) have been echoed by others.

Trouton and Eysenck concluded from a review of experiments on drugs, using volunteer subjects, that

> much of the literature on hallucinogens, particularly on mescaline, is subject to the same criticism (i.e., the atypicality of

volunteer subject responses). If it is not possible to use a random sample, it is clearly important to have some measure of the personality of volunteers, and the type and degree of abnormality that may characterize them.

Lasagna and Felsinger (1954) similarly suggested with respect to volunteer subjects in drug research that "regardless of whether *specific* volunteers can be categorized as 'normal,' the personality of such subjects or their reasons for volunteering, or both, may be important determinants of their responses in the experimental situation."

The findings of Riggs and Kaess (1955) that volunteers for an experiment to be "conducted by the clinical staff" had higher scores on Guilford's T and C scales led them to suggest that associated volunteer characteristics would be potent influences in investigations involving "hostility, authority, stress, level of aspiration, memory for failures, self-perception, dreams, fantasies, etc." Differences between volunteers and non-volunteers in scores on Guilford's A, G, R, and S scales suggested to Frey and Becker (1958) the possibility that volunteer bias would "enter most studies of conformity behaviour, group dynamics and anxiety."

Studies of attitude to sex and sexual behaviour appear to be susceptible to bias from the use of volunteer subjects (Maslow & Sakoda, 1952). Siegman (1956), too, has suggested that "although no difference was found . . . in regard to personality characteristics . . . the two groups (i.e., volunteers and non-volunteers for a Kinsey interview) nevertheless differ in their attitude to sexual behaviour . . . (and that) . . . values and attitudinal factors . . . are important determinants of behaviour."

Although Frye and Adams (1959) concluded that "results suggest that, as far as personality variables measured by the Edwards' Personal Preference Schedule are concerned, the volunteer variable does not bias leaderless group discussion experiments," Burdick (1956) has suggested that volunteers bias may indeed influence simulated group discussion experiments. Newman (1957) who found no significant differences in scores on the Edwards' PPS between volunteers and non-volunteers for perception and personality experiments nevertheless concluded that the two groups were "not sufficiently equal to justify indiscriminate and unqualified use of volunteers as representative of the total population in every respect."

Studies of time estimation may be subject to bias from use of volunteer subjects. Eysenck (1959) and Costello (1961) have reported a relationship between time estimation and introversion-extraversion. Bell and Provins (1962) have found that higher emotional maladjustment scores on the Heron Two-Part Personality Measure were associated with higher verbal estimates of time-passed. Both introversion and emotional maladjustment have been used in descriptions of volunteer personality characteristics.

Finally, Brower (1948) studied the performance of 148 control subjects and 59 volunteer subjects (44 percent of those asked) on a maze-tracing task. He found significant differences between the two groups in both time taken and number of errors scores. In a "blindfolded" condition the task was significantly better performed by the volunteer group than by the control group. Though Brower (1948) did not examine his subject groups for personality differences he concluded that there were volunteer variables which

> may all contribute to produce a situation in which a large body of psychological data derived from the university laboratory represent widely heterogeneous and skewed groups . . . (and that) . . . these data strongly suggest that differential motivation may be operative in groups of college students who are used for psychological research.

There is, unfortunately, insufficient evidence, as yet, to enable an investigator to predict that the use of volunteer subjects from a given population would produce a known degree of bias in a known direction on a particular kind of performance. At most, an investigator may be able to extrapolate the findings of studies of volunteer personality characteristics in other kinds of investigations to his own experimental situation. At least, an investigator may become aware that volunteer bias may be a factor relevant to his particular investigation and take steps to assess or control it in the experimental situation with which he is concerned.

5. DISCUSSION AND CONCLUSIONS

Scheier (1959) has emphasized that "volunteers must be compared on precise, valid measurements." Validation of some of the tests used to study volunteers may have been based on clinical assessments of patients rather than on studies of random samples of the normal or college populations from which volunteers are usually drawn. A comparison of volunteers and non-volunteers from a non-clinical population may not be as precise and valid as a comparison of two groups of patients on those tests on which higher scores are indicative of pathological conditions. There is insufficient evidence to support an assumption that volunteers are the pre-morbid personality members of the general population. In many of the studies cited as investigations of volunteer bias, clinically orientated tests may not have provided the most relevant measuring instruments—and may therefore have produced apparently negative results of comparisons of volunteers and non-volunteers where more appropriate tests would have given more positive information.

A second difficulty in assessing studies of personality characteristics of "volunteers" is related to the distinction which may be drawn, in studies of volunteers for laboratory investigations, between subjects who express willingness to participate and subjects who actually do participate in the experiment; and in surveys, between respondents who are available and acquiescent and those who come from their homes with a desire to participate in the enquiry. For the laboratory investigator this distinction is perhaps more important than for the survey investigator. The latter has the problem of assessing how different those who have not been contacted differ from his data-providers in terms of distributions of opinions, attitude etc. The laboratory investigator, however, is concerned to know how the personality characteristics of volunteer subjects may directly affect the data he collects in the experimental situation. If expressed willingness and actual participation characteristics do not correspond, the distinction is an important one, when most studies of volunteer personality characteristics have been concerned with the expressed-willingness stage of volunteering.

It would appear that the problem of volunteer bias in psychological studies falls into two parts. The first lies in the difficulty of generalizing results of volunteer based studies to parent populations who have not been adequately represented by the volunteers. The second lies in the danger that volunteer personality characteristics are such that, although no difference may emerge between volunteer and non-volunteer subjects in the control condition of an experimental routine, the volunteers may be differentially susceptible to the experimental variable itself and may produce a distorted impression of its effect.

The amount of consistent, well-supported information about volunteer personalities and their effects in specific experimental fields of study is obviously insufficient for adequate safeguards to be introduced immediately into all psychological investigations. Nevertheless, it does appear from the studies examined in this report that the problem of volunteer bias in psychological investigations may be an important one. An awareness in experimenters of the potential danger of bias in findings resulting from the use of volunteer subjects is perhaps a necessary first step towards a more complete and useful delineation of the parameters of volunteer bias—not only in terms of the highest common factor of many studies, but also in relation to effect of volunteers taken from specified subject populations for use in specified fields of psychological enquiry.

REFERENCES

Adorno, T. W., Frenkel-Brunswik, E., Levinson, D. J., & Sanford, R. N. *The authoritarian personality*. New York: Harper & Row, 1950.

Atkinson, J. W. The achievement motive and recall of interrupted and completed tasks. *J. exp. Psychol.*, 1953, **46**, 381–390.

Atkinson, J. W. Personality dynamics. *Ann. Rev. Psychol.*, 1960, **11**, 255–290.

Bair, J. T., & Gallagher, T. J. Volunteering for extra-hazardous duty. *J. appl. Psychol.*, 1960, **44**, 329–331.

Bell, C. R. Psychological versus sociological variables in studies of volunteer bias in surveys. *J. app. Psychol.*, 1961, **45**, 80–85.

Bell, C. R., & Provins, K. A. The influence of oral temperature, activity, personality, and method of estimation, on time judgements. 1962, to be published.

Belson, W. A. Volunteers bias in test-room groups. *Publ. Opin. Quart.*, 1960, **24**, 115–126.

Bennett, E. B. Discussion, decision, commitment, and consensus in "group decision." *Hum. Rel.*, 1955, **8**, 251–273.

Bernreuter, R. G. *The personality inventory*. Stanford, Calif.: Stanford Univ. Press, 1935.

Blake, R. R., Berkowitz, H., Bellamy, R. Q., & Mouton, J. S. Volunteering as an avoidance act. *J. abnorm. soc. Psychol.*, 1956, **53**, 154–156.

Brower, D. The role of incentive in psychological research. *J. gen. Psychol.*, 1948, **39**, 145–147.

Burchinal, L. G. Personality characteristics and sample bias. *J. appl. Psychol.*, 1960, **44**, 172–174.

Burdick, H. A. The relationship of attraction, need achievement and certainty to conformity under conditions of simulated group atmosphere. *Dissertation Abstracts*, 1956, **16**, 1518.

Buros, O. K. (Ed.) *3rd mental measurements yearbook*. Highland Park, N.J.: Gryphon Press, 1949, pp. 103–110.

Buros, O. K. (Ed.) *4th mental measurements yearbook*. New Jersey: Gryphon Press, 1953, pp. 126–131.

Cattell, R. B. *Handbook for the I.P.A.T. anxiety scale*. Champaign Ill.: Institute of Personality and Ability Testing, 1957.

Christie, R. W., & Budnitzky, S. A short forced-choice anxiety scale. *J. consult. Psychol.*, 1957, **21**, 501.

Clausen, J. A., & Ford, R. N. Controlling bias in mail questionnaires. *J. Amer. statist. Ass.*, 1947, **42**, 497–511.

Costello, C. G. The effects of meprobamate on time perception. *J. ment. Sci.*, 1961, **107**, 67–73.

Dahlstrom, W. G., & Welsh, G. S. *An M.M.P.I. handbook: A guide to use in clinical practice and research*. Minneapolis: Univ. Minnesota Press, 1960.

Davids, A. Comparison of three methods of personality assessment: Direct, indirect, and projective. *J. Pers.*, 1955, **23**, 423–440.

Edwards, A. L. *Personal preference schedule*. New York: Psychol. Corp., 1954.

Eysenck, H. J. *The structure of human personality*. New York: John Wiley, 1953.

Eysenck, H. J. Personality and the estimation of time. *Percept. mot. Skills*, 1959, **9**, 405–406.

Ferber, R. The problem of bias in mail returns: A solution. *Publ. Opin. Quart.*, 1948, **12**, 669–676.

Ferber, R. More on bias in mail surveys (with rejoinder by R. N. Ford & H. Zeisel, and comment by R. Ferbert. *Publ. Opin. Quart.*, 1950, **14**, 193–197.

Frey, A. H., & Becker, W. C. Some personality correlates of subjects who failed to appear for experimental appointments. *J. consult. Psychol.*, 1958, **22**, 164.

Frye, R. L., & Adams, H. E. Effect of the volunteer variable on leader-less group discussion experiments. *Psychol. Rep.*, 1959, **5**, 184.

Gough, H. G. Predicting social participation. *J. soc. Psychol.*, 1952, **35**, 227–233.

Greenberg, A. L. Respondent ego-involvement in large scale surveys. *J. Market.*, 1956, **20**, 390–393.

Guilford, J. P. *Personality.* New York: McGraw-Hill, 1959.

Hathaway, S. R., & McKinley, J. C. *Manual for the Minnesota Multiphasic Personality Inventory.* New York: Psychol. Corp., 1951.

Heron, A. A two-part personality measure for use as a research criterion. *Brit. J. Psychol.*, 1956, **47**, 243–251.

Himelstein, P. Taylor Scale characteristics of volunteers and non-volunteers for psychological experiments. *J. abnorm. soc. Psychol.*, 1956, **52**, 138–139.

Howe, E. S. Quantitative motivational differences between volunteers and non-volunteers for a psychological experiment. *J. appl. Psychol.*, 1960, **44**, 115–120.

Kruglov, L. P., & Davidson, H. H. The willingness to be interviewed: A selective factor in sampling. *J. soc. Psychol.*, 1953, **38**, 39–47

Lasagna, L., & Felsinger, J. M. von. The volunteer subject in research. *Science*, 1954, **120**, 359–361.

Lazarus, R. Motivation and personality in psychological stress. *U.S. Office of Naval Res.*, Progress report No. 2. Clark University, 1956.

Levitt, E. E., Lubin, B., & Zuckerman, M. Note on the attitude toward hypnosis of volunteers and non-volunteers for an hypnosis experiment. *Psychol. Rep.*, 1959, **5**, 712.

Martin, R. M., & Marcuse, F. L. Characteristics of volunteers and non-volunteers in psychological experimentation. *J. consult. Psychol.*, 1958, **22**, 475–479.

Maslow, A. H. A test for dominance feeling (self-esteem). *J. soc. Psychol.*, 1940, **12**, 255–270.

Maslow, A. H. Self-esteem (dominance feeling) and sexuality in women. *J. soc. Psychol.*, 1942, **16**, 259–262.

Maslow, A. H., Birsh, E., Stein, M., & Honigmann, I. A clinically derived test for measuring psychological-insecurity. *J. gen. Psychol.*, 1945, **33**, 21–41.

Maslow, A. H., & Sakoda, J. M. Volunteer-error in the Kinsey study. *J. abnorm. soc. Psychol.*, 1952, **47**, 259–262.

McClelland, D. C. Methods of measuring human motivations. Chapter I in J. W. Atkinson, *Motives in fantasy, action and society.* Princeton, N.J.: Van Nostrand, 1958.

McClelland, D. C., Atkinson, J. W., Clark, R. A., & Lowell, E. L. *The achievement motive.* New York: Appleton-Century-Crofts, 1953.

Murray, H. A. *Exploration in personality.* New York: Oxford Univ. Press, 1938.

Newman, M. Personality differences between volunteers and non-volunteers for psychological investigation; self-actualization of volunteers and non-volunteers for researches in personality and perception.*Dissert. Abstr.*, 1957, **17**, 684.

Norman, R. D. A review of some problems related to the mail questionnaire. *Educ., psychol. Measmt.*, 1948, **8**, 235–247.

Riggs., M. M., & Kaess, W. Personality differences between volunteers and non-volunteers. *J. Psychol.*, 1955, **40**, 229–245.

Rorschach, H. *Psychodiagnostics; a diagnostic test based on perception* (trans. by P. Lemkau, & B. Kronenburg). Bern: Huber, 1942.

Rosen, E. Differences between volunteers and non-volunteers for psychological studies. *J. appl. Psychol.*, 1951, **35**, 185–193.

Rosenbaum, M. E. The effect of stimulus and background factors on the volunteering response. *J. abnorm. soc. Psychol.*, 1956, **53**, 118–121.

Rosenbaum, M., & Blake, R. R. Volunteering as a function of field structure. *J. abnorm. soc. Psychol.*, 1955, **50**, 193–196.

Schachter, S. *The psychology of affiliation.* Palo Alto, Calif.: Stanford Univ. Press, 1959.

Schachter, S., & Hall, R. Group-derived restraints and audience persuasion. *Hum. Rel.*, 1952, **5**, 397–406.

Scheier, I. H. To be or not to be a guinea pig: Preliminary data on anxiety and the volunteer for experiment. *Psychol. Rep.*, 1959, **5**, 239–240.

Scott, C. Research on mail surveys. *J. R. statist. Soc.* Series A, 1961, **124**, 143–205.

Siegman, A. W. Responses to a personality questionnaire by volunteers and non-volunteers to a Kinsey interview. *J. abnorm. soc. Psychol.*, 1956, **52**, 280–281.

Strong, E. K. *Vocational interests of men and women.* Palo Alto, Calif.: Stanford Univ. Press, 1943.

Taylor, J. A. A personality scale of manifest anxiety. *J. abnorm. soc. Psychol.*, 1953, **48**, 285–290.

Thurstone, T. G., & Thurstone, L. L. *American Council on Education psychological examination for college freshmen.* New York: Educ. Testing Service, 1953.

Trouton, D., & Eysenck, H. J. The effects of drugs on behaviour. In H. J. Eysenck (Ed.), *Handbook of Abnormal Psychology.* London: Pitman, 1960.

6

ON THE SOCIAL PSYCHOLOGY OF THE PSYCHOLOGICAL EXPERIMENT: THE EXPERIMENTER'S HYPOTHESIS AS UNINTENDED DETERMINANT OF EXPERIMENTAL RESULTS

Robert Rosenthal

Scientists are aware of the fact that they are imperfect instruments in the quest for lawful relationships (Wilson, 1952). Errors of observation and of interpretation have been discussed systematically from the time of the discovery of the personal equation among the astronomers Bessel, Kinnebrook, and Maskelyne *et al.* (Boring, 1950). A lively interest in these problems is to be found today among medical researchers and particularly among those working with drugs. Various techniques, such as the "double-blind" method, have been developed in which neither patient nor physician is to be aware of the nature of the substance ingested by the patient (Beecher, 1959). One purpose of this technique, of course, is to avoid errors of observation[1] and interpretation in both subject (patient) and experimenter (physician).

For many of the sciences, there seems to be little danger that

From R. Rosenthal, *Amer. Scient.*, 1963, **51**, 268–283. With permission of author and publisher

This paper is an expanded and revised version of one presented at the symposium: *On the Social Psychology of the Psychological Experiment.* Henry W. Riecken, Chairman, Amer. Psychol. Ass., New York; Sept., 1961. I am particularly grateful for the personal encouragement and intellectual stimulation provided by Donald T. Campbell, Harold B. Pepinsky, and Henry W. Riecken.

Preparation of this paper and most of the investigations summarized were supported by research grants (G-17685 and G-24826) from the division of Social Sciences of the National Science Foundation.

[1] Papers with fairly extensive bibliographies dealing with these and other types of experimenter effects have been prepared for publication.

the act of observation itself may change the object of study, if the object be macroscopic (Reichenbach, 1951). For the behavior sciences, however, when humans or animals are the object of study, the act of observation may very well change the object of study. Research in the assessment of personality has shown that the personality and behavior of the assessor (observer) can change the response of the subject (Masling, 1960). The interviewer in the public opinion survey has been very systematically studied for his effect upon his respondents (Hyman *et al.*, 1954). The experimental psychologist, working in his laboratory rather than the clinic or the field, has been less systematically investigated. Nevertheless, studies have shown that different psychological experimenters (Es) may obtain, statistically, significantly different data from comparable human subjects (Ss) (McGuigan, 1961; Mulry, 1962; Pflugrath, 1962). Further evidence suggests that different Es may obtain statistically significantly different data from comparable Ss even when Ss are planaria (an invertebrate organism placed low on the phylogenetic scale) (Rosenthal & Halas, 1962).

Findings such as those presented, and the conceptualization of the psychological experiment as a social situation led Riecken (originally in 1958, now in press) to state clearly the need for a social psychology of the psychological experiment. Orne (1961) and White (1962) have studied the role of S in the E-S dyad and shown that certain features of an experimental situation may cue S as to what responses may be desired. The purpose of this paper is to consider the role of E as a partial determinant of the outcome of his experiments. More specifically we will consider E outcome-orientation bias; that is, the notion that Es obtain from their Ss, human or animal, the data they want and/or expect to obtain (Rosenthal, 1956).

When an E undertakes an experiment, even if it is not very explicitly formulated, he has some hypothesis or expectancy about the outcome. The expectancy may be vague, indeed it may be a family of expectancies; but the fact of having selected one or more particular variables for study rather than other variables serves as a clue to the nature of the expectancy. To the extent that this expectancy (and motivational variables associated with it) is a determinant of experimental results, we must re-evaluate most carefully the results of those experiments of the past and those proposed for the future which may not have been controlled adequately for the operation of this phenomenon.

We will first present some of the evidence for the occurrence of this phenomenon and for its generality. We will then turn to a consideration of what is known about the sources and mediation of this phenomenon and finally consider some implications of our findings for research methodology in the behavioral sciences.

EVIDENCE FOR THE OCCURRENCE OF EXPERIMENTER BIAS

The basic paradigm for the study of this phenomenon has been to create two or more groups of Es with different hypotheses, or expectations about the data they would obtain from their Ss. In those of our studies where Es ran human Ss, their experimental task has been to obtain ratings of photos from their Ss. These photos were of faces cut from a weekly news magazine and standardized in such a way that most Ss would normally regard them as occupying a neutral position on a rating scale of success or failure. The actual rating scale employed ran from −10 (extreme failure) to +10 (extreme success) with intermediate labeled points. In three different experiments (Rosenthal & Fode, 1961; Fode, 1963) there was a group of Es who was told that they would probably obtain mean ratings of +5 from their Ss while another group of Es of equal size was told that they would probably obtain mean ratings of −5 from their Ss. All Es read identical instructions to their Ss (see Appendix). In the three studies, a total of 30 Es ran about 375 Ss. In every one of these studies the lowest mean rating obtained by *any* E expecting high ratings was higher than the highest mean rating obtained by *any* E expecting low ratings from his Ss. The three p levels were .004, .001, and .004.

Pavlov was aware of the fact that Es could influence their animal Ss. In speaking of experiments on the inheritance of acquired characteristics, he suggested that noted increase in learning ability of successive generations of mice was really more an increase in teaching ability on the part of the experimenter (Gruenberg, 1929, p. 327).

Two studies in experimenter outcome-orientation bias have

been conducted using animal Ss (Rosenthal & Fode, 1960; Rosenthal & Lawson, 1961). In each study, half the Es were told that the rats they would be running had been specially bred for brightness, while the remaining Es were told that their Ss had been specially bred for dullness. The actual learning problems for the rats involved both maze learning and Skinner-box situations. In both studies, Es believing their Ss to be bred for brightness obtained better learning from their rats than did Es believing their Ss to have been bred for dullness (ps were .01 and .02).

At the conclusion of one of these studies, we told all Es of the nature of the experiment which had lasted the entire quarter. Their reaction was most interesting. When Es who had run "dull" rats were told that their Ss were really not dull at all, their uniform reaction was: "How very interestingly you took in those other Ss our rat, however, was obviously *really* dull."

Several other studies, some of which will be discussed later, have also shown the occurrence of the experimenter outcome-bias phenomenon.

GENERALITY OF THE PHENOMENON

The five studies summarized above yield some evidence bearing on the question of the generality of the phenomenon under discussion. Within the framework of Brunswik's (1956) notion of the representative design of experiments, a more complete statement of the sampling domains involved in our research program seems indicated.

A total of twenty studies has been conducted within our research program, of which twelve could be analyzed to determine the occurrence of experimenter outcome-orientation bias. The phenomenon occurred in varying degrees in all twelve studies, the weakest p level being .08, and the median p level being .02.

There have been altogether 250 Es (90 percent of them males) running over 1700 human Ss (approximately 50 percent males, 50 percent females). Fifty different Es (85 percent males) ran 80 rat Ss, about two-thirds of whom were females. Most of the Es and Ss were attending the University of North Dakota and the Ohio State University with smaller samples being drawn from two smaller universities in Ohio. Several of the studies done at the University of North Dakota were conducted during summer sessions.

Volunteer and non-volunteer populations of Es have been drawn from advanced undergraduate courses in experimental, industrial, and clinical psychology and from graduate courses in psychology and education. Volunteer and non-volunteer Ss have been drawn from introductory psychology courses for the most part, but also from other undergraduate courses in psychology, education, and the humanities. Animal Ss were varied as to strains and home colonies.

Spatial-temporal characteristics were also varied. Some of the studies lasted only a few days, one lasted several months. Experimental room characteristics varied from a large armory, in which Es ran groups of Ss simultaneously, to small rooms where Es ran individual Ss, which was the more common procedure. Some of these rooms had one-way vision mirrors and microphones in view, others did not.

In view of the wide variety of E, S, and context domains sampled, we may conclude that experimenter outcome-orientation bias is both a fairly general and a fairly robust phenomenon.[2]

SOURCES OF EXPERIMENTER BIAS

E-Expectation

As described earlier, we have in general systematically varied E's expectations in most of our experiments. Expectation has been one of our major independent variables and, from the studies reported earlier, it is a clearly significant one. Since statistical significance is no guarantee of practical significance, we may ask what proportion of the variance of E's obtained data is determined by his pre-experimental expectation. Four

---

[2] A recent well-done master's thesis by Ursula Ekren (1962) utilizing 8 Es and 32 Ss found no outcome-orientation effects determining Ss' performance on an intelligence test task. In this study there was some question, however, whether individual Es actually were aware of the differential expectancies to be induced in them.

of the experiments included an expectancy statement by Es before they actually ran their Ss (Rosenthal & Fode, 1960; Rosenthal, Fode, & Vikan-Kline, 1960, Rosenthal, Friedman et al., 1964; Rosenthal, Persinger, Vikan-Kline, & Fode, 1961). These statements of expectancy were quite restricted in range and clustered closely around the values E had already been given as an expectancy by the investigators. Correlations between Es' specific expectancies and their subsequently obtained data were computed separately for each treatment group of Es. Considering now only the five groups of Es who were either unpaid for their participation, or paid only nominally, and not explicitly instructed to bias, we find correlations ranging from .31 to .99, with a median Rho of .43. The total N of this group of Es was 36 and, for them, expectancy accounted for 18 percent of the variance of their subsequently obtained data. Had we corrected for the restriction of range of E-expectancies caused by our giving them specific expectations, the proportion of variance accounted for would have been at least doubled. Considering now only the five groups of Es ($N = 30$) who were offered more incentive to bias, or who were more explicitly instructed to bias, we find correlations ranging from .00 to −.31 with a median Rho of −.21. While for these Es, this obtained correlation accounted for only 4 percent of the variance (uncorrected for restriction of range) it is significantly opposite to that obtained by our other set of Es. This finding will be interpreted in the next section. We may conclude that under the more usual conditions of a psychological experiment, E's expectation determines, to a significant extent, the magnitude of the data he will obtain.

E-Motivation

We saw in the last section that E-expectancy interacts with motivation in determining the phenomenon of experimenter bias. Apparently, when E is motivated to the point where he feels he is being bribed to bias, or when he is very aware of his own motivation to obtain certain data from Ss, he tends to show a significant reverse bias effect (Rosenthal & Fode, 1960; Rosenthal, Friedman et al., 1964). In some cases, it may be E's need for autonomy that leads to the reverse bias as though he wanted to say "You can't influence me." In other cases, it may be E's scientific integrity which leads him to obtain data significantly opposite to that hypothesized.

Can anything be said about the relative power of intrinsic E-motivation versus E-expectancy in determining the degree of E-bias? Two of our studies have some bearing on this question (Rosenthal & Fode, 1960; Rosenthal & Lawson, 1961). These studies employed a group of experimental psychology laboratory students who were all intrinsically motivated to have their animals perform well so that they could complete the experiment and go on to the next one. It was for them, phenomenologically, rather important to get good learning from their Ss. Yet, in both these studies, those Es expecting dull performance from their Ss obtained dull performance, suggesting that expectancy effects may be more powerful than motivation effects.

Early Data Returns

That the "early returns" of psychological research studies can have an effect on experimenters was noted and well discussed by Ebbinghaus (1885). After saying that investigators notice the results of their studies as they progress, he stated: "Consequently it is unavoidable that, after the observation of the numerical results, suppositions should arise as to general principles which are concealed in them and which occasionally give hints as to their presence. As the investigations are carried further, these suppositions, as well as those present at the beginning, constitute a complicating factor which probably has a definite influence upon the subsequent results [p. 28]." He went on to speak of the pleasure of finding expected data, and surprise at obtaining unexpected data and continued by stating the hypothesis of the present study: where "average values" were obtained initially, subsequent data would tend to be less extreme and where "especially large or small numbers are expected it would tend to further increase or decrease the values [p. 29]."

Ebbinghaus was, of course, speaking of himself as both E and S. Nevertheless, on the basis of his thinking and of more contemporary observations, it was decided to test Ebbinghaus's hypothesis of the effect of early data returns on data subsequently obtained by Es.

Twelve experimentally biased *E*s, each running six *S*s on a photo-rating task, were equally and randomly divided into three treatment conditions. One group of *E*s obtained "good" or expected data from their first two *S*s (who were actually accomplices), another group of *E*s obtained "bad" or unexpected data from their first two *S*s (who were also accomplices), while the third group, utilizing only naïve *S*s, served as a control. Comparisons were made of the mean data obtained by *E*s from the last four *S*s run. These were all naïve and were randomly assigned to *E*s.

Results indicated that *E*s obtaining "*good*" initial data obtained better subsequent data. *E*s obtaining "bad" initial data obtained worse subsequent data. This effect appeared to be stronger when female *S*s were run. In addition, the effect showed a slight "delayed action effect," appearing to be stronger later in the series of test *S*s run (Rosenthal, Persinger, Vikan-Kline, & Fode, 1961a).

How may the effect of early data returns be explained? Early returns probably affect *E*'s expectation of the nature of the data he will subsequently obtain. We have already seen the powerful role played by *E*-expectancy effects. In addition, early data returns tend to affect *E*'s mood as has been autobiographically and disarmingly documented by Griffith (1961).

The improved mood of that *E* who can look forward to having his original (or newly revised) hypothesis successfully confirmed, may lead to more effective biasing, by affecting his behavior toward his *S*s (Rosenthal, Fode, Friedman, & Vikan-Kline, 1960). The darkened mood of that *E* who hypothesized incorrectly, and who did not revise his hypothesis, would likely lead to less effective biasing, by affecting his behavior toward his *S*s. In a later section, we shall summarize what we know about the effect on *E*-bias of *E*-attitudes and behavior in the *E-S* interaction.

Bias Origin

We have only one experiment specifically dealing with the question of the origin of the bias or the source of the hypothesis (Marcia, 1961). In that study, half the *E*s were allowed to formulate their own hypothesis about the data they would obtain from their *S*s. The remaining *E*s were matched on relevant personality variables and assigned the same hypothesis which the other pair member had evolved for himself. There was a tendency (not statistically significant) for the Es whose hypothesis had been assigned to show greater bias. Jim Marcia, who ran this study, hypothesized that an expectancy induced by a more prestigeful figure might be for E more credible than E's own expectancy or hypothesis.

Modeling Effects

In any behavioral experiment, S is asked to perform some task. E may request S to answer some questions, perform verbal or motor exercises, or simply allow his autonomic nervous system to generate a set of functions on a moving tape. The extent to which a given E's own performance of a certain experimental task determines his Ss' performance of the same task is the extent to which E "models" S (in his own image). In practice, we can speak of E modeling effects (or bias) if a set of Es' performances correlate significantly with their randomly assigned Ss' performances. Modeling effects of Es are independent of E-expectancy or -motivation effects (or bias) only to the extent that E's performance of an experimental task is unrelated to his expectancies or wishes regarding the data he obtains from his Ss.

Eight of our experiments were designed to assess the existence and magnitude of E modeling effects. All of these studies employed the photo-rating task described earlier. Es themselves rated the photos before running their Ss. Modeling effects were defined by the correlation between the mean ratings of the photos given by different Es and the mean ratings subsequently obtained by Es from their randomly assigned Ss. The number of Es per study (and therefore the N per correlation coefficient) ranged from 10 to 26. The number of Ss per study ranged from 55 to 206. The number of Ss per E ranged from 4 to 20. In all, 145 Es ran more than 800 Ss.

The correlations obtained were remarkably inconsistent: the highest two being +.65 and +.52, and the lowest being −.32 and −.49. Taken individually, only the correlation of +.65 differed very significantly from zero ($p = .001$).[3] Considered as

[3] Hinkle, D. N., Personal communication, 1961. The data on which this correlation was based were not made available to us for closer study.

a set, however, the correlations did differ significantly ($p = .01$) among themselves. It seems more likely than not that, in different experiments utilizing a person-perception task, there will be significantly different magnitudes of modeling effects which for any single experiment might often be regarded as a chance fluctuation from a correlation of zero.

Somewhat puzzling was the statistically significant ($p = .03$) trend for the correlations to become more negative in the later-conducted experiments. The only possibly relevant systematic difference between the earlier and later-run experiments was the increasing probability that Es suspected themselves to be objects of study. This recognition might have put Es on their guard to avoid biasing their S with a consequent reversal of the direction of bias. Evidence for a reversal of bias effect has been put forth elsewhere (Rosenthal, Friedman et al., 1964).

Mediation of Experimenter Bias

The question which we will ask in this section is: Granting the occurrence and some generality of the phenomenon, how does it work? Cheating cannot reasonably account for the observed effect since at least those instances of cheating of which we have become aware, tended on the whole to diminish the biasing effect, as when Es who believed their rat Ss to be dull, prodded them, and, in a few cases, presented fraudulent data. Es' data recording and computations were checked, and while the number of net recording and computational errors was very small it was not always randomly distributed. In general, more biased Es tended to make more and larger recording and computational errors in the direction of their hypothesis (Rosenthal, Friedman et al., 1964). All of our own calculations were of course based on the raw data rather than on Es' computation. If neither cheating nor honest errors could account for our findings, what might?

Verbal Conditioning

The most obvious hypothesis seemed to be some form of verbal conditioning. If an E expects to obtain high ratings of photographs, might he not subtly reinforce this type of response? Conversely, if E expects low ratings of photos, might he not reinforce subtly those responses which are low? He might be capable of this system of subtle reinforcement even without any implication of dishonesty, for it might be an unintended response on his part. Fortunately, we were able to test this hypothesis. If indeed verbal conditioning were mediating the phenomenon, we might expect to find that biasing increases as a function of the number of photos rated. Certainly, we would not expect to find any biasing on the very first photos rated by Ss run by different groups of Es. There had, after all, been no reinforcement possible prior to the very first response. In a test of this hypothesis (Rosenthal, Fode, Vikan-Kline, & Persinger, 1961) we found, if anything, that biasing decreased over the course of the photo ratings. Furthermore, there was a significant biasing effect in evidence on the first photo alone, thus ruling out verbal conditioning as a necessary mediator or even as an augmentor of the phenomenon. An important implication of this finding is our need to pay special attention, in our search for the mediators of the bias phenomenon, to the brief pre-data-gathering interaction during which E greets S, seats S, "sets" S, and instructs S.

A subsequent study (Fode, Rosenthal, Vikan-Kline, & Persinger, 1961) was conducted to learn whether operant conditioning could drive the ratings of photos up or down according to the will of the E. Results showed clearly that this was possible, and that it worked best with certain types of Ss. We may therefore conclude, that while verbal conditioning is neither a necessary nor a necessarily frequent antecedent of biasing, it nevertheless could be.

Although not strictly relevant to our discussion of mediating factors in the biasing phenomenon, one of our most recent findings may be of interest (Rosenthal, Persinger, Vikan-Kline, & Fode, 1961b). Recent workers have been much concerned with the role of awareness in verbal conditioning (Matarazzo, Saslow, & Pareis, 1960; Levin, 1961). In keeping with our more general paradigm of experimenter bias studies, we had 18 Es condition their Ss to give high positive photo ratings. Half the Es were told that their Ss would not be aware of having been conditioned. All Es used identically programmed procedures but those Es, expecting their Ss to be aware, did have significantly more aware Ss than did the group of Es expecting non-awareness. Ss were not tested for awareness by their Es but filled out questionnaires which could be reliably ($r = .98$) scored for awareness, by members of our research group, working under blind conditions.

Modality of Cue Communication

Are visual or verbal cues, such as tone, more important for the mediation of bias? Fode (1960) studied this question by using a group of Es behind screens to eliminate visual cues, and a group of Es who remained silent throughout the experiment to eliminate verbal cues. He found that verbal cues of tone are probably sufficient to mediate the biasing but that the effect can be greatly augmented by visual cues. Restriction of visual cues accounted for about 80 percent of the variance of bias magnitude.

In the case of the studies using rat Ss, the picture is less clear. According to Es' self ratings, those who though their rats were bright tended to handle them more, and more gently, than did the Ss who thought their Ss to be dull. In addition, these latter Es rated themselves as seeing their Ss as less pleasant and themselves as less enthusiastic and friendly. We propose very tentatively that Es' attitudes towards their animal Ss were mediated to their animals via their handling patterns, and that their expectations thus were in the nature of self-fulfilling prophecies.

Personal Characteristics of Es and Ss

E's need for approval as measured by the MMPI and by the Marlowe-Crowne Social Desirability Scale (M-C SD) appears to predict E bias rather well. In five samples (Fode, 1963; Marcia, 1961; Rosenthal, Persinger et al., 1963) E's SD score was correlated with his degree of biasing. For a total of 35 Es of medium anxiety level (or unselected for anxiety) the obtained correlations averaged .74 ($p = .001$). For a total of 33 Es scoring very high or very low on the Taylor Manifest Anxiety Scale (MAS) the analogous correlation was negative but not very statistically significant. Preliminary findings suggest no relationship between Ss' need for approval and bias-ability.

E's anxiety level (MAS) has been found related to magnitude

of E's bias in a remarkably inconsistent manner. One experiment found least anxious Es to bias most (Persinger, 1962). A second experiment found medium anxious Es to bias most (Fode, 1963). A third experiment found most anxious Es to bias most (Rosenthal, Persinger et al., 1963). Since each of these three findings could have occurred by chance only rarely, we are forced to conclude that E-anxiety is related to E-biasing, but in an as yet unpredictable manner. A similar conclusion must be drawn from the relationship between S's anxiety and susceptibility to E bias. Persinger (1962) found least anxious Ss, Fode (1963) found medium anxious Ss, and Rosenthal, Persinger et al. (1963), found most anxious Ss to be most susceptible to E-bias. It is of interest to note that in each of the three studies cited, the level of E-anxiety associated with most biasing is also the level of S-anxiety associated with most susceptibility to bias. While this finding may be coincidental ($p = .17$), it suggests the possibility that Ss are more biasable by those biasing Es who are most like them in certain personality characteristics.

We had hypothesized that female Es might be more biasable by male Es because of their role assignment in our culture. In most of our studies sex comparisons were made and typically revealed no sex effect. One of our studies (Rosenthal, Persinger et al., 1961) did, however, show females to be more biasable than male Ss.

One of our studies (Rosenthal, Fode, Friedman, and Vikan-Kline, 1960) suggests that Es who bias more, but without having been virtually bribed to do so, are seen by their Ss as more likeable, more personal, more interested, more honest, slower speaking, and more given to the use of hand, head, and leg gestures than are Es who bias their Ss less. These ratings tended to be intercorrelated and a median Rho with degree of bias was therefore computed and found to be .56 (see also Rosenthal and Persinger, 1962). On the other hand, those Es who, so to speak, accepted the bribe and did not bend over backwards to avoid biasing, were seen as significantly less honest by their Ss. Incidentally, Ss' ratings of their Es' "honesty" during the E-S interaction predicted significantly well the direction and magnitude of Es' subsequent computational errors. Those Es who were rated as less honest made more and larger errors in favor of their hypothesis (Rosenthal, Friedman et al., 1964).

Prior acquaintanceship between male Es and their Ss seemed to facilitate the biasing phenomenon. In one experiment this appeared to be true for both male and female Ss (Rosenthal, Persinger *et al.*, 1963), but in a second study (Persinger, 1962) it appeared true only for female Ss.

The perceived status of the experimenter was found to be related to his degree of biasing. Vikan-Kline (1962) found higher status Es better able to bias their Ss' responses. We have some preliminary data which suggest that Es rated by observers as more professional are the Es who bias their Ss most.

If, on the basis of the data available to date, we were forced to describe the paradigm fostering maximal E-bias, we would postulate an E with a high need for social approval, with an anxiety level neither very high nor very low but similar to the anxiety level of his Ss. E would have high status, be gesturally inclined, and behave in a friendly, interested manner vis-à-vis his Ss. Ss might best be acquainted with Es and perhaps be female rather than male.

The pattern described might be understood best by considering the E-S dyad as a signal exchange system. The signals under discussion are, of course, unintentional. Es high in need for social approval may typically be more precise in their signaling behavior. The business of impression management (Goffman, 1956), or signal editing, is more important to them in their everyday life. Their motivation for biasing may also be greater because of their need to please the source of the hypothesis. The high status and friendly manner may serve to focus Ss' attention on the signal source and increase the likelihood of E's unintentional message being understood.

METHODOLOGICAL IMPLICATIONS OF STUDIES OF EXPERIMENTER BIAS

It seemed reasonable to conclude from our findings that systematic E biasing effects might be eliminated by employing as data collectors, research assistants (As) who did not know Es' hypothesis or expectancy. Not only did this technique seem logically implied by our data, but it would be practical as well. More and more data collection is actually carried out for Es by research assistants. We decided, however, to test the soundness of this methodological suggestion in an empirical manner.

We began by conducting a by now fairly standard experiment in experimenter bias. Fourteen Es ran a total of 76 Ss in the photo rating task with half of the Es led to expect +5, and half the Es led to expect −5 mean ratings of the success of perons pictured in photos. At the conclusion of this experiment, each E was awarded a "research grant" from which he could draw a small salary and also hire two research assistants (E's As). As were randomly assigned to Es who then trained and supervised their two As. Each A then ran five or six randomly assigned Ss of his own (A's Ss). Unlike the original instructions to Es, instructions to As did not inform them as to what perceptions to expect from their Ss. Es, however, were subtly led, by their printed instructions, to expect their As to obtain data of the same sort they had themselves obtained from their own Ss.

Es biased their Ss, and Es' As in turn biased their Ss. The correlation between magnitude of Es' bias and their respective pair of assistants' bias was .67 ($p = .01$). Apparently, E's hypothesis or expectancy may be communicated to his research assistants without E's ever telling As the nature of his hypothesis or expectancy.

What methodological suggestions remain then which might serve to reduce or eliminate E outcome-orientation effects? For those studies in which it is possible to do so, E might eliminate himself and his surrogates from the interaction with Ss. Automated setups make this feasible for some kinds of behavioral research, but not for others. Any technique of instruction of data collectors by E which would eliminate the possibility of the subtle communication of expectancies from E to his A would be a methodological improvement. This would be no easy matter and no perfect solution. The too frequent failure of the double-blind method in medical research attests to this. It is a failure not of "double-blindness" but of maintenance of "blindness." During the E-S interaction each may learn too much about the other to insure "blindness-maintenance."

Not only because of the danger of bias, but also because of the general nature of E-effect, it would be desirable to employ samples of Es drawn as randomly as possible from a relevant population of relevantly uninformed E. Following Brunswik (1956), this would greatly increase the generality of our findings and thus be of benefit even if no bias were ever operating. Alternatively, there may be value in employing samples of Es with known distributions of bias as Mosteller (1944) has suggested in the case of interviewers. The particular biases, however, need not be pre-existing ones, and it may be useful *purposefully* to induce different biases in our sample of Es, giving us better control over the nature and degree of experimenters' biases.

SOME SUBSTANTIVE IMPLICATIONS OF STUDIES OF EXPERIMENTER BIAS

The findings presented lead us to a consideration of the sociology and psychology of science and of scientists. But perhaps the most compelling and the most general conclusion to be drawn is that human beings can engage in highly effective and influential unprogrammed and unintended communication with one another. The subtlety of this communication is such that casual observation of human dyads is unlikely to reveal the nature of this communication process. Sound motion pictures may provide the necessary opportunity for more leisurely, intensive, and repeated study of subtle influential communication processes. We have obtained sound motion picture records of 28 experimenters each interacting with several subjects. Preliminary analyses have given us cause to hope that we may be able to learn something of consequence about the mediation of the E-bias phenomenon in particular, and about subtle communication processes in general. In these films, all Es read identical words to their Ss so that the burden of communication falls on the gestures, expressions, and intonations which accompany the highly programmed aspects of Es' inputs into the E-S interaction.

The study of the mediation of E's bias via his research assistants has particularly interesting implications for social psychology. It appeared from that study that in a two-party interaction (A-S) there may be a non-present third party (E) who operates through one of the participants but without necessarily having simply made that participant a surrogate for himself. The participant serving as "carrier" for the non-present influencer may still be able to exert his own influence in a manner additive to the influence of the non-present participant. Furthermore, interpersonal influence once removed does not appear to be an all-or-none phenomenon. The more a person is able to influence others subtly, the more he seems able to make others carriers of his subtle influence (Rosenthal, Persinger *et al.*, in press).

Some interesting practical questions arise from these considerations. When an experienced physician or psychotherapist tells the neophyte therapist that the neophyte's patient has a poor or good prognosis, is the experienced clinician only assessing or is he actually "causing" the poor or good prognosis? When the master teacher tells his apprentice that a pupil appears to be a slow learner, is this prophecy then self-fulfilled? When the employer tells the employee that a task cannot be accomplished, has the likelihood of its accomplishment thereby been reduced? More subtly, might these phenomena occur even if the supervisors never verbalized their beliefs? The experiment cited suggests that they may.

SUMMARY

In the normal course of behavioral research, different experimenters (*E*s) often obtain different data from comparable groups of subjects. We may call this *E*-effect or gross "error" (Eckler and Hurwitz, 1957). That portion of *E*-effect which is non-canceling or specifically predictable we regard as *E* net error or bias. In this paper we have summarized a program of research on *E*-bias. We presented experimental evidence for the occurrence and generality of the phenomenon. *E*-expectation and -motivation were shown to be partial determinants of the results of behavioral research. Verbal conditioning was rejected as a necessary mode of mediation of the biasing phenomenon. *E* and *S* correlates of *E* biasing and *S* susceptibility to *E*-bias were summarized. Methodological and substantive implications of our research program were discussed.

REFERENCES

Beecher, H. K. *Measurement of subjective responses: Quantitative effects of drugs.* New York: Oxford Univ. Press, 1959.

Boring, E. G. *A history of experimental psychology.* 2nd ed. New York: Appleton-Century-Crofts, 1950.

Brunswik, E. *Perception and the representative design of psychological experiment.* Berkeley, Calif.: Univ. Calif. Press, 1956.

Ebbinghaus, H. *Memory: A contribution to experimental psychology.* (1885) Trans. by H. A. Ruger, & C. E. Bussenius. New York: Teachers College, Columbia Univ., 1913.

Eckler, A. R., & Hurwitz, W. N. Response variance and biases in censuses and surveys. Unpublished manuscript, U.S. Bureau of the Census, June, 1957.

Ekren, U. The effect of experimenter knowledge of a subject's scholastic standing on the performance of a reasoning task. Unpublished master's thesis, Marquette Univ., 1962.

Fode, K. L. The effect of non-visual and non-verbal interaction on experimenter bias. Unpublished master's thesis, Univ. No. Dakota, 1960.

Fode, K. L. The effect of experimenters' and subjects' level of anxiety and need for approval on experimenter outcome-bias. Unpublished doctoral dissertation, Univ. No. Dakota, 1963.

Fode, K. L., Rosenthal, R., Vikan-Kline, L. L., & Persinger, G. W. Susceptibility to influence in a verbal conditioning situation. Unpublished data, Univ. No. Dakota, 1961.

Goffman, E. *The presentation of self in everyday life.* Univ. Edinburgh Soc. Sci. Res. Centre, Monogr. 2, 1956.

Griffith, R. Rorschach water percepts: A study in conflicting results. *Amer. Psychologist,* 1961, **16,** 307–311.

Gruenberg, B. C. *The story of evolution.* New York: Van Nostrand, 1929.

Hyman, H. H., Cobb, W. J., Feldman, J. J., Hart, C. W., & Stember, C. H. *Interviewing in social research.* Chicago: Univ. Chicago Press, 1954.

Levin, S. M. The effects of awareness on verbal conditioning. *J. exp. Psychol.,* 1961, **61,** 67–75.

Marcia, J. Hypothesis-making, need for social approval, and their effects on conscious experimenter bias. Unpublished master's thesis, Ohio State Univ., 1961.

Masling, J. The influence of situational and interpersonal variables in projective testing. *Psychol. Bull.,* 1960, **57,** 65–85.

Matarazzo, J. D., Saslow, G., & Pareis, E. N. Verbal conditioning of two response classes: Some methodological considerations. *J. abnorm. soc. Psychol.,* 1960, **61,** 190–206.

McGuigan, F. J. The experimenter: A neglected stimulus object. Paper based on a contribution to the symposium: *On the Social Psychology of the Psychological Experiment,* Henry W. Riecken, Chairman, Amer. Psychol. Assn., New York: Sept., 1961.

Mosteller, F. Correcting for interviewer bias. In H. Cantril, *Gauging public opinion*. Princeton, N.J.: Princeton Univ. Press, 1944, pp. 286–288.

Mulry, R. C. The effects of the experimenter's perception of his own performance on subject performance in a pursuit motor task. Unpublished master's thesis, Univ. No. Dakota, 1962.

Orne, M. T. On the social psychology of the psychological experiment: With particular reference to demand characteristics and their implications. *Amer. Psychologist*, 1962, **17**, 776–783.

Persinger, G. W. The effect of acquaintanceship on the mediation of experimenter bias. Unpublished master's thesis, Univ. No. Dakota, 1962.

Pflugrath, J. Examiner influence in a group testing situation with particular reference to examiner bias. Unpublished master's thesis, Univ. No. Dakota, 1962.

Reichenbach, H. *The rise of scientific philosophy*. Berkeley & Los Angeles: Univ. Calif. Press, 1951.

Riecken, H. W. A program for research on experiments in social psychology. In *Decisions, values and groups*. Vol. II. New York: Pergamon Press, 1962.

Rosenthal, R. The hypothesis of unconscious experimenter bias. In: An attempt at the experimental induction of the defense mechanism of projection. Unpublished doctoral dissertation, UCLA, 1956, pp. 65–72.

Rosenthal, R., & Fode, K. L. The effect of experimenter bias on the performance of the albino rat. Unpublished manuscript, Harvard Univ., 1960.

Rosenthal, R. & Fode, K. L. The problem of experimenter outcome-bias. In Ray, D. P. (Ed.) *Series research in social psychology*. Symposia studies series no. 8, Wash., D.C. Natl. Inst. Soc. Behav. Sci., 1961.

Rosenthal, R., Fode, K. L., Friedman, C. J., & Vikan-Kline, L. L. Subjects' perception of their experimenter under conditions of experimenter bias. *Percept. mot. Skills*, 1960, **11**, 325–331

Rosenthal, R., Fode, K. L., & Vikan-Kline, L. L. The effect on experimenter bias of varying levels of motivation of Es and Ss. Unpublished manuscript. Harvard Univ., 1960.

Rosenthal, R., Fode, K. L., Vikan-Kline, L. L., & Persinger, G. W. The role of verbal conditioning in the mediation of experimenter outcome-bias. Unpublished manuscript, Harvard Univ., 1961.

Rosenthal, R., Friedman, C. J., Johnson, C. A., Fode, K. L., Schill, T. R., White, C. R., & Vikan-Kline, L. L. Variables affecting experimenter bias in a group situation. *Genet. Psychol. Monogr.,* 1964, **70,** 271–296.

Rosenthal, R., & Halas, E. S. Experimenter effect in the study of invertebrate behavior. *Psychol. Rep.,* 1962, **11,** 251–256.

Rosenthal, R., & Lawson, R. A longitudinal study of the effects of experimenter bias on the operant learning of laboratory rats. Unpublished manuscript, Harvard Univ., 1961.

Rosenthal, R., & Persinger, G. W. Let's pretend: Subjects' perception of imaginary experimenters. *Percept. mot. Skills,* 1962, **14,** 407–409.

Rosenthal, R., Persinger, G. W., & Fode, K. L. Experimenter bias, anxiety, and social desirability. *Percept. mot. Skills,* 1962, **15,** 73–74.

Rosenthal, R., Persinger, G. W., Vikan-Kline, L. L., & Fode, K. L. The effect of early data returns on data subsequently obtained by outcome-biased experimenters. Unpublished manuscript, Harvard Univ., 1961   (a)

Rosenthal, R., Persinger, G. W., Vikan-Kline, L. L., & Fode, K. L. The effect of experimenter bias and subject set on awareness in verbal conditioning. Unpublished manuscript, Harvard Univ., 1961.   (b)

Rosenthal, R., Persinger, G. W., Vikan-Kline, L. L., & Mulry, R. C. The role of the research assistant in the mediation of experimenter bias. *J. Pers.,* 1963, **31,** 313–335.

Vikan-Kline, L. L. The effect of an experimenter's status on the mediation of experimenter bias. Unpublished master's thesis, Univ. No. Dakota, 1962.

White, C. R. The effect of induced subject expectations on the experimenter bias situation. Unpublished doctoral dissertation, Univ. No. Dakota, 1962.

Wilson, E. B. *An introduction to scientific research.* New York: McGraw-Hill, 1952.

APPENDIX

SAMPLE INSTRUCTIONS TO *Es* AND *Ss*[4]

Instructions to *Es*

You have been asked to participate in a research project developing a test of empathy. The reason for your participation

[4] Instructions varied from study to study. These are presented as fairly typical.

in this project is to standardize results of experiments of this type. There is the problem in psychological research of different examiners getting somewhat different data on the same tests as a function of individual differences. Therefore, to standardize the tests it is better methodological procedure to use groups of experimenters.

You will now be asked to run a series of Ss and obtain from each ratings of photographs. The experimental procedure has been typed out for you and is self-explanatory.

According to preceding research of this nature, the type of subjects that you will be using have averaged a +5 rating.[5] Therefore, the Ss you are running should also average about a +5 rating.

Just read the instructions to the Ss. Say nothing else to them except hello and goodbye. If for any reason you should say anything to an S other than that which is written in your instructions, please write down the exact words you used and the situation which forced you to say them.

GOOD LUCK!

Experimental Procedure for Es

In front of you, you will find the instructions you are to read to your Ss, a sheet of paper for recording each S's rating for each photo and a set of 20 numbered photos.

After recording data from each subject at the top of the recording sheet and reading instructions to the E, you are ready to begin.

Take photo #1 and say: "This is photo #1" and hold it in front of the S until he tells you his rating, which you will write down on the recording sheet. Continue this procedure through the 20 photos. Do not let any S see any photo for longer than 5 seconds.

After each subject, total the ratings of the 20 photos and find the average (mean).

Instructions to Ss

I am going to read you some instructions. I am not permitted to say anything which is not in the instructions nor can I answer any questions about this experiment. OK?

[5] For half the Es this read "−5."

We are in the process of developing a test of empathy. This test is designed to show how well a person is able to put himself into someone else's place. I will show you a series of photographs. For each one I want you to judge whether the person pictured has been experiencing success or failure. To help you make more exact judgments you are to use this rating scale. As you can see, the scale runs from −10 to +10. A rating of −10 means that you judge the person to have experienced extreme failure. A rating of +10 means that you judge the person to have experienced extreme success. A rating of −1 means that you judge the person to have experienced mild failure while a rating of +1 means that you judge the person to have experienced mild success. You are to rate each photo as accurately as you can. Just tell me the rating you assign to each photo. All ready? Here is the first photo. (No further explanation may be given although all or part of the instructions may be repeated.)

THE EXPERIMENTER:
A NEGLECTED STIMULUS OBJECT

F. J. McGuigan

In single E experiments it is not possible to generalize to a population of Es. There are 3 cases for multi-E experiments: In Case I different Es do not differentially affect the results; in Case II one E obtains higher scores for all groups than does a second E; and in Case III E characteristics interact with treatment conditions. Results are potentially generalizable for Cases I and II, but not for Case III. Evidence indicates that multi-E experiments are common, but that reports of procedure and results for different Es are almost nonexistent. It is essential that we explicitly attempt to generalize to a population of Es; specify techniques of controlling the E variable; and accumulate knowledge in a variety of experimental situations about the effects of Es on their Ss.

To say that behavior is a function of a fantastically large number of stimulus variables is to understate the immensity of the problem facing the psychologist. Clearly, the sustained laboratory dissection of our environment has produced considerable information about the relationship between behavior and a number of classes of stimulus variables, but just as clearly much more remains to be accomplished. In assessing our status, it is

From F. J. McGuigan, *Psychol. Bull.*, 1963, **60**, 421–428. With permission of author and publisher.

Modification of a paper presented at the American Psychological Association meetings, 1961, in a symposium entitled "The Social Psychology of the Psychological Experiment."

The author expresses appreciation to Sherman Ross for his valuable suggestions concerning the presentation of this paper.

well to emphasize the presence of one particular stimulus object of the complex environment in which we immerse subjects —the experimenter himself. While we have traditionally recognized that the characteristics of an experimenter may indeed influence behavior, it is important to observe that we have not seriously attempted to study him as an independent variable. Rather, we have typically regarded the experimenter as necessary, but undesirable, for the conduct of an experiment. Accordingly, in introductory textbooks on experimental psychology we provide prescriptions for controlling this extraneous variable; but seldom do we consider the experimenter variable further, and the extent to which we actually control it in our experimentation can be seriously questioned. As documentation for this statement, consider some findings based on an analysis of 37 usable articles from three recent issues (selected at random) of the *Journal of Experimental Psychology*. These articles were classified according to the number of possible data collectors and number of authors. In Table 1 we can see that 10 of the 37

Table 1 Number of Possible Data Collectors in a Sample of Articles from the *Journal of Experimental Psychology*

NO. OF AUTHORS	NO. OF ARTICLES	NO. OF POSSIBLE DATA COLLECTORS			
		1	2	3	4
1	16	10	3	1	2
2	17	0	14	2	1
3	4	0	0	4	0
Total	37	10	17	7	3

articles had only one possible data collector. It is reasonable to assume that at least a majority of the other 27 experiments employed more than one data collector. In no article was any mention made of techniques of controlling the experimenter variable and in only one of the articles was the number of data collectors actually specified. Furthermore, in no article was a statistical analysis of results as a function of experimenters reported. It seems quite clear that we are deficient in the write-up and analysis, if not in the design of our experiments as far as the experimenter variable is concerned. The possibility is alarming that in multidata collector experiments adequate control is not exercised. Especially is this so for those psychologists who have witnessed in amazement the conduct of experiments by some of their colleagues in which one experimenter collects data for a while, after which he is relieved by another experimenter, with no plan for balancing the subjects in the groups over the experiments. Such an experiment is totally indefensible. But it is, optimistically, assumed to be relatively rare. Where pains *have* been taken to control the experimenter variable in multiexperimenter experiments, it is unreasonable to request that results be presented as a function of experimenters. This request has three bases: (a) it will justify the control procedures used, (b) it will help indicate the extent to which the results are generalizable to a population of experimenters, and (c) it will provide much needed information on the extent and nature of the experimenter's influence on the subjects. Point a needs no further elaboration. But points c and b can profitably be developed.

SAMPLING FROM A POPULATION OF EXPERIMENTERS

Assume that in a given experiment it was possible to control the experimenter variable in a completely adequate fashion by holding that variable constant. This means that the numerous stimuli emanating from the experimenter-stimulus object have assumed the same constant, but unspecified, value for all the subjects throughout the experiment. Whatever the intensity and other values of these experiment-produced stimuli, we are assuming that they have not differentially affected the behavior of the subjects.

Clearly such a technique of controlling the experimenter variable is not practical. But that is not the worst of it. For controlling any variable by holding it constant is only defensible in the long run if the one experiment concerned exhausts the universe of investigations on the problem posed. And never would a universe of experiments be limited to one. Hence, let us consider that our hypothetical experiment in which the experimenter variable is held constant is repeated by another experimenter, one who takes pains to duplicate all of the conditions of our experiment that have been specified. And there is the rub. In the original experiment we have held the experimenter variable constant, but it simply was not possible to specify the intensity and other values of that complex variable. While in the replication of our hypothetical experiment we may assume that the experimenter variable was similarly held constant, it is also safe to assume that it was held constant at different values than obtained in our original experiment.

Let us take a particular, measurable characteristic of the experimenter as an illustration. Suppose that the experimenter in one experiment manifests what we call a high degree of anxiety, whereas the second experimenter has a low degree of anxiety. We can well expect that the stimuli emitted by these two experimenters will either be different in nature, or in value. Will these two classes of stimuli differentially affect the dependent variable measures of the subjects in the two experiments? This question gives us the opportunity to make sure that we are in agreement with respect to the place of the experimenter variable in psychological research.

The problems arising in the sampling of subjects for experimenters have received considerable attention—the undergraduate psychology major who is not aware of the mechanics of obtaining a random sample from a well-defined population of subjects is probably a rare specimen. While the way was paved some years ago, particularly by Brunswik (e.g., 1947), however, the same cannot be said with regard to other populations relevant to experimentation. Brunswik emphasized the importance of sampling stimulus populations, but rarely are such populations actually systematically sampled in psychology today —especially is this true of the subclass of stimulus variables emitted by the experimenter who faces the subjects. On any given problem, we could define a population of experimenters, although admittedly not easily in an unambiguous fashion. In our conduct of an experiment on that problem, then, strictly speaking we should employ a design (such as a complete factorial design) that allows us to vary experimenters—we should randomly sample from a population of experimenters and replicate the experiment for each experimenter used.

Now let us return to our question: Does the fact that two experimenters who differ only in regard to a single characteristic affect the performance of subjects in two otherwise identical experiments? There are three general answers possible.

CASE I

First, the stimulus characteristic in question is totally unrelated to the dependent variable being measured. In this event essentially the same scores would be obtained by both experimenters. Clearly in this case, we need not be concerned in the slightest as to whether or not experimenters in our hypothetical population differ—their respective characteristics have no differential effects on the dependent variable. There is but one remaining point: we could not possibly know this unless we had designed and analyzed our experiment to find it out.

CASE II

The second general possibility is that the variable for which the two experimenters differ does affect the dependent variable, but it affects all subjects in the same way, regardless of the experimental condition to which those subjects were assigned. For example, we might suppose that subjects assigned to the anxious experimenter perform at a higher level on the average, than do those assigned to the nonanxious experimenter.

Typically, we are interested in whether or not one group of subjects performs higher or lower than a second group on a given dependent variable measure. Since in this second case we are able to reach the same conclusion with regard to our hypothesis regardless of which experimenter conducted the experiment, we are not immediately interested in the experimenter difference. As an adjunct to this experiment, however, we note that a particular kind of behavior *is* influenced by this experimenter characteristic, information that is potentially valuable.

CASE III

The first two possible answers to our question do not greatly concern us. The third, however, can be rather important. To take an extreme case, let us say that the performance of an experimental group is superior to that of a control group for the anxious experimenter, but that the reverse is true for the nonanxious experimenter. In short, suppose that there is an interaction between the characteristics with which the experimenters differ and the independent variable of the experiment.

As an example of a Case III experiment, briefly consider an interaction reported by Kanfer (1958). Two experimenters who had "minimal gross differences" participated in a verbal conditioning experiment. The subjects were required to say words continually and the verbs that they emitted were reinforced by flashing a light according to one of three reinforcement schedules. The experimenter's task was simple—to discriminate between verbs and nonverbs, and flash a light. The results indicated a significant Method × Experimenter interaction—there was more frequent reinforcement of words for one schedule than for the others, the frequency varying for the experimenters. The experimenters evidently differed from each other in their ability to perceive verbs as a function of reinforcement schedule. The reason for this seems obscure, but the lesson to the investigator is again driven home—if our results are a function of experimenter characteristics, then they are highly specific and cannot be generalized.

It should be emphasized that interactions involving experimenters may not only be unexpected, but quite obscure. In general we simply have not had enough experience with experimenter interactions to know where to look for them. To further emphasize the obscurity of this type of interaction, consider some results from a study involving four methods of learning and nine experimenters (McGuigan, 1960). The analysis of variance indicated that there was a significant difference among methods but that experimenters did not differ, and particularly that the methods by experimenter interaction was not significant. According to our normal procedure, we would conclude that the results with regard to methods is not a function of experimenters. But now let us study the interexperimenter variability more closely. We can note that there is considerable variability among experimenters for Methods P and VIW in Figure 1, but that there is relatively little interexperimenter variability for Methods IW and W. The variance for each method was computed and it was found that they differ significantly. Furthermore, the variability among the experimenters is a function of methods when methods are ordered from P to VIW to IW and to W.

In Figure 1 we arranged the experimenters on the horizontal axis in a random fashion. Lines of best fit are approximately

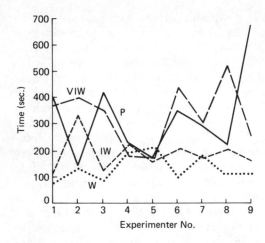

Figure 1   Dependent variable scores for four methods plotted as a function of experimenters (after McGuigan, 1960).

parallel. In Figure 2, however, we have arranged the experimenters according to intraexperimenter variability. Now lines of best fit appear to deviate rather markedly from being parallel. Particularly note that the relative proficiency due to the various methods is a function of the experimenters. Here we have a single experiment replicated nine times. Suppose that we had conducted the experiment only once using, say, Experimenter Number 9. This experimenter yielded a clear set of results due to methods. But had we chosen Experimenter Number 8, a different set of results would have obtained. And contrast these results with those obtained by Experimenter Number 4 where no significant differences among methods appear. The problem posed by Figure 2 is: What are the characteristics of the experimenters that cause them to be ordered along the horizontal axis in this particular fashion? There are two possible answers: First, that the experimenters varied in their techniques of administering the independent variables and recording the dependent variable. In this case the solution is quite clear and we have long been aware of the problem—precise adherence to experimental procedure as we report it in detail in our publications. That this principle is not strictly adhered to can be made manifestly clear by conducting interexperimenter analyses. The re-

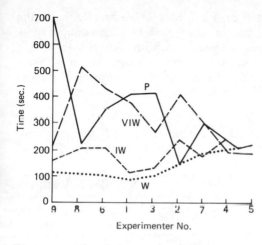

Figure 2 The data points of Figure 1 ordered according to intra-experimenter variability.

cent work of Azrin, Holz, Ulrich, and Goldiamond (1961) on operant conditioning of conversations by student experimenters indicated considerable variation in reinforcement techniques as well as downright distortion. Stories of violation of proper data collection procedures by graduate assistants are legion, if somewhat suppressed. Analyses to determine differences among experimenters on dependent variable scores can serve to at least stimulate investigation of procedural problems in a given experiment. The second possible difference among experimenters in Figure 2 concerns what we might call personality characteristics of the experimenters—we have a possible ordering of experimenters along some personality dimension. The only question is what is it and how might we discover it? One thing we could do when we find this sort of interaction is to administer a battery of personality tests to our experimenters, in an effort to determine personality differences that differentially influenced a given dependent variable. Hints can thus be obtained that can lead to additional experiments in which characteristics of the experimenters are varied in an effort to better understand the nature of these interactions that concern us. We actually did this for the experimenters of Figure 2. Table 2 shows a sample of the correlations between trait scores of the experimenters and dependent variable scores of their subjects. None of the correlations was significant, but several were high enough to be somewhat suggestive even without significant differences among experimenters, and with such a limited sample. As an illustration: the more neurotic (B1-N scale of the Bernreuter) the experimenter the poorer the performance of the subject.

Table 2 r's Between Personality Characteristics of Nine Experimenters and Dependent Variable Scores (Time to Perform a Task) of Their Subjects

BERNREUTER		BELL		MANIFEST ANXIETY
B1-N:	.35	A:	.15	.04
B2-S :	.19	B :	.15	
B3-I :	.24	C :	.09	
B4-D:	.14	D:	.08	
F1-C :	.16			
F2-S :	.23			

Experiments in which experimenters with different personality characteristics were deliberately used are few in number. One such study was a verbal conditioning experiment using the response class of hostile words emitted in sentences (Binder, McConnell, & Sjoholm, 1957). Whenever the subject used a hostile word in a sentence the experimenter reinforced that response by saying "good." Two groups were used, a different experimenter for each group. The two experimenters differed in gender, height, weight, age, appearance, and personality:

> The first . . . was . . . an attractive soft-spoken, reserved young lady . . . 5'½" in height, and 90 pounds in weight. The . . . second . . . was very masculine, 6'5" tall, 220 pounds in weight, and had many of the unrestrained personality characteristics which might be expected of a former marine captain—perhaps more important than their actual age difference of about 12 years was the difference in their age appearance: the young lady could have passed for a high school sophomore while the male experimenter was often mistaken for a faculty member [Binder et al., 1957, p. 309].

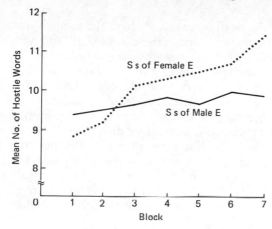

Figure 3 Learning curves for two groups treated the same except for experimenters. (The steeper slope for the subjects of the female experimenter illustrates an interaction involving exprimenters—after Binder *et al.*, 1957.)

The results of this experiment are shown in Figure 3. We can see that the rate of emitting hostile words increases with trials for both groups—saying "good" reinforced the response for both experimenters. But of particular significance to us now is the fact that the rates of learning for the two groups differed significantly—the slope is steeper for the female experimenter's group. Clearly the differences between the two experimenters are numerous, so it is difficult to specify just what experimenter characteristic or combination of characteristics is responsible for this difference in learning rate for the two groups. But this research is a promising start. A follow-up of it might be aimed at testing the authors' speculation as to the important difference: that the female experimenter "provided a less threatening environment, and the *S*s consequently were less inhibited in the tendency to increase their frequency of usage to hostile words" (Binder *et al.*, 1957, p. 313).

An interesting experiment by Spires (1960) is illustrative of how characteristics of the subjects can interact with perceived characteristics of the experimenter. Spires selected a group of subjects high on the *Hy* scales of the MMPI and a second high on the *Pt* scale. The subjects entered the experimental situation with one of two sets: the positive set was where the subject was told the experimenter was a "warm, friendly person, and you should get along very well"; the negative set was where the subject was told that the experimenter may "irritate him a bit, that he's not very friendly, in fact kind of cold." This was a verbal conditioning study in which a class of pronouns was reinforced by saying "good." An analysis of variance for Spire's results indicated that there was a significant difference between positive and negative sets for the experimenters (the positive set leading to better conditioning), and that the interaction between set for the experimenter and MMPI score of the subject was significant. This interaction is illustrated by the learning curves shown in Figure 4. There we can see that the hysterics,

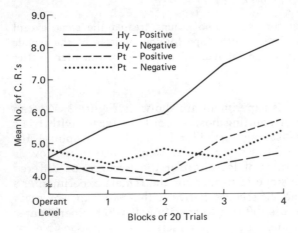

Figure 4 Learning curves for four conditions. (The marked departure of the *Hy*-positive-set group—solid line—illustrates an interaction between set for the experimenter and personality characteristic of the subjects—after Spires, 1960.)

who had a positive set for their experimenter, condition remarkably better than the other three groups. While apparently this is the only study which shows that a rather well-defined personality characteristic of the subject interacts with a perceived characteristic of the experimenter, further investigation would undoubtedly yield additional interactions of this nature.

Conclusions

1. Where one data collector is used in an experiment, the best that can be done is to attempt to hold his influence on the subjects constant. The results, in this instance, cannot strictly speaking be generalized to the relevant population of experimenters—if they are, the generalization must be extended exceedingly cautiously, at best. While it is not possible to adequately specify the experimenter's characteristics in the report of the experiment, it should be recognized that this inability does not remove the problem—it persists and for a worker in a particular area the question of generalization from a single-experimenter experiment can assume nightmarish proportions.

2. Where more than one data collector has been used (a) techniques of control should be specified, (b) the data should be analyzed and reported as a function of experimenters, and (c) interactions between experimenters and treatments should be tested. Should the results indicate that the experiment is an instance of Cases I or II, the results are generalizable to a population of experimenters to the extent to which such a population has been sampled. Granted that completely satisfactory sampling can seldom occur, at least some sampling is better than none. And it is beneficial to *know* and to be able to *state* that, within those limitations, the results appear to be instances of Cases I or II. If the experiment turns out to be an instance of Case III, the extent to which the results can be generalized is sharply limited. One can only say, for instance, that Method A will be superior to Method B when experimenters similar to Experimenter Number 1 are used, but that the reverse is the case when experimenters similar to Experimenter Number 2 are used. This knowledge is of course valuable, but only in a negative sense since we do not know what the characteristics of the two experimenters are—to understate the matter, the interaction tells us to proceed with considerable caution.

3. It is important to contribute to our general fund of knowledge of the experimenter variable, for it is indeed small at this time. That this request to collect relevant data will not excessively burden us is indicated by the frequency with which more than one experimenter already participates in an experiment (see Table 1; further, note that in a sample of 722 articles from journals concerned primarily with experiments, 48 percent had

two or more authors [Woods, 1961]). Quite clearly we already have enough information to safely assert that interactions between experimenters and treatments do occur. But there is a paucity of data about their frequency of occurrence as a function of type of experimental situation. By designing more experiments to test for differences between experimenters and for interactions involving experimenters we may eventually be able to handle the problems indicated in Number 1 above and by instances of Case III.

As with all other variables with which we are concerned, determining the effects of the experimenter variable is a long, energy-consuming project. But we must face up to our task. Recognizing the enormity of this project, one can well ask whether or not there is a more efficient approach. The only other possibility that occurs at present is to eliminate the experimenter from the experiment. For some problems that we study, this would be relatively easy, but it is hard to visualize how this could be accomplished in other experiments. For instance, a number of completely automated devices have been developed and successfully used in running rats—the subjects are never exposed to a human experimenter. Automation has also entered psychology at the human level, but in neither case is automation very general, and certainly it is not standardized. In a number of experiments it seems reasonable to have the subject enter the experimental room and be directed completely by taped instructions, thus removing all visual cues, olfactory stimuli, etc., emitted by the experimenter. If eventually the human experimenter is replaced by devices which automatically run the subject through his routine, we must be careful not to select values of stimuli emanating from these devices that themselves interact with the treatments that we are studying.

REFERENCES

Azrin, N. H., Holz, W., Ulrich, R., & Goldiamond, J. The control of conversation through reinforcement, *J. exp. anal. Behav.*, 1961, **4**, 25–30.

Binder, A., McConnell, D., & Sjoholm, N. A. Verbal conditioning as a function of experimenter characteristics. *J. abnorm. soc. Psychol.*, 1957, **55**, 309–314.

Brunswik, E. *Systematic and representative design of psychological experiments*. Berkeley: Univer: California Press, 1947.

Kanfer, F. H. Verbal conditioning: Reinforcement schedules and experimenter influence. *Psychol. Rep.*, 1958, **4**, 443–452.

McGuigan, F. J. Variation of whole-part methods of learning. *J. educ. Psychol.*, 1960, **51**, 213–216.

Spires, A. M. Subject-experimenter interaction in verbal conditioning, Unpublished doctoral dissertation, New York University, 1960.

Woods, P. J. Some characteristics of journals and authors. *Amer. Psychologist*, 1961, **16**, 699–701.

8

EXPERIMENTER ATTRIBUTES AS DETERMINANTS OF SUBJECTS' RESPONSES

Robert Rosenthal

More than thirty years ago (e.g., Marine, 1929) we began as *clinical* psychologists to examine experimentally our personal effect upon our patients' performance in a clinical test or task. We are still very much interested in this problem (Turner & Coleman, 1962). As *research* psychologists we have generally been much slower to examine our effects upon our subjects' performance in an experimental task.

We, as researchers, have then run the risk of unawareness of important sources of response error variance. One reason for our slowness to study ourselves as researchers compared to our willingness to study ourselves as clinicians may lie in a collective illusion about the experimenter (*E*) as non-person.. The beginning clinician is quickly taught about his role in interacting with patients (e.g., countertransference). The beginning researcher is given only the most casual, if any, instruction about his role as a person in the interaction with subjects.[1]

From R. Rosenthal, *J. proj. Tech. pers. Assess.*, 1963, **27**, 324–331. With permission of author and publisher.

Preparation of this paper was facilitated by a research grant (G-24826) from the Division of Social Sciences of the National Science Foundation.
[1] While the clinical interaction of *E* (examiner) with *Pt* certainly differs in many ways from the experimental interaction of *E* (experimenter) with *S*, these interactions nevertheless have a great deal of communality. Both involve dyadic human relationships, both are status-ordered with one participant more or less in control of the dyad. In both situations the "one-in-charge" has in some way arranged for the meeting to occur, has certain general goals to guide him and certain specific goals. It is his responsibility to structure the interaction and its origination, and to set the clinical and experimental interaction the "other" (*Pt* or *S*) requires structuring, instruction, and motivation. Furthermore, the "other" is often, if not always, concerned with what it is the *E* wants from him *really*

Our purpose here is to bring together a good bit of what is now known about the effect of specific E attributes on the responses E obtains from Ss.[2] We seem due for such a summary so that we may consolidate what is substantively known about the problem, and remind ourselves of the interpersonally meaningful nature of the experimenter-subject dyad. Finally, it is to be hoped that experiments will be designed with the findings reviewed in mind so that we may decrease the response error variance of our experiments and achieve a greater degree of generality of our research findings.

ATTRIBUTES INVESTIGATED

Experimenters' Sex

In a study of verbal conditioning, Binder, McConnell, and Sjoholm (1957) found that a male experimenter and a female experimenter obtained different rates of learning from their subjects. These experimenters differed not only in sex, but in height, weight, age, appearance (other than secondary sex characteristics), and personality. Therefore, the obtained differences in learning, while associated with a sex difference, could hardly be attributed to that difference rather than some other. Ferguson and Buss (1960) did not find the sex of their two experimenters to make a difference in their operant conditioning study.

Working with preschool children, Stevenson (1961) found that female experimenters were better able to control their subjects' responses than were male experimenters. Female experimenters were more influential than males when working with six- and seven-year-old boys. For the same age children, male experimenters tended to be more influential when the subjects

---

and what sanctions may be imposed if he does not comply. Both E and Pt (or S) are trying to learn something about each other (Riecken, 1962). Perhaps E's wish to learn about Pt (or S), to be a data-collector, and his socially derived right to these activities are the chief communalities between the clinical and the experimental interaction.

[2] Most of the studies discussed are from what would generally be regarded as the "experimental literature" although we have included some of the findings of research on clinicians and survey research interviewers. (See footnote 1 for the rationale underlying this procedure.)

were girls. For children aged nine and ten, neither experimenters' sex nor subjects' sex was a determinant of influence. Stevenson was also able to cite two other studies which showed that for young children, at least, sex of experimenter was a partial determinant of subject response, especially in interaction with the sex of the subject.

In a survey research situation, Bradley (1953) found female data collectors better able to initiate interviews, but male data collectors were better able to maintain rapport and collect "personal" data. Rorschach responses of a sexual nature were not significantly altered by the use of male and female examiners in a study by Alden and Benton (1951). However, Masling (1960) cites several Rorschach and related studies which did find subjects' responses affected by the sex of the examiner, and several studies which did not. It seems safe to conclude that, at least sometimes, the sex of the experimenter can determine in part the response made by the experimental subjects.

Experimenters' Religion

An important relevant study was conducted by Robinson and Rohde (1946) who dealt with the "Jewishness" of the interviewer, and responses to a survey about anti-Semitism. These authors used the following four groups of interviewers: (a) a Jewish-looking group, (b) a non-Jewish-looking group, (c) a Jewish-looking group with Jewish names, and (d) a non-Jewish-looking group with non-Jewish names. Subjects made more anti-Semitic responses when the interviewer did not seem to be Jewish. Lower economic and educational groups' responses were more affected by the apparent Jewishness of the interviewer than were higher economic and educational groups.

Experimenters' Race

An opinion survey by Williams and Cantril (1945) was carried out among Negro subjects using both white and Negro data collectors. On a number of political questions, respondents' replies were not affected by the interviewer's skin color. However, subjects more often told Negro rather than white interviewers that American Negroes would not be worse off than they were at present in case Japan should conquer the United States.

Rankin and Campbell (1955) employed both a Negro and a white experimenter in an experiment employing a galvanic skin response shift as the dependent variable. During the time the experimenters were adjusting the apparatus on the subject, it was found that subjects' galvanic skin responses showed a greater increase when the experimenter was Negro. In this study, as in the study reported earlier, (Binder, McConnell, & Sjoholm, 1957), there were a number of dimensions other than the postulated one along which the experimenters differed and which could have accounted for the obtained differences.

One study will serve to illustrate the negative findings of the effects of skin color of the experimenter upon the behavior of his subjects. Canady (1936) used both Negro and white examiners in giving intelligence tests to white and Negro students. Overall, he did not find any reliable effects of experimenters' skin color on subjects' test performances.

In a study of the control of verbal behavior of fifth-grade children, Prince (1962) employed two experimenters differing markedly in prestige. He found that subjects' responses were controlled more by the more prestigeful experimenter. Ekman and Friesen (1960) also investigated the effect of experimenter's status on subjects' responses. These workers found no effects of status on the absolute amount of conditioning of hostile responses to peer photographs. However, they did find that rate of conditioning was related not only to experimenter status but to experimenter personality as well. Only one additional study of the effect of experimenter status on subjects' responses in a verbal conditioning situation will be cited. Military rank appeared to make some difference in the amount of verbal conditioning occurring when the subjects were "unaware" that they were being reinforced for certain verbal responses. While none of the studies cited can claim to be definitive ones, the overall impression derived is that higher-status experimenters obtain different verbal responses from lower-status experimenters and that where the responses may be viewed as a measure of susceptibility to interpersonal influence, higher-status experimenters are more influential.

Birney (1958) employed three experimenters to test subjects for need achievement. He found experimenters who were faculty members to obtain higher need achievement scores than the experimenter who was a student. It seems reasonable to assume that faculty experimenters have a higher status in the eyes of students than do student experimenters. Birney's study also is non-definitive to the extent that, in addition to the status difference, there may have been age, appearance, manner, and intellectual differences which might have accounted for the obtained difference. Other workers who have illustrated or discussed the effect of the status of the experimenter (including student-faculty status) on the subjects' responses include Matarazzo, Saslow, and Pareis (1960) and McTeer (1953).

Experimenters' "Warmth"

The degree of warmth or coldness the experimenter radiates to his subject has been shown to affect often the nature of the data the subject produces in the experiment. It seems most likely that for most populations of subjects for behavioral research, warmth and likeability of experimenter are associated. Warm experimenters or experimenters establishing a warm climate as context for the interaction with their subjects are more likely to be liked. In several experiments, however, experimenter warmth has been sufficiently differently defined from likeability of experimenter that we may discuss them separately, keeping in mind the very probable association.

A friendly permissive experimenter persuaded seventeen out of twenty Army reservists to try eating grasshoppers. At the same time a more official, formal experimenter persuaded only ten out of twenty subjects to do so (Smith, 1961). This difference in obtained compliance could have occurred by chance less than one in 100 times. (In fairness to the dissonance theory under test in this study, it must be added that the "cooler" experimenter, while obtaining less behavior change, did obtain greater attitude change in favor of eating grasshoppers [at least among the subjects who complied] than did the "warmer" experimenter.)

In a Rorschach experiment, Lord (1950) experimentally varied the warmth of her experimenters and found this to be a partial determinant of subjects' Rorschach responses. Gordon and Durea (1948) found that a cool climate, created by experimenters making derogatory and discouraging remarks to subjects, led to a lowering of over six points on an intelligence test. Relative to these performances were those of subjects who were more warmly treated as required by the standardization requirements of the test. Masling (1960) has further discussed the effects of warm and cold examiners on the data as produced by subjects and interpreted by clinical psychologists.

Verbal responses can be increased by the manipulation of the warmth of the experimenter. Reece and Whitman (1962) defined warm experimenter behavior in terms of the experimenter's leaning toward the subject, looking directly at him, smiling, and keeping his hands still. Cold behavior was defined in terms of the experimenter leaning away from the subject, looking around the room, not smiling, and drumming his fingers. In another verbal learning experiment, Ferguson and Buss (1960) found that when an experimenter played an aggressive role he retarded subjects' learning relative to a more neutral experimenter.

Experimenters' Likeability

At least in certain types of experimental situations, experimenters who are better liked by their subjects tend to obtain different data from them than do less-liked experimenters. In a national survey conducted by the National Opinion Research Center, respondents were asked to rate their interaction with the interviewer. Better interviewing or better rapport with the interviewer was associated with fewer "don't know" responses in the poll being conducted. Better rapport was also related to the number of usable responses given to more open-ended questions (Brown, 1955).

In a verbal conditioning experiment Sapolsky (1960) found that better-liked experimenters were more effective in increasing the production of subjects' "I" and "we" pronouns than were less-liked experimenters. When experimenter-subject dyads were constructed on the dimension of compatibility (as defined by Schutz' FIRO-B method), more compatible dyads showed more conditioning of subjects' verbal responses than did less compatible dyads. These findings that better-liked experimenters are more successful influencers of subjects' behavior has been borne out by the work of Sampson and French (1960).

Experimenters' Acquaintanceship

Experimenters' acquaintanceship with their subjects has also been related to the data obtained from subjects. Working with three-year-old children, Sacks (1952) established three treatment groups of ten children each. For the first group (A) she spent one hour each day for ten days with the children in a nursery school participating as a good, interested teacher. For the second group (B) her procedure was similar except that she played the part of an uninterested, dull-appearing teacher. For the third group (C) she avoided prior acquaintanceship. The dependent variable was change in intelligence test scores from before to after treatment. Group A gained 14.5 IQ points on re-examination, an improvement which could have occurred only once in 100 times by chance alone. Group B gained 5.0 IQ points on re-examination, an improvement which could have occurred five in 100 times by chance alone. Group C gained only 1.6 IQ points, an improvement easily attributable to chance alone. These results suggest that prior acquaintance with an intelligence test examiner can significantly improve test performance, at least for pre-school children. Furthermore, when the nature of the prior acquaintanceship was more "favorable," i.e., the examiner was more interested, the magnitude of improvement was greater by 9.5 IQ points ($p = .02$). Sacks' study, therefore, has relevance not only to the effect of acquaintanceship on data obtained, but very likely also on the effect of likeability on subjects' responses.

Working with somewhat older school children, Marine (1929) employed two groups of subjects. For one group she spent twenty minutes per day for four days with the children. For the other group she avoided contact. Unlike Sacks, she found no difference in improved IQ test performance between her two groups.

In a more recent study of verbal conditioning, Kanfer and Karas (1959) employed four types of experiences for subjects before the experimental conditioning trials began. One type of experience called for the experimenter's complimenting the subjects in order to create a feeling of success or satisfaction. Another type of experience called for the experimenter's offending the subjects in order to create a feeling of failure or dissatisfaction. A third type of experience involved a neutral interaction with subjects. Finally, the fourth condition involved no contact whatever with subjects. All three groups which had prior contact with their experimenter conditioned faster than did the group with no prior contact. Interestingly, there were no differences in susceptibility to experimenter influence among the three different conditions of prior acquaintance.

Experimenters' Personality

Depending on our definition of personality, several of the experimenter attributes discussed so far might be considered personality variables. This might be particularly true of the variable "likeability." Our reason for not including this variable in this section is that in most of the work on this variable, likeability was defined in terms of subjects' perceptions of their particular experimenter. In this section we will restrict our discussion of personality variables to those studies or situations in which experimenter personality was assessed independently of the experimenter's relationship to his subjects.

In the area of Rorschach research, Cleveland (1951) and Sanders and Cleveland (1953) found a relationship between examiner personality and responses obtained from subjects. Experimenters measured as having more covert anxiety obtained from their subjects more "hostile" content responses, more "passive" trends, more "fantasy," and more "self-awareness" than did less covertly anxious experimenters. Similar findings from other studies involving projective techniques have been reported by Masling (1960) and Turner and Coleman (1962).

Working in the controversial research area of extra-sensory perception, Schmeidler and McConnell (1958) discussed the role of the experimenter's personality in the occurrence of ESP phenomena. These workers found a difference in ESP ability between those subjects who believed ESP was possible ("sheep") and those who believed it impossible ("goats"). The researchers suggested that the personality and manner of the experimenter might influence the subject's self-classification as sheep or goat. They cite additional evidence that two different investigators had obtained contradictory findings in an ESP study conducted jointly by them. Schmeidler and McConnell felt that many disparate results of ESP investigations might be attributable to personality factors in the experimenters conducting them.

Before discussing some rather well-controlled studies of the effects of experimenter personality on data obtained from subjects, it might be instructive to consider some more anecdotal but not at all atypical data. Maier (1956) presents the following anecdote:

> A further point of interest and possible importance is mentioned here in the hope that it may encourage other experimenters to report similar observations. This is the role of the experimenter in influencing the behavior of animals, particularly under stress. Some years ago two research assistants were working in adjacent rooms on related problems each with three groups of twelve or more rats from the same colony, over a period of a semester. One of them obtained the usual number of fixated position responses (over 50 percent) in each of the successive groups with which he worked; the other was unable to obtain a single fixation. Although they compared procedures on preliminary training, methods of testing, and other general routines, they were unable to determine the reason for the differences. Motivational consideration also failed to throw light on the matter. The researcher who was unable to obtain fixations required them for his doctoral dissertation, so that his results did not correspond with his motives. However, it was discovered that he felt sorry for the rats, and this may have caused him to pet the rats between trials somewhat more than other researchers. This possible influence might be analogous to feeding after shock, which reduced the number of fixated rats in Farber's experiment [pp. 375–376].

In two personal communications (1960, 1961), E. Philip Trapp has related his finding that experimenters reflecting self-confidence and a proper professional air are much better able to ego-involve subjects in studies of the effect of ego-involvement on incidental learning.

Using the Worchel Self-Activity Inventory as a measure of personality, Young (1959) selected a number of introductory psychology students who served as experimenters. Each one administered a memory-for-digits test to peers. More "poorly-adjusted" experimenters' subjects performed better at the assigned task than did subjects whose experimenters were "well adjusted."

An experiment by Mulry (1962) is most relevant here. In his study, each of twelve male experimenters tested six subjects on a pursuit rotor task. He found a tendency for those experimenters with a higher need for social approval to obtain superior performances from their subjects. In this study, need for social approval was defined by scores on the Marlowe-Crowne Social Desirability Scale. The higher need-for-approval experimenters obtained especially high performance scores from their subjects when the subjects were males and when the experimenters felt themselves to be good at a pursuit rotor task. In addition, those of Mulry's experimenters who scored as low authoritarians (defined by scores on the California F Scale), and who felt they were themselves not good at a pursuit rotor task, obtained higher performance scores than did other combinations of experimenters' authoritarianism and perception of adequacy on the pursuit rotor task. Finally, less intelligent experimenters running male subjects obtained better performance scores from their subjects than did any other combination of experimenter intelligence and sex of subject. Intelligence was defined by Mulry in terms of scores on the Shipley-Hartford Test. The statistical significance of the relationships just discussed ranged from a p of .01 to .10 .

Peggy Cook-Marquis (1958) employed nine male experimenters and fifty-four subjects in her study of experimenter effects. Both her experimenter and her subject groups were subdivided into those who were high authoritarian, low authoritarian, and acquiescent. The California F Scale was the basis for these divisions. The author found no effect of experimenter's personality on subject's performance on the Einstellung Water Jar Test of problem solving. Nor did she find an interaction between experimenters' and subjects' personalities to be a determinant of performance. However, the low authoritarian and the acquiescent experimenters were significantly more effective in changing their subjects' attitudes about teaching methods than were high authoritarian experimenters. The author's interpretation of this result was that since high authoritarians might not themselves believe in unstructured teaching techniques, they were therefore less convincing in trying to change their subjects' attitude in favor of these techniques.

In a recent study by Sarason (1962) twenty experimenters (ten male and ten female) reinforced the choice of mildly hostile verbs in a sentence construction task. Subjects' and experimenters' general level of hostility was obtained. More hostile experimenters, especially when running more hostile subjects, elicited more hostile verbs, a relationship holding particularly when experimenters were males.

Finally, we will report the results of an experiment employing 40 experimenters (almost all male) and 230 subjects, about half of them male and half of them female, (Rosenthal, Persinger, Vikan-Kline, & Mulry, 1963). In this study, each experimenter requested about six subjects to rate the apparent success or failure of twenty persons pictured in photographs. For 31 of the 40 experimenters we had scores on both the Marlowe-Crowne Social Desirability Scale and the Taylor Manifest Anxiety Scale. A correlation of .48 ($p = .02$) was obtained between the experimenters' anxiety scores and the degree of success their subjects saw in the photos of faces. For these same thirty-one experimenters, the correlation between their need for social approval as measured by the Marlowe-Crowne Scale and the ratings of success of the photos obtained from their subjects was $-.32$ ($p = .10$). Thus, subjects rated photos as more successful when in the presence of experimenters who were more anxious and had a lower need for social approval. (For this sample of experimenters, the correlation between experimenters' need for social approval and their anxiety was $-.14$). For a smaller sample size of experimenters, Marcia (1961) provided tentatively corroborative data of the relationship between experimenters' need for social approval and their subjects' perception of the success or failure of persons pictured in photos. Among seven male experimenters the correlation obtained was $-.27$ which, while not statistically different from zero, was a close approximation to our obtained correlation of $-.32$. Suggesting the possible complexity of the phenomenon was his additional finding for six female experimenters of a correlation of $+.43$. This latter correlation, while not differing statistically from zero, raises the possibility that correlation between experimenter personality attributes and subjects' responses may be partially determined by experimenters' sex.

SUMMARY

We have tried to show how a variety of experimenter attributes can be partial determinants of the responses given the experimenter by his subjects in a variety of data-collecting situations. The attributes discussed have included the experimenter's sex, religion, race, status, likeability, acquaintanceship, warmth, and a number of personality variables. A more superordinate set of constructs to account for the many findings has yet to be empirically developed. If, in the absence of such unifying empirical work, some summary statement were needed now, we would postulate the following:

That experimenters will obtain different data from their subjects as a function of how the experimenter is regarded by his subjects on the attributes of (a) likeability, (b) prestige, (c) professional skill, (d) trust, and (e) sex.

REFERENCES

Alden, P., & Benton, A. L. Relationship of sex of examiner to incidence of Rorschach responses with sexual content. *J. proj. Tech.*, 1951, **15**, 231–234.

Binder, A., McConnell, D., & Sjoholm, N. A. Verbal conditioning as a function of experimenter characteristics. *J. abnorm. soc. Psychol.*, 1957, **55**, 309–314.

Birney, R. C. The achievement motive and task performance: A replication. *J. abnorm. soc. Psychol.*, 1958, **56**, 133–135.

Bradley, J. E. Survey bias as a function of respondent-interviewer interaction. *Dissert. Abstr.*, 1953, **16**, 530–535.

Brown, J. M. Respondents rate public opinion interviewers. *J. appl. Psychol.*, 1955, **39**, 96–102.

Canady, H. G. The effect of "rapport" on the I.Q.: A new approach to the problem of racial psychology. *J. Negro Educ.*, 1936, **5**, 209–219.

Cleveland, S. The relationship between examiner anxiety and subjects' Rorschach scores. *Microfilm Abstr.*, 1951, **11**, 415–416.

Cook-Marquis, P. Authoritarian or acquiescent: Some behavioral differences. Paper read at APA, Washington, D.C., Sept. 1958.

Ekman, P., & Friesen, W. V. Status and personality of the experimenter as a determinant of verbal conditioning. *Amer. Psychologist*, 1960, **15**, 430. (Abstract)

Ferguson, D. C., & Buss, A. H. Operant conditioning of hostile verbs in relation to experimenter and subject characteristics. *J. consult. Psychol.*, 1960, **24**, 324–327.

Glucksberg, S., & Lince, D. L. The influence of military rank of experimenter on the conditioning of a verbal response. *Tech.*

Mem. 10–62 Human engineering Lab. Aberdeen proving ground, Maryland, 1962.

Gordon, L. V., & Durea, M. A. The effect of discouragement on the revised Stanford Binet Scale. *J. genet. Psychol.*, 1948, **73**, 201–207.

Kanfer, F. H., & Karas, S. C. Prior experimenter-subject interaction and verbal conditioning. *Psychol. Rep.*, 1959, **5**, 345–353.

Lord, E. Experimentally induced variations in Rorschach performance. *Psychol. Monogr.*, 1950, **64**, No. 10.

Maier, N. R. F. Frustration theory: restatement and extension. *Psychol. Rev.*, 1956, **63**, 370–388.

Marcia J. Hypothesis-making, need for social approval, and their effects on unconscious experimenter bias. Unpublished master's thesis, Ohio State Univ., 1961.

Marine, Ed. L. The effect of familiarity with the examiner upon Stanford-Binet test performance. *Teach. Coll. contr. Educ.*, 1929, **381**, 42.

Masling, J. The influence of situational and interpersonal variables in projective testing. *Psychol. Bull.*, 1960, **57**, 65–85.

Matarazzo, J. D., Saslow, G., & Pareis, E. N. Verbal conditioning of two response classes: Some methodological considerations. *J. abnorm. soc. Psychol.*, 1960, **61**, 190–206.

McTeer, W. Observational definitions of emotion. *Psychol. Rev.*, 1953, **60**, 172–180.

Mulry, R. C. The effects of the experimenter's perception of his own performance on subject performance in a pursuit rotor task. Unpublished master's thesis, Univ. North Dakota, 1962.

Prince, A. I. Relative prestige and the verbal conditioning of children. *Amer. Psychologist*, 1962, **17**, 378. (Abstract)

Rankin, R., & Campbell, D. Galvanic skin response to Negro and white experimenters. *J. abnorm. soc. Psychol.*, 1955, **51**, 30–33.

Reece, M. M., & Whitman, R. N. Expressive movements, warmth, and verbal reinforcements. *J. abnorm. soc. Psychol.*, 1962, **64**, 234–236.

Riecken, H. W. A program for research on experiments in social psychology. In: *Decisions, values and groups*, Vol. II. New York: Pergamon Press, 1962, pp. 25–41.

Robinson, D., & Rohde, S. Two experiments with an anti-Semitism poll. *J. abnorm. soc. Psychol.*, 1946, **41**, 136–144.

Rosenthal, R., Persinger, G. W., Vikan-Kline, L. L., & Mulry, R. C. The role of the research assistant in the mediation of experimenter bias. *J. Pers.*, 1963, **31**, 313–335.

Sacks, E. L. Intelligence scores as a function of experimentally established social relationships between child and examiner. *J. abnorm. soc. Psychol.*, 1952, **47**, 354–358.

Sampson, E. E., & French, J. R. P. An experiment on active and passive resistance to social power. *Amer. Psychologist*, 1960, **15**, 396. (Abstract)

Sanders, R., & Cleveland, S. E. The relationship between certain examiner personality variables and subject's Rorschach scores. *J. proj. Tech.*, 1953, **17**, 34–50.

Sapolsky, A. Effect of interpersonal relationships upon verbal conditioning. *J. abnorm. soc. Psychol*, 1960, **60**, 241–246.

Sarason, I. G. Individual differences, situational variables and personality research. *J. abnorm. soc. Psychol.*, 1962, **65**, 376–380.

Schmeidler, G., & McConnell, R. A. *ESP and personality patterns.* New Haven: Yale Univ. Press, 1958.

Smith, E. E. Relative power of various attitude change techniques. Paper read at APA, New York, Sept. 1961.

Stevenson, H. W. Social reinforcement with children as a function of CA, sex of E, and sex of S. *J. abnorm. soc. Psychol.*, 1961, **63**, 147–154.

Turner, G. C., & Coleman, J. C. Examiner influence on thematic apperception test responses. *J. proj. Tech.*, 1962, **26**, 478–486.

Williams, F., & Cantril, H. The use of interviewer rapport as a method of detecting differences. *J. soc. Psychol.*, 1945, **22**, 171–175.

Young, R. K. Digit span as a function of the personality of the experimenter. *Amer. Psychologist*, 1959, **14**, 375. (Abstract)

9

HUMAN USE OF HUMAN SUBJECTS: THE PROBLEM OF DECEPTION IN SOCIAL PSYCHOLOGICAL EXPERIMENTS

Herbert C. Kelman

Though there is often good reason for deceiving Ss in social psychological experiments, widespread use of such procedures has serious (a) ethical implications (involving not only the possibility of harm to S, but also the quality of the E-S relationships, (b) methodological implications (relating to the decreasing naiveté of Ss), and (c) implications for the future of the discipline. To deal with these problems, it is necessary (a) to increase active awareness of the negative implications of deception and use it only when clearly justified, not as a matter of course; (b) to explore ways of counteracting and minimizing negative consequences of deception when it is used; and (c) to develop new experimental techniques that dispense with deception and rely on S's positive motivations.

In 1954, in the pages of the *American Psychologist*, Edgar Vinacke raised a series of questions about experiments—particularly in the area of small groups—in which "the psychologist conceals the true purpose and conditions of the experiment, or positively misinforms the subjects, or exposes them to painful, embarrassing, or worse, experiences, without the subjects'

From H. C. Kelman, *Psychol. Bull.*, 1967, **67**, 1–11. With permission of author and publisher.

Paper read at the symposium on "Ethical and Methodological Problems in Social Psychological Experiments," held at the meetings of the American Psychological Association in Chicago, September 3, 1965. This paper is a product of a research program on social influence and behavior change supported by United States Public Health Service Research Grant MH-07280 from the National Institute of Mental Health.

knowledge of what is going on [p. 155]." He summed up his concerns by asking, "What . . . is the proper balance between the interests of science and the thoughtful treatment of the persons who, innocently, supply the data? [p. 155]." Little effort has been made in the intervening years to seek answers to the questions he raised. During these same years, however, the problem of deception in social psychological experiments has taken on increasingly serious proportions.[1]

The problem is actually broader, extending beyond the walls of the laboratory. It arises, for example, in various field studies in which investigators enroll as members of a group that has special interest for them so that they can observe its operations from the inside. The pervasiveness of the problem becomes even more apparent when we consider that deception is built into most of our measurement devices, since it is important to keep the respondent unaware of the personality or attitude dimension that we wish to explore. For the present purposes, however, primarily the problem of deception in the context of the social psychological experiment will be discussed.

The use of deception has become more and more extensive, and it is now a commonplace and almost standard feature of social psychological experiments. Deception has been turned into a game, often played with great skill and virtuosity. A considerable amount of the creativity and ingenuity of social psychologists is invested in the development of increasingly elaborate deception situations. Within a single experiment, deception may be built upon deception in a delicately complex structure. The literature now contains a fair number of studies in which second- or even third-order deception was employed.

One well-known experiment (Festinger & Carlsmith, 1959), for example, involved a whole progression of deceptions. After the subjects had gone through an experimental task, the investigator made it clear—through word and gesture—that the experiment was over and that he would now "like to explain what

---

[1] In focusing on deception in *social* psychological experiments, I do not wish to give the impression that there is no serious problem elsewhere. Deception is widely used in most studies involving human subjects and gives rise to issues similar to those discussed in this paper. Some examples of the use of deception in other areas of psychological experimentation will be presented later in this paper.

this has been all about so you'll have some idea of why you were doing this [p. 205]." This explanation was false, however, and was designed to serve as a basis for the true experimental manipulation. The manipulation itself involved asking subjects to serve as the experimenter's accomplices. The task of the "accomplice" was to tell the next "subject" that the experiment in which he had just participated (which was in fact a rather boring experience) had been interesting and enjoyable. He was also asked to be on call for unspecified future occasions on which his services as accomplice might be needed because "the regular fellow couldn't make it, and we had a subject scheduled [p. 205]." These newly recruited "accomplices," of course, were the true subjects, while the "subjects" were the experimenter's true accomplices. For their presumed services as "accomplices," the true subjects were paid in advance—half of them receiving $1, and half $20. When they completed their service, however, the investigators added injury to insult by asking them to return their hard-earned cash. Thus, in this one study, in addition to receiving the usual misinformation about the purpose of the experiment, the subject was given feedback that was really an experimental manipulation, was asked to be an accomplice who was really a subject, and was given a $20 bill that was really a will-o'-the-wisp. One wonders how much further in this direction we can go. Where will it all end?

It is easy to view this problem with alarm, but it is much more difficult to formulate an unambiguous position on the problem. As a working experimental social psychologist, I cannot conceive the issue in absolutist terms. I am too well aware of the fact that there are good reasons for using deception in many experiments. There are many significant problems that probably cannot be investigated without the use of deception, at least not at the present level of development of our experimental methodology. Thus, we are always confronted with a conflict of values. If we regard the acquisition of scientific knowledge about human behavior as a positive value, and if an experiment using deception constitutes a significant contribution to such knowledge which could not very well be achieved by other means, then we cannot unequivocally rule out this experiment. The question for us is not simply whether it does or does not use deception, but whether the amount and type of deception are justified by the significance of the study and the unavailability of alternative (that is, deception-free) procedures.

I have expressed special concern about second-order deceptions, for example, the procedure of letting a person believe that he is acting as experimenter or as the experimenter's accomplice when he is in fact serving as the subject. Such a procedure undermines the relationship between experimenter and subject even further than simple misinformation about the purposes of the experiment; deception does not merely take place *within* the experiment, but encompasses the whole definition of the relationship between the parties involved. Deception that takes place while the person is within the role of subject for which he has contracted can, to some degree, be isolated, but deception about the very nature of the contract itself is more likely to suffuse the experimenter-subject relationship as a whole and to remove the possibility of mutual trust. Thus, I would be inclined to take a more absolutist stand with regard to such second-order deceptions—but even here the issue turns out to be more complicated. I am stopped short when I think, for example, of the ingenious studies on experimenter bias by Rosenthal and his associates (e.g., Rosenthal & Fode, 1963; Rosenthal, Persinger, Vikan-Kline, & Fode, 1963; Rosenthal, Persinger, Vikan-Kline, & Mulry, 1963). These experiments employed second-order deception in that subjects were led to believe that they were the experimenters. Since these were experiments about experiments, however, it is very hard to conceive of any alternative procedures that the investigators might have used. There is no question in my mind that these are significant studies; they provide fundamental inputs to present efforts at reexamining the social psychology of the experiment. These studies, then, help to underline even further the point that we are confronted with a conflict of values that cannot be resolved by fiat.

I hope it is clear from these remarks that my purpose in focusing on this problem is not to single out specific studies performed by some of my colleagues and to point a finger at them. Indeed, the finger points at me as well. I too have used deception, and have known the joys of applying my skills and ingenuity to the creation of elaborate experimental situations that the subjects would not be able to decode. I am now making active attempts to find alternatives to deception, but still I have not forsworn the use of deception under any and all circumstances. The questions I am raising, then, are addressed to myself as well as to my colleagues. They are questions with which all of us who are committed to social psychology must come to grips, lest we leave their resolution to others who have no understanding of what we are trying to accomplish.

What concerns me most is not so much that deception is used, but precisely that it is used without question. It has now become standard operating procedure in the social psychologist's laboratory. I sometimes feel that we are training a generation of students who do not know that there is any other way of doing experiments in our field—who feel that deception is as much *de rigueur* as significance at the .05 level. Too often deception is used not as a last resort, but as a matter of course. Our attitude seems to be that if you can deceive, why tell the truth? It is this unquestioning acceptance, this routinization of deception, that really concerns me.

I would like to turn now to a review of the bases for my concern with the problem of deception, and then suggest some possible approaches for dealing with it.

IMPLICATIONS OF THE USE OF DECEPTION IN SOCIAL PSYCHOLOGICAL EXPERIMENTS

My concern about the use of deception is based on three considerations: the ethical implications of such procedures, their methodological implications, and their implications for the future of social psychology.

1. Ethical Implications

Ethical problems of a rather obvious nature arise in the experiments in which deception has potentially harmful consequences for the subject. Take, for example, the brilliant experiment by Mulder and Stemerding (1963) on the effects of threat on attraction to the group and need for strong leadership. In this study—one of the very rare examples of an experiment conducted in a natural setting—independent food merchants in a number of Dutch towns were brought together for group meetings, in the course of which they were informed that a large organization was planning to open up a series of super-markets in the Netherlands. In the High Threat condition, subjects were told that there was a high probability that their town would be selected as a site for such markets, and that the advent of these markets would cause a considerable drop in their business. On the advice of the executives of the shop-keeepers' organizations, who had helped to arrange the group meetings, the investigators did not reveal the experimental manipulations to their subjects. I have been worried about these Dutch merchants ever since I heard about this study for the first time. Did some of them go out of business in anticipation of the heavy competition? Do some of them have an anxiety reaction every time they see a bulldozer? Chances are that they soon forgot about this threat (unless, of course, supermarkets actually did move into town) and that it became just one of the many little moments of anxiety that must occur in every shopkeeper's life. Do we have a right, however, to add to life's little anxieties and to risk the possibility of more extensive anxiety purely for the purposes of our experiments, particularly since deception deprives the subject of the opportunity to choose whether or not he wishes to expose himself to the risks that might be entailed?

The studies by Bramel (1962, 1963) and Bergin (1962) pro-vide examples of another type of potentially harmful effects arising from the use of deception. In the Bramel studies, male undergraduates were led to believe that they were homosexually aroused by photographs of men. In the Bergin study, subjects of both sexes were given discrepant information about their level of masculinity or femininity; in one experimental condi-tion, this information was presumably based on an elaborate series of psychological tests in which the subjects had partici-pated. In all of these studies, the deception was explained to the subject at the end of the experiment. One wonders, how-ever, whether such explanation removes the possibility of harm-ful effects. For many persons in this age group, sexual identity is still a live and sensitive issue, and the self-doubts generated by the laboratory experience may take on a life of their own and linger on for some time to come.

Yet another illustration of potentially harmful effects of de-ception can be found in Milgram's (1963, 1965) studies of obedience. In these experiments, the subject was led to believe that he was participating in a learning study and was instructed to administer increasingly severe shocks to another person who after a while began to protest vehemently. In fact, of course, the victim was an accomplice of the experimenter and did not receive any shocks. Depending on the conditions, sizable proportions of the subjects obeyed the experimenter's instructions and continued to shock the other person up to the maximum level, which they believed to be extremely painful. Both obedient and defiant subjects exhibited a great deal of stress in this situation. The complexities of the issues surrounding the use of deception become quite apparent when one reads the exchange between Baumrind (1964) and Milgram (1964) about the ethical implications of the obedience research. There is clearly room for disagreement, among honorable people, about the evaluation of this research from an ethical point of view. Yet, there is good reason to believe that at least some of the obedient subjects came away from this experience with a lower self-esteem, having to live with the realization that they were willing to yield to destructive authority to the point of inflicting extreme pain on a fellow human being. The fact that this may have provided, in Milgram's (1964) words, "an opportunity to learn something of importance about themselves, and more generally, about the conditions of human action [p. 850]" is beside the point. If this were a lesson from life, it would indeed constitute an instructive confrontation and provide a valuable insight. But do we, for the purpose of experimentation, have the right to provide such potentially disturbing insights to subjects who do not know that this is what they are coming for? A similar question can be raised about the Asch (1951) experiments on group pressure, although the stressfulness of the situation and the implications for the person's self-concept were less intense in that context.

While the present paper is specifically focused on social psychological experiments, the problem of deception and its possibly harmful effects arises in other areas of psychological experimentation as well. Dramatic illustrations are provided by two studies in which subjects were exposed, for experimental purposes, to extremely stressful conditions. In an experiment designed to study the establishment of a conditioned response in a situation that is traumatic but not painful, Campbell, Sanderson, and Laverty (1964) induced—through the use of a drug

—a temporary interruption of respiration in their subjects. "This has no permanently harmful physical consequences but is nonetheless a severe stress which is not in itself painful . . . [p. 628]." The subjects' reports confirmed that this was a "horrific" experience for them. "All the subjects, in the standard series said that they thought they were dying [p. 631]." Of course the subjects, "male alcoholic patients who volunteered for the experiment when they were told that it was connected with a possible therapy for alcoholism [p. 629]," were not warned in advance about the effect of the drug, since this information would have reduced the traumatic impact of the experience.[2] In a series of studies on the effects of psychological stress, Berkun, Bialek, Kern, and Yagi (1962) devised a number of ingenious experimental situations designed to convince the subject that his life was actually in danger. In one situation, the subjects, a group of army recruits, were actually "passengers aboard an apparently stricken plane which was being forced to 'ditch' or crash-land [p. 4]." In another experiment, an isolated subject in a desolate area learned that a sudden emergency had arisen (accidental nuclear radiation in the area, or a sudden forest fire, or misdirected artillery shells—depending on the experimental condition) and that he could be rescued only if he reported his position over his radio transmitter, "which has quite suddenly failed [p. 7]." In yet another situation, the subject was led to believe that he was responsible for an explosion that seriously injured another soldier. As the authors pointed out, reactions in these situations are more likely to approximate reactions to combat experiences or to naturally occurring disasters than are reactions to various laboratory stresses, but is the experimenter justified in exposing his subjects to such extreme threats?

So far, I have been speaking of experiments in which deception has potentially harmful consequences. I am equally concerned, however, about the less obvious cases, in which there

[2] The authors reported, however, that some of their other subjects were physicians familiar with the drug; "they did not suppose they were dying but, even though they knew in a general way what to expect, they too said that the experience was extremely harrowing [p. 632]." Thus, conceivably, the purposes of the experiment might have been achieved even if the subjects had been told to expect the temporary interruption of breathing.

is little danger of harmful effects, at least in the conventional sense of the term. Serious ethical issues are raised by deception per se and the kind of use of human beings that it implies. In our other interhuman relationships, most of us would never think of doing the kinds of things that we do to our subjects— exposing others to lies and tricks, deliberately misleading them about the purposes of the interaction or withholding pertinent information, making promises or giving assurance that we intend to disregard. We would view such behavior as a violation of the respect to which all fellow humans are entitled and of the whole basis of our relationship with them. Yet we seem to forget that the experimenter-subject relationship—whatever else it is—is a *real* interhuman relationship, in which we have responsibility toward the subject as another human being whose dignity we must preserve. The discontinuity between the experimenter's behavior in everyday life and his behavior in the laboratory is so marked that one wonders why there has been so little concern with this problem, and what mechanisms have allowed us to ignore it to such an extent. I am reminded, in this connection, of the intriguing phenomenon of the "holiness of sin," which characterizes certain messianic movements as well as other movements of the true-believer variety. Behavior that would normally be unacceptable actually takes on an aura of virtue in such movements through a redefinition of the situation in which the behavior takes place and thus of the context for evaluating it. A similar mechanism seems to be involved in our attitude toward the psychological experiment. We tend to regard it as a situation that is not quite real, that can be isolated from the rest of life like a play performed on stage, and to which, therefore, the usual criteria for ethical interpersonal conduct become irrelevant. Behavior is judged entirely in the context of the experimenter's scientific contribution and, in this context, deception—which is normally unacceptable—can indeed be seen as a positive good.

The broader ethical problem brought into play by the very use of deception becomes even more important when we view it in the light of present historical forces. We are living in an age of mass societies in which the transformation of man into an object to be manipulated at will occurs "on a mass scale, in a systematic way, and under the aegis of specialized institutions deliberately assigned to this task [Kelman, 1965]." In institutionalizing the use of deception in psychological experiments, we are, then, contributing to a historical trend that threatens values most of us cherish.

2. Methodological Implications

A second source of my concern about the use of deception is my increasing doubt about its adequacy as a methodology for social psychology.

A basic assumption in the use of deception is that a subject's awareness of the conditions that we are trying to create and of the phenomena that we wish to study would affect his behavior in such a way that we could not draw valid conclusions from it. For example, if we are interested in studying the effects of failure on conformity, we must create a situation in which the subjects actually feel that they have failed, and in which they can be kept unaware of our interest in observing conformity. In short, it is important to keep our subjects naïve about the purposes of the experiment so that they can respond to the experimental inductions spontaneously.

How long, however, will it be possible for us to find naïve subjects? Among college students, it is already very difficult. They may not know the exact purpose of the particular experiment in which they are participating, but at least they know, typically, that it is *not* what the experimenter says it is. Orne (1962) pointed out that the use of deception "on the part of psychologists is so widely known in the college population that even if a psychologist is honest with the subject, more often than not he will be distrusted." As one subject pithily put it, " 'Psychologists always lie!' " Orne added that "This bit of paranoia has some support in reality [pp. 778–779]." There are, of course, other sources of human subjects that have not been tapped, and we could turn to them in our quest for naïveté. But even there it is only a matter of time. As word about psychological experiments gets around in whatever network we happen to be using, sophistication is bound to increase. I wonder, therefore, whether there is any future in the use of deception.

If the subject in a deception experiment knows what the experimenter is trying to conceal from him and what he is really after in the study, the value of the deception is obviously nullified. Generally, however, even the relatively sophisticated subject does not know the exact purpose of the experiment; he only has suspicions, which may approximate the true purpose of the experiment to a greater or lesser degree. Whether or not he knows the *true* purpose of the experiment, he is likely to make an effort to figure out its purpose, since he does not believe what the experimenter tells him, and therefore he is likely to operate in the situation in terms of his own hypothesis of what is involved. This may, in line with Orne's (1962) analysis, lead him to do what he thinks the experimenter wants him to do. Conversely, if he resents the experimenter's attempt to deceive him, he may try to throw a monkey wrench into the works; I would not be surprised if this kind of Schweikian game among subjects became a fairly well-established part of the culture of sophisticated campuses. Whichever course the subject uses, however, he is operating in terms of his own conception of the nature of the situation, rather than in terms of the conception that the experimenter is trying to induce. In short, the experimenter can no longer assume that the conditions that he is trying to create are the ones that actually define the situation for the subject. Thus, the use of deception, while it is designed to give the experimenter control over the subject's perceptions and motivations, may actually produce an unspecifiable mixture of intended and unintended stimuli that make it difficult to know just what the subject is responding to.

The tendency for subjects to react to unintended cues—to features of the situation that are not part of the experimenter's design—is by no means restricted to experiments that involve deception. This problem has concerned students of the interview situation for some time, and more recently it has been analyzed in detail in the writings and research of Riecken, Rosenthal, Orne, and Mills. Subjects enter the experiment with their own aims, including attainment of certain rewards, divination of the experimenter's true purposes, and favorable self-presentation (Riecken, 1962). They are therefore responsive to demand characteristics of the situation (Orne, 1962), to unintended communications of the experimenter's expectations (Rosenthal, 1963), and to the role of the experimenter within the social system that experimenter and subject jointly constitute (Mills, 1962). In any experiment, then, the subject goes beyond the description of the situation and the experimental manipulation introduced by the investigator, makes his own interpretation of the situation, and acts accordingly.

For several reasons, however, the use of deception especially encourages the subject to dismiss the stated purposes of the experiment and to search for alternative interpretations of his own. First, the continued use of deception establishes the reputation of psychologists as people who cannot be believed. Thus, the desire "to penetrate the experimenter's inscrutability and discover the rationale of the experiment [Riecken, 1962, p. 34]" becomes especially strong. Generally, these efforts are motivated by the subject's desire to meet the expectations of the experimenter and of the situation. They may also be motivated, however, as I have already mentioned, by a desire to outwit the experimenter and to beat him at his own game, in a spirit of genuine hostility or playful one-upmanship. Second, a situation involving the use of deception is inevitably highly ambiguous since a great deal of information relevant to understanding the structure of the situation must be withheld from the subject. Thus, the subject is especially motivated to try to figure things out and likely to develop idiosyncratic interpretations. Third, the use of deception, by its very nature, causes the experimenter to transmit contradictory messages to the subject. In his verbal instructions and explanations he says one thing about the purposes of the experiment; but in the experimental situation that he has created, in the manipulations that he has introduced, and probably in covert cues that he emits, he says another thing. This again makes it imperative for the subject to seek his own interpreation of the situation.

I would argue, then, that deception increases the subject's tendency to operate in terms of his private definition of the situation, differing (in random or systematic fashion) from the definition that the experimenter is trying to impose; moreover, it makes it more difficult to evaluate or minimize the effects of this tendency. Whether or not I am right in this judgment, it can, at the very least, be said that the use of deception does not resolve or reduce the unintended effects of the experiment as a social situation in which the subject pursues his private aims. Since the assumptions that the subject is naive and that he sees the situation as the experimenter wishes him to see it are unwarranted, the use of deception no longer has any special obvious advantages over other experimental approaches. I am not suggesting that there may not be occasions when deception may still be the most effective procedure to use from a methodological point of view. But since it raises at least as many methodological problems as any other type of procedure does, we have every reason to explore alternative approaches and to extend our methodological inquiries to the question of the effects of using deception.

3. Implications for the Future of Social Psychology

My third concern about the use of deception is based on its long-run implications for our discipline and combines both the ethical and methodological considerations that I have already raised. There is something disturbing about the idea of relying on massive deception as the basis for developing a field of inquiry. Can one really build a discipline on a foundation of such research?

From a long-range point of view, there is obviously something self-defeating about the use of deception. As we continue to carry out research of this kind, our potential subjects become more and more sophisticated, and we become less and less able to meet the conditions that our experimental procedures require. Moreover, as we continue to carry out research of this kind, our potential subjects become increasingly distrustful of us, and our future relations with them are likely to be undermined. Thus, we are confronted with the anomalous circumstance that the more research we do, the more difficult and questionable it becomes.

The use of deception also involves a contradiction between our experimental procedures and our long-range aims as scientists and teachers. In order to be able to carry out our experiments, we are concerned with maintaining the naïveté of the population from which we hope to draw our subjects. We are all familiar with the experimenter's anxious concern that the introductory course might cover the autokinetic phenomenon, need achievement, or the Asch situation before he has had a chance to complete his experimental runs. This perfectly understandable desire to keep procedures secret goes counter to the traditional desire of the scientist and teacher to inform and enlighten the public. To be sure, experimenters are interested only in temporary secrecy, but it is not inconceivable that at some time in the future they might be using certain procedures on a regular basis with large segments of the population and thus prefer to keep the public permanently naïve. It is perhaps not too fanciful to imagine, for the long run, the possible emergence of a special class, in possession of secret knowledge —a possibility that is clearly antagonistic to the principle of open communication to which we, as scientists and intellectuals, are so fervently committed.

DEALING WITH THE PROBLEM OF DECEPTION IN SOCIAL PSYCHOLOGICAL EXPERIMENTS

If my concerns about the use of deception are justified, what are some of the ways in which we, as experimental social psychologists, can deal with them? I would like to suggest three steps that we can take: increase our active awareness of the problem, explore ways of counteracting and minimizing the negative effects of deception, and give careful attention to the development of new experimental techniques that dispense with the use of deception.

1. Active Awareness of the Problem

I have already stressed that I would not propose the complete elimination of deception under all circumstances, in view of the genuine conflict of values with which the experimenter is confronted. What is crucial, however, is that we always ask ourselves the question whether deception, in the given case, is necessary and justified. How we answer the question is less important than the fact that we ask it. What we must be wary of is the tendency to dismiss the question as irrelevant and to accept deception as a matter of course. Active awareness of the problem is thus in itself part of the solution, for it makes the use of deception a matter for discussion, deliberation, investigation, and choice. Active awareness means that, in any given case, we will try to balance the value of an experiment that uses deception against its questionable or potentially harmful effects. If we engage in this process honestly, we are likely to find that there are many occasions when we or our students can forego the use of deception—either because deception is not necessary (that is, alternative procedures that are equally good or better are available), because the importance of the study does not warrant the use of an ethically questionable procedure, or because the type of deception involved is too extreme (in terms of the possibility of harmful effects or of seriously undermining the experimenter-subject relationship).

2. Counteracting and Minimizing the Negative Effect of Deception

If we do use deception, it is essential that we find ways of counteracting and minimizing its negative effects. Sensitizing the apprentice researcher to this necessity is at least as fundamental as any other part of research training.

In those experiments in which deception carries the potential of harmful effects (in the more usual sense of the term), there is an obvious requirement to build protections into every phase of the process. Subjects must be selected in a way that will exclude individuals who are especially vulnerable; the potentially harmful manipulation (such as the induction of stress) must be kept at a moderate level of intensity; the experimenter must be sensitive to danger signals in the reactions of his subjects and be prepared to deal with crises when they arise; and, at the conclusion of the session, the experimenter must take time not only to reassure the subject, but also to help him work through his feelings about the experience to whatever degree may be required. In general, the principle that a subject ought not to leave the laboratory with greater anxiety or lower self-esteem than he came with is a good one to follow. I would go beyond it to argue that the subject should in some positive way be enriched by the experience, that is, he should come away from it with the feeling that he has learned something, understood something, or grown in some way. This, of course, adds special importance to the kind of feedback that is given to the subject at the end of the experimental session.

Postexperimental feedback is, of course, the primary way of counteracting negative effects in those experiments in which the issue is deception as such, rather than possible threats to the subject's well-being. If we do deceive the subject, then it is our obligation to give him a full and detailed explanation of what we have done and of our reasons for using this type of procedure. I do not want to be absolutist about this, but I would suggest this as a good rule of thumb to follow: Think very carefully before undertaking an experiment whose purposes you feel unable to reveal to the subjects even after they have completed the experimental session. It is, of course, not enough to give the subject a perfunctory feedback, just to do one's duty. Postexperimental explanations should be worked out with as much detail as other aspects of the procedure and, in general, some thought ought to be given to ways of making them meaningful and instructive for the subject and helpful for rebuilding his relationship with the experimenter. I feel very strongly that to accomplish these purposes, we must keep the feedback itself inviolate and under no circumstances give the subject false feedback or pretend to be giving him feedback while we are in fact introducing another experimental manipulation. If we hope to maintain any kind of trust in our relationship with potential subjects, there must be no ambiguity that the statement "The experiment is over and I shall explain to you what it was all about" means precisely that and nothing else. If subjects have reason to suspect even that statement, then we have lost the whole basis for a decent human relationship with our subjects and all hope for future cooperation from them.

3. Development of New Experimental Techniques

My third and final suggestion is that we invest some of the creativity and ingenuity, now devoted to the construction of elaborate deceptions, in the search for alternative experimental techniques that do not rely on the use of deception. The kind of techniques that I have in mind would be based on the principle of eliciting the subject's positive motivations to contribute to the experimental enterprise. They would draw on the subject's active participation and involvement in the proceedings and encourage him to cooperate in making the experiment a success—not by giving the results he thinks the experimenter wants, but by conscientiously taking the roles and carrying out the tasks that the experimenter assigns to him. In short, the kind of techniques I have in mind would be designed to involve the subject as an active participant in a joint effort with the experimenter.

Perhaps the most promising source of alternative experimental approaches are procedures using some sort of role playing. I have been impressed, for example, with the role playing that I have observed in the context of the Inter-Nation Simulation (Guetzkow, Alger, Brody, Noel, and Snyder, 1963), a laboratory procedure involving a simulated world in which the subjects take the roles of decision-makers of various nations. This situation seems to create a high level of emotional involvement and to elicit motivations that have a real-life quality to them. Moreover, within this situation—which is highly complex and generally permits only gross experimental manipulations—it is possible to test specific theoretical hypotheses by using data based on repeated measurements as interaction between the simulated nations develops. Thus, a study carried out at the Western Behavioral Sciences Institute provided, as an extra, some interesting opportunities for testing hypotheses derived from balance theory, by the use of mutual ratings made by decision-makers of Nations A, B, and C, before and after A shifted from an alliance with B to an alliance with C.

A completely different type of role playing was used effectively by Rosenberg and Abelson (1960) in their studies of cognitive dilemmas. In my own research program, we have been exploring different kinds of role-playing procedures with varying degrees of success. In one study, the major manipulation consisted in informing subjects that the experiment to which they had just committed themselves would require them (depending on the condition) either to receive shocks from a fellow subject, or to administer shocks to a fellow subject. We used a regular deception procedure, but with a difference: We told the subjects before the session started that what was to follow was make-believe, but that we wanted them to react as if they really found themselves in this situation. I might mention that some subjects, not surprisingly, did not accept as true the information that this was all make-believe and wanted to know when they would show up for the shock experiment to which they had committed themselves. I have some question about the effectiveness of this particular procedure. It did not do enough to create a high level of involvement, and it turned out to be very complex since it asked subjects to role-play subjects, not people. In this sense, it might have given us the worst of both worlds, but I still think it is worth some further exploration. In another experiment, we were interested in creating differently structured attitudes about an organization by feeding different kinds of information to two groups of subjects. These groups were then asked to take specific actions in support of the organization, and we measured attitude changes resulting from these actions. In the first part of the experiment, the subjects were clearly informed that the organization and the information that we were feeding to them were fictitious, and that we were simply trying to simulate the conditions under which attitudes about new organizations are typically formed. In the second part of the experiment, the subjects were told that we were interested in studying the effects of action in support of an organization on attitudes toward it, and they were asked (in groups of five) to role-play a strategy meeting of leaders of the fictitious organization. The results of this study were very encouraging. While there is obviously a great deal that we need to know about the meaning of this situation to the subjects, they did react differentially to the experimental manipulations and these reactions followed an orderly pattern, despite the fact that they knew it was all make-believe.

There are other types of procedures, in addition to role playing, that are worth exploring. For example, one might design field experiments in which, with the full cooperation of the subjects, specific experimental variations are introduced. The advantages of dealing with motivations at a real-life level of intensity might well outweigh the disadvantages of subjects' knowing the general purpose of the experiment. At the other extreme of ambitiousness, one might explore the effects of modifying standard experimental procedures slightly by informing the subject at the beginning of the experiment that he will not be receiving full information about what is going on, but asking him to suspend judgment until the experiment is over.

Whatever alternative approach we try, there is no doubt that it will have its own problems and complexities. Procedures effective for some purposes may be quite ineffective for others, and it may well turn out that for certain kinds of problems there is no adequate substitute for the use of deception. But there *are* alternative procedures that, for many purposes, may be as effective or even more effective than procedures built on deception. These approaches often involve a radically different set of assumptions about the role of the subject in the experiment: They require us to *use* the subject's motivation to cooperate rather than to bypass it; they may even call for increasing the sophistication of potential subjects, rather than maintaining their naïveté. My only plea is that we devote some of our energies to active exploration of these alternative approaches.

REFERENCES

Asch, S. E. Effects of group pressure upon the modification and distortion of judgments. In H. Guetzkow (Ed.), *Groups, leadership, and men*. Pittsburgh: Carnegie Press, 1951, pp. 177–190.

Baumrind, D. Some thoughts on ethics of research: After reading Milgram's "Behavioral study of obedience." *Amer. Psychologist*, 1964, **19**, 421–423.

Bergin, A. E. The effect of dissonant persuasive communications upon changes in a self-referring attitude. *J. Pers.*, 1962, **30**, 423–438.

Berkun, M. M., Bialek, H. M., Kern, R. P., & Yagi, K. Experimental studies of psychological stress in man. *Psychol. Monogr.*, 1962, **76**(15, Whole No. 534).

Bramel, D. A dissonance theory approach to defensive projection. *J. abnorm. soc. Psychol.*, 1962, **64**, 121–129.

Bramel, D. Selection of a target for defensive projection. *J. abnorm. soc. Psychol.*, 1963, **66**, 318–324.

Campbell, D., Sanderson, R. E., & Laverty, S. G. Characteristics of a conditioned response in human subjects during extinction trials following a single traumatic conditioning trial. *J. abnorm. soc. Psychol.*, 1964, **68**, 627–639.

Festinger, L., & Carlsmith, J. M. Cognitive consequences of forced compliance. *J. abnorm. soc. Psychol.*, 1959, **58**, 203–210.

Guetzkow, H., Alger, C. F., Brody, R. A., Noel, R. C., & Snyder, R. C. *Simulation in international relations*. Englewood Cliffs, N. J.: Prentice-Hall, 1963.

Kelman, H. C. Manipulation of human behavior: An ethical dilemma for the social scientist. *J. soc. Issues*, 1965, **21**(2), 31–46.

Milgram, S. Behavioral study of obedience. *J. abnorm. soc. Psychol.*, 1963, **67**, 371–378.

Milgram, S. Issues in the study of obedience: A reply to Baumrind. *Amer. Psychologist*, 1964, **19**, 848–852.

Milgram, S. Some conditions of obedience and disobedience to authority. *Hum. Rel.*, 1965, **18**, 57–76.

Mills, T. M. A sleeper variable in small groups research: The experimenter. *Pac. sociol. Rev.*, 1962, **5**, 21–28.

Mulder, M., & Stremerding, A. Threat, attraction to group, and need for strong leadership. *Hum. Rel.*, 1963, **16**, 317–334.

Orne, M. T. On the social psychology of the psychological experiment: With particular reference to demand characteristics and their implications. *Amer. Psychologist*, 1962, **17**, 776–783.

Riecken, H. W. A program for research on experiments in social psychology. In N. F. Washburne (Ed.), *Decisions, values and Groups*. Vol. 2. New York: Pergamon Press, 1962, pp. 25–41.

Rosenberg, M. J., & Abelson, R. P. An analysis of cognitive balancing. In M. J. Rosenberg et al. (Ed.), *Attitude organization and change*. New Haven: Yale Univ. Press, 1960, pp. 112–163.

Rosenthal, R. On the social psychology of the psychological experiment: The experimenter's hypothesis as unintended determinant of experimental results. *Amer. Scient.*, 1963, **51**, 268–283.

Rosenthal, R., & Fode, K. L. Psychology of the scientist: V. Three experiments in experimenter bias. *Psychol. Rep.*, 1963, **12**, 491–511. (Monogr. Suppl. 3-V12)

Rosenthal, R., Persinger, G. W., Vikan-Kline, L. L., & Fode, K. L. The effect of early data returns on data subsequently obtained by outcome-biased experimenters. *Sociometry*, 1963, **26**, 487–498.

Rosenthal, R., Persinger, G. W., Vikan-Kline, L. L., & Mulry, R. C. The role of the research assistant in the mediation of experimenter bias. *J. Pers.*, 1963, **31**, 313–335.

Vinacke, W. E. Deceiving experimental subjects. *Amer. Psychologist*, 1954, **9**, 155.

10

ON THE ECOLOGICAL VALIDITY OF LABORATORY DECEPTIONS

Martin T. Orne and Charles H. Holland

"O what a tangled web we weave,
When first we practise to deceive!"
Sir Walter Scott, 1808

In any psychological experiment, the subject's knowledge and beliefs about the study may have significant effects upon his behavior. In order to obtain undistorted responses, it is often felt necessary to disguise the purpose of an experiment, and to do this investigators have used misinformation, confederates, and other forms of deception. Milgram's studies in obedience are analyzed as an example of significant research where the importance of the theoretical, social and moral implications has tended to obscure these methodological issues. How the subject perceives the experiment in general, and how plausible the deception manipulation is for him in particular, must be evaluated before meaningful inference can be drawn from the experiment to life outside the laboratory.

In the last half of this century social psychology has gained increasing significance and importance. In an age when tech-

From M. T. Orne and C. H. Holland, *Inter. J. Psychiat.*, 1968, **6**, 282–293. With permission of authors and publisher.

For further reference see author's more recent articles: in R. Rosenthal & R. Rosnow (Eds.), *Artifact in behavioral research.* New York: Academic Press, 1969; in *Nebraska Symposium on Motivation.* Lincoln, Neb.: Univ. of Nebraska Press, 1970.

The substantive work upon which the theoretical outlook presented in this paper was based was supported in part by contract # Nonr 4731 from the Group Psychology Branch of the Office of Naval Research.

We wish to thank our colleagues, Frederick J. Evans, Edgar P. Nace, Emily C. Orne, David A. Paskewitz, and David L. Rosenhan, for their helpful comments and criticisms.

nology has made the sudden extinction of man an all too real possibility, when we are witnessing a world-wide crisis of values and the only remaining social certainty is continuing change, the prospect of bringing relevant social psychological processes under scientific scrutiny is of major concern to all of us. The impressionistic, quasi-philosophical approaches which had long characterized writings about crowd behavior and group processes were not sufficient to form the body of a science, nor could the technology of evaluating attitudes and public opinion, regardless of its methodological sophistication, provide for the development of basic new insights into the nature of man. Rather the pioneering work, particularly by Lewin, Asch, and Sherif, showed how the techniques of experimental psychology could also be applied to the study of social psychological phenomena. The use of the psychological experiment as a tool has made it possible to systematically manipulate a wide range of variables, and increasing ingenuity has been devoted to the application of this tool to an ever wider range of problems. The experiments by Festinger and his students (e.g., Brehm & Cohen, 1962) in support of the cognitive dissonance theory are particularly ingenious examples of what has recently become known as experimental social psychology.

Conceptual and methodological issues that had been skirted by much of the research in this exciting new discipline have been brought to a head by Milgram's studies in obedience. He has addressed himself to one of the most compelling questions of our time: What are the conditions under which man will inflict pain and suffering upon another individual? In a series of apparently crucial experiments Milgram seems to have shown that subjects (hereinafter designated Ss) can be required to inflict pain up to and beyond intensities clearly designated as dangerous merely by legitimizing this behavior as part of a scientific experiment. Such findings are uncomfortably reminiscent of the concentration camp "medical experiments" reported to have been carried out by Schumann, Mengele, and others (Manvell & Fraenkel, 1967). Milgram has also tried to demonstrate that this behavior is lawful in that it can be shown to vary, depending upon the proximity between the S and his victim and the extent to which the experimental situation as a whole is legitimized, i.e., carried out within the confines of a university campus versus a rented office in a slightly disreputable office building.

The implications of Milgram's work are clear. It would appear that with little effort most individuals can be induced to carry out destructive and aggressive actions bringing severe pain, possibly permanent injury or even death to their victim. The fact that the S's behavior is in the name of science provides little reassurance and suggests at the very least a horrifying callousness as a characteristic of modern man. The studies seem to provide convincing empirical support for Freud's belief in the death instinct and the philosophic position on man put forth by Hobbes, Nietzsche, and others. One may even conceive of these studies as laboratory analogs to the Genovese murder (Rosenthal, 1964).

As has often been pointed out, the extent to which scientific findings become generally accepted is only partly a function of the care with which they are obtained. In large part acceptance depends upon the extent to which results fit the *Zeitgeist* and the prejudices of the scientific community. The flair with which Milgram presents his findings and the effects they generate tend to obscure serious questions about their validity. In evaluating research which has broad implications and is of practical importance, there is a tendency to minimize concern for methodological rigor. Yet it is because of its importance that this research demands thoughtful consideration.

ECOLOGICAL VALIDITY OF DECEPTION STUDIES

In some areas, the bases for evaluating the methodological adequacy of research have been worked out in considerable detail. A judgment is usually made by evaluating the controls, the manner in which data are collected and how they are handled statistically. By these criteria, Milgram's work appears to have been carefully carried out. Unfortunately there is an entirely different set of problems requiring consideration, which Brunswik (1947) has subsumed under the concept of ecological validity.

Experiments are carried out to make inferences to other— usually nonexperimental—situations. They make it possible to observe events in a standard situation, ideally holding constant everything other than the particular independent variable under investigation. For this technique to allow valid inference it is essential that the experimental situation adequately reflect the process under investigation. This crucial step is taken when the general process is translated into specific experimental terms by an operational definition. Milgram, for example, has operationally defined the concept of obedience as whether or not in the experiment the S continues to administer exer-increasing levels of electric shock. Then by studying the conditions under which the specific behavior may be obtained, the ease with which it can be elicited, the percentage of individuals who obey, etc., he tries to investigate the generic problem of obedience. The validity of his findings for legitimate generalizations to non-experimental contexts where the concept of obedience applies depends upon the appropriateness of the experimental situation and the adequacy of the operational definition—questions central to the issue of ecological validity. Unfortunately, while the rules of statistical inference have received a great deal of attention in recent years, no such consensus exists about how to evaluate the ecological validity of research findings.

As a solution to the problem of ecological validity, Brunswik suggested running Ss with differing demographic, personality, and IQ characteristics and extending the study to a wide variety of contexts. Milgram's work is of special interest because he, more than most other investigators, has systematically tried to vary both subject population and the institutional setting in which his studies are carried out, implicitly recognizing the crux of the issues confronting his work. These attempts do not, however, successfully deal with the two issues addressed in this discussion: the methodological problems common to all psychological deception studies and the unique social psychological attributes of the psychological experiment itself.

PROBLEMS OF DECEPTION STUDIES

Conceptually, the Milgram situation is closely related to the conformity situation developed by Asch. In his classic research on conformity, Asch (1952) placed Ss in a group situation, ostensibly to investigate perception. The Ss were required to carry out simple perceptual tasks such as judging the length of lines and to reach agreement about their perceptions. Starting out with very ambiguous stimuli, the perceptual qualities became more and more clear-cut. The situation was so devised, however, that there was only one real S while the other Ss were confederates. They were instructed to agree on perceptions which were in fact inaccurate, and matters were so arranged that the actual S was required to make his judgment after most of the others. In the beginning, with stimuli which were very ambiguous, it was not difficult for him to agree but, as the experiment continued, he found himself confronted with agreement among his peers about perceptions that were clearly at odds with his own, an experience which many Ss found extremely frightening and disturbing. They were forced either to conform to group pressure and deny what they could plainly see or to maintain their perceptual judgment against the group.

Asch used this situation to explore the kinds of factors that determined the S's conformity response. Recognizing the importance of not allowing the S to suspect that the other Ss were actually confederates, he was careful to keep the situation plausible. The stimuli were chosen to be ambiguous at first, and only gradually was the S forced to recognize the increasing discrepancy between his perceptions and those of his peers. The extent to which Ss accepted the situation was checked by careful postexperimental interviews which allowed Asch to evaluate their degree of suspicion. In this way he was able to determine the limits within which the experiment had to be conducted without becoming obvious—a formidable problem when Swarthmore students were used as Ss!

The development of a new paradigm of this kind is usually followed by a large number of studies using the technique in order to relate conformity to a wide variety of other parameters. While Asch himself paid close attention to the plausibility of his situation, later investigators showed less concern about this problem, often changing the perceptual stimuli abruptly and excessively. Rather than checking carefully whether Ss were taken in by the deception they tended to define conformity in simple behavioral terms, either omitting postexperimental discussion or carrying it out in a perfunctory fashion.

Unless a postexperimental inquiry is carried out with great persistence and sensitivity a "pact of ignorance" tends to develop (Orne, 1962b). It is important to Ss that their experimental participation prove useful. If the S sees through the deception in an experiment, he may also realize that this might destroy the value of his performance. Since neither he nor the experimenter (E) wants to discard his data, their interests collaborate to make the S appear naïve even after extremely transparent procedures.

The use of deception in social psychological studies has become extremely popular in recent years.[1] It is obviously felt that deception is needed to make it possible to explore the process under investigation. Experimenters implicitly realize that Ss are active, sentient beings who are influenced not only by the immediate stimuli in the experimental situation but also by their symbolic meaning in a broader sense: the context in which the studies are carried out, their aims, purposes and so forth. The deception, then, is an attempt on the part of the investigator to circumvent those cognitive processes of the S which would interfere with his research. When such an experiment is carried out, however, it is vital that the investigator determine whether it is the S or himself who is being deceived!

Milgram's studies use deception to create what seems to be a compelling conflict situation. Because of the ingenuity of the deception, the reader is drawn to assume with Milgram that Ss accepted the situation at face value. It is unfortunate that no data are presented to indicate whether this was in fact the case. Yet the extent to which the deception actually was accepted by the S determines how the results should be interpreted. Had quasi-control procedures been included in the obedience studies, they would have shed light on the adequacy of the deception manipulation, but in the absence of data on this crucial issue, the only way we can evaluate the experiment's plausibility is to analyze the congruence of the cues available to the S.

THE MILGRAM DESIGN

In all the variations of Milgram's obedience research, Ss are told that they are participating in an experiment to study the effect of punishment on memory. Each S always draws straws with the other S (confederate) and by "chance" ends up with the teacher's role. The other "S" is always strapped into an awesome looking electric chair and both are always shown a shock generator by means of which shocks from a very low voltage up to 450 volts can be administered. This machine is

---

[1] For an excellent discussion of the ethical problems as well as other issues concerning the use of deception in psychological studies see Kelman, "Human Use of Human Subjects," 1967.

made all the more awesome by labeling the high end of the scale in red letters, "Danger—Severe Shock—XXX."

Before beginning the experiment a shock described as 45 volts is administered to the S, presumably so that he knows what the shocks are like. This, incidentally, is an extremely uncomfortable shock. The teacher's role is then explained to the S— how to present a paired-associates learning task to the learner, how it is the teacher who determines the duration of the punishment, and how a higher level of shock must be administered for each failure. Initially the learner is able to answer correctly two out of three times, but he rapidly begins to fail more and more frequently, requiring the S to administer ever higher levels of shock to the victim. "Starting with 75 volts the learner begins to grunt and moan. At 150 volts he demands to be let out of the experiment. At 180 volts he cries out that he can no longer stand the pain. At 300 volts he refuses to provide any more answers to the memory test, insisting that he is no longer a participant in the experiment and must be freed [Milgram, 1965, p. 60]."

The E throughout this procedure remains calm and instructs the S to continue. If the teacher says that the learner is no longer responding and therefore there is no point in going on, he is told, "Treat the absence of an answer as equivalent to a wrong answer, and follow the usual shock procedure." If the S does not wish to do so, he is told, "You have no other choice, you must go on!" Regardless of the degree of agitation shown by the S or the anguished screams of the victim, the E remains imperturbable and demands that the S continue.

HOW PLAUSIBLE IS THIS PARADIGM?

Ss participating in psychological experiments have considerable awareness of the implicit rules which govern the situation. They have learned to distrust the E because they know that the true purpose of the experiment may be disguised. Many Ss view their task as a problem-solving situation which requires them to determine the "real" situation and respond appropriately. This process has been analyzed elsewhere (Orne, 1962b; Riecken, 1962). Of particular relevance here is that the S's perception of the purpose of an experiment will depend only in part on what he is told explicitly. He will then evaluate this information in terms of his prior knowledge, using whatever cues are available in the situation. These cues include not only the manner in which instructions are communicated but also scuttlebutt about the experiment, the setting in which it is carried out, the person of the E and, most important of all, the experimental procedure itself. The congruence of all of these cues with the instructions that the S is explicitly given will determine the plausibility of the experimental situation. When the procedure suggests one experimental intent and the explicit instructions another, what the S believes becomes difficult to determine and very slight changes in the procedure may lead to radical changes in the S's hypotheses and subsequent behavior. In a conflict situation when the instructions are at odds with other cues, the S is apt, however, to rely preferentially on those cues stemming from the experimental procedure because, as the old adage says, "Actions speak louder than words."

To successfully carry out a deception study is exceedingly difficult because subtle practical problems, often dealt with in some fashion by research assistants, assume crucial importance. In arranging the schedule, for example, the S may inquire whether he might be run at the same time as a friend. Considerable ingenuity is required to explain in a plausible fashion why no suitable time exists for the Ss to be run together in a study apparently requiring two Ss. The task of preventing Ss from communicating with each other is also formidable, especially in an experiment that makes such ideal cocktail party conversation. There are moreover innumerable subtle cues that can give away the true status of a confederate, stemming not only from the confederate's behavior but also from that of the E. (It is exceedingly difficult to treat the confederate and the S in a similar fashion.) In the absence of evidence it does not seem justified to assume that the performance was carried out flawlessly in each instance. Plausible deceptions are not easily achieved, but no hint of difficulties or S disqualifications appears in any of Milgram's reports.

Beside the myriad technical problems, even if we were to assume that everybody played his role to perfection, the experimental procedure itself contains serious incongruities. The experiment is presented as a study of the effect of punishment on memory. The investigator presumably is interested in determining how the victim's rate of learning is affected by punishment, yet there is nothing that he requires of the S (teacher) that he could not as easily do himself. Those Ss who have some scientific training would also be aware that experimental procedures require more care and training in administering stimuli than they have been given. The way in which the study is carried out is certainly sufficient to allow some Ss to recognize that they, rather than the victim, are the real Ss of the experiment.

The most incongruent aspect of the experiment, however, is the behavior of the E. Despite the movie image of the mad scientist, most Ss accept the fact that scientists—even behavioral scientists—are reasonable people. No effort is made to emphasize the world-shaking importance of the learning experiment; rather it is presented as a straightforward, simple study. Incongruously the E sits by passively while the victim suffers, demanding that the experiment continue despite the victim's demands to be released and the possibility that his health may be endangered. This behavior of the E, which Milgram interprets as the demands of legitimate authority, can with equal plausibility be interpreted as a significant cue to the true state of affairs—namely that no one is actually being hurt. Indeed, if the S believes that the experiment is a legitimate study, the very fact that he is being asked to continue a relatively trivial experiment while inflicting extreme suffering upon his victim clearly implies that no such suffering or danger exists.

The incongruity between the relatively trivial experiment and the imperturbability of the E on the one hand, and the awesome shock generator able to present shocks designated as "Danger —Severe Shock" and the extremity of the victim's suffering on the other, should be sufficient to raise serious doubts in the minds of most Ss.

ANOTHER WAY TO CONCEPTUALIZE MILGRAM'S FINDINGS

In considering the incongruities of the situation, one may wonder how different this experiment is from the stage magician's trick where a volunteer from the audience is strapped into the guillotine and another volunteer is required to trip the release lever. The magician is careful to do a professional job of deception. He demonstrates that the guillotine will split a head of cabbage and allows the volunteer to satisfy himself about the genuineness of the guillotine. Though releasing the lever will lead to the apparently inevitable decapitation of the victim, he has little difficulty in obtaining "obedience" because the S knows full well that everything is going to be all right. This does not, of course, prevent the S from being somewhat uncomfortable, perhaps showing nervous laughter, when he is actually required to trip the lever, if only because such behavior is appropriate in this context.

The lawfulness which Milgram demonstrates in the relationship of obedience to physical proximity can be accounted for by the cues that different procedures communicate to the S— albeit implicitly—that things are not what they seem. Sixty-six percent obedience is obtained when the victim is in another room and the only communication between him and the teacher is his banging the wall at 300 volts, ostensibly wanting to be let out. When we consider the most striking cues available to the S at this point—the victim's protestations and the E's calmly continuing to take notes and ignoring these pleas—it would seem more plausible to assume not that the E is some fanatic with a cause which justifies his behavior but rather that the E is still a responsible scientist whose behavior is clearly communicating that the alleged victim is not really a victim at all. One need not assume undue intellectual ability on the part of the S to postulate that he may be able to surmise the true state of affairs. To us the high rate of compliance would seem less due to the S's "putting the victim out of mind" (as Milgram suggests) than to the relatively low cue value of the victim's behavior when compared with that of the E's unswerving imperturbability. The addition of auditory feedback (the victim's screams) results in a remarkably small decrement in obedience —to 62.5 percent. We would suspect this is partly due to the technical problems; namely, the S tends to scream only in response to the immediate punishing stimuli while sitting quietly and continuing to cooperate in response to the verbal stimuli. Regardless of the quality of the screams, the situation is not very plausible. Apparently by using good actors in close proximity it is easier to convince Ss that the situation might be real. Here the degree of compliance drops to 40 percent, and when the S is required to actually hold the victim's hand, to 30 percent.

In contrast to many other investigators, Milgram is aware of some of the difficulties inherent in social psychological laboratory research and, for this reason, he used the ingenious modification of renting an office in downtown Bridgeport and making the research appear unrelated to a major university. Under these circumstances the cue value of the E's imperturbability would diminish and, as one might expect, the degree of obedience also diminishes. Even in this situation, however, the E is still carrying out an experiment in an apparently professional manner.

RELEVANT DATA FROM OTHER STUDIES

The problems inherent in this research are illustrated in the long-standing controversy about whether Ss in hypnosis can be compelled to carry out antisocial actions. Already, in 1889, Janet reports that before a distinguished group of jurists and medical men a deeply hypnotized patient stabbed individuals with rubber daggers, poisoned their tea with sugar, and carried out any other type of murder or mayhem required of her. This demonstration was very impressive, and after the distinguished guests had left, the S was left to be awakened by students who wished to end the experiment on a lighter note. They suggested to the patient that she was alone, about to take a bath, and should undress. Her response to the suggestion was to awaken immediately, greatly disturbed. It is one thing to "kill" people during an experimental situation with means that cannot really do damage; it is quite another to be asked to undress in a context that transcends the experimental situation.

More recently, Rowland (1939) carried out a seemingly definitive experiment by showing that Ss in deep hypnosis could be compelled to carry out antisocial and destructive acts, such as throwing fuming nitric acid at a research assistant, a finding which was subsequently replicated by P. C. Young (1952). In both studies Ss were "obedient" in deep hypnosis, but when asked in the waking state whether they would carry out these actions, they indicated in horror that they would not. In a careful replication of these experiments, Orne and Evans (1965) found that five out of six deeply hypnotized Ss could in fact be compelled to carry out an action as antisocial as throwing fuming nitric acid at another individual. In addition, however, it was found that six out of six nonhypnotized individuals, who had been required to simulate hypnosis for a "blind" E, would also carry out these actions. Depending upon the degree of social pressure, moreover, various degrees of "obedience" were obtained from other groups of Ss who were merely asked to participate in a previously unspecified experiment. The crucial difference seemed to be that instead of *asking* Ss whether they would carry out the action, the E clearly communicated to them that they *were* to do so. In an experiment, when it is clearly communicated to the S that he is to carry out an action which appears very destructive and dangerous, it is thereby concurrently communicated that it will be safe to do so. In contrast, when the S is questioned as to whether he would carry out such an action, it does nothing to alter what is patently obvious—that someone would be severely hurt—thereby eliciting vehement denial.

Thus far we have only described the part of the experiment which is analogous to the seeming antisocial aspects of Milgram's work. More illuminating perhaps is that Ss were also required to carry out apparently self-destructive actions; in particular, to pick up and place in a bag a snake known to be poisonous and to remove a penny from the jar of fuming nitric acid with their bare fingers. In Milgram's terms, there was little trouble in eliciting obedience from our Ss. Our findings in this regard did not, however, lead us to conclude that outside the experimental situation Ss can be instructed to walk off the roof, in some other way to injure themselves or even to commit suicide. On the contrary, when we asked our Ss about their behavior, they clearly indicated that despite perceptual evidence to the contrary they did not have the slightest doubt that every care had been taken to protect them from serious harm. Without having to be told, Ss were quite aware of the reality constraints governing research in our society and, correctly we might add, assumed that as long as we really intended them to carry out these behaviors, we would have made certain no serious injury would befall anyone—neither them nor our research assistants.

It was essential for the S to be in an actual subject-experimenter relationship in order to have him carry out these actions; despite repeated attempts, not one of our colleagues could be induced to attempt any of these acts. We would like to attribute their refusal not to a lack of trust in us, but to the absence of the experimental relationship that legitimized the behavior. Our colleagues were also convinced, much like the group of psychiatrists polled by Milgram, that few if any Ss would comply with the demands of the experiment. It would appear that even expertise in nonexperimental human behavior does not allow accurate prediction of what Ss will do in an actual experimental situation.

Holland (1967) extended Milgram's studies in an attempt to explore the demand characteristics of the situation. The substantive findings will be reported elsewhere and only some observations are relevant here. Initially it was intended to replicate precisely the verbal feedback condition where the victim refuses to answer further after having received a 300-volt shock. It became clear, however, that it would be necessary to add additional auditory feedback in the form of moans or groans each time a substantial shock was administered because during the pilot studies Ss run in the original condition indicated after the experiment that they had been certain that the victim had either escaped or been released! Even with additional auditory feedback and meticulous attention to perfecting the deception aspects of the situation, three-quarters of the Ss run in the analog of Milgram's situation indicated that they did not really believe the deception when carefully questioned after the experiment.

Holland added two additional groups of Ss in his study and a "blind" second E. The first E told one group that they were control Ss and suggested that there would be something "fishy" about the experiment in which they were about to participate. They were instructed not to "let on" but rather to act as though they were regular Ss. In this manner it was hoped to raise their level of suspicion, making it virtually certain that they would become aware of the incongruities of the situation. The other group was told before the experiment that the level of shock which would be administered to the S was really only onetenth of what was indicated on the shock generator. Though the experimental manipulation made certain that these latter two groups would be relatively aware that things were not as they seemed, their obedience behavior was not significantly different from the group run under the Milgram condition. Other aspects of their behavior also failed to separate these groups: Ss exposed to each treatment appeared to become uncomfortable and show signs of severe anxiety conflict. As a result, the "blind" E was unable to judge at better than chance levels the experimental group to which Ss belonged. These findings suggest that Ss run in the Milgram condition could easily have become aware of the deception and still behave as if they were naive. Neither the extent of the S's obedience nor his objective signs of discomfort necessarily reflect what he experiences. Thus, in the final post-experimental inquiry it became clear that much of the S's disturbed behavior was purposive and occurred because the individual felt that such behavior was demanded by the situation.

It would seem that the simple behavioral response of obeying instructions cannot tell us much about why the S obeys. We are dealing with a highly complex situation where Ss may perceive that no real hurt is being inflicted upon anyone and yet not be certain what constitutes the desired response on their part. They are placed in a dilemma where the only definitely appropriate response seems to be discomfort. Whether continued obedience or conformity is seen as the successful response seems to depend upon many as yet obscure and subtle aspects of the total situation.

It seems that in the Milgram-type experiment one may encounter two groups of Ss that do not necessarily differ in their overt behavior. Usually the majority of Ss assume that the situation is essentially safe while a much smaller group may accept the situation at its face value. Logically these two groups of Ss take part in quite different experiments. Obedience by the first group that is (correctly) convinced the situation is essentially safe allows inference about what they would do in other experimental situations but not about what they would do outside of such a context. For the experiment to have any significance for other contexts, it is essential that the Ss believe in its reality. To ignore the Ss' perceptions and merely focus upon their overt behavior by saying it matters only whether the S is in fact obedient according to an arbitrary operational definition ignores a vital issue: To what are they obedient? Only by answering this question can an experiment of this kind have broader meaning.

THE PSYCHOLOGY OF THE PSYCHOLOGICAL EXPERIMENT

For most psychological studies involving deception it is sufficient to make certain that the situation is accepted, but Milgram's paradigm raises an additional problem. There are some issues which cannot readily be examined in an experimental context since they are context-specific or at least context-related. This is particularly true when an experimental situation is used to study compliance or obedience.

Milgram appropriately points out that we expose our neck to the barber and remove our shoes in the shoe store because these constitute legitimate requests. In everyday life the individual is able to determine what constitutes a legitimate request and rather clearly defined, implicit rules govern what one individual may ask of another. However, the agreement to participate in an experiment gives the E carte blanche about what may legitimately be requested. In asking the S to participate in an experiment, the E implicitly says, "Will you do whatever I ask for a specified period of time? By so doing you may earn a fee, contribute to science, and perhaps even learn something of value to yourself. In return I promise that no harm will befall you. At the completion of the experiment you will be no better or worse off than you are now and though you may experience temporary inconvenience, this is justified by the importance of the undertaking." A corollary to this agreement is that the S may not ask why certain things are required of him. He must assume that these actions are legitimate and appropriate for the needs of the experiment.

The S's willingness to comply with unexplained or unreasonable requests in an experimental context does not permit inference to be drawn beyond this context. For example, a study required Ss to carry out a boring and tedious task—serial addition. After completing each page of work Ss were instructed to destroy their own product and continue working (Orne, 1962b). To our surprise, Ss were willing to carry out this task for long periods of time and do so with a high rate of speed and accuracy. Anyone who believes direct inference about obedience in real life can be drawn from an experimental context should ask his secretary to type a letter, and after making certain there are no errors, ask her to tear it up and retype it. With rare exceptions, two or three such trials should be sufficient to ensure that the E will require a new secretary! It should be noted that the activity required of the secretary is no different in kind from what she is normally required to do. She is paid for the work at her usual rate, no one is hurt and yet as long as she has an option, there is little question about her behavior in real life. Incidentally, the same individual would likely be "obedient" if she had agreed to participate in an experiment.[2]

The S's unquestioning compliance with the E's requests depends in part upon his awareness of the total experimental situation and the safeguards built into it. The Milgram paradigm runs, therefore, into an inevitable paradox. There are some things which the S would not do, but there are behaviors that he knows the E cannot require of him. Therefore, when the E asks him to carry out an action which would lead to serious harm either to himself or to someone else and communicates that the S is intended to carry out these actions, he inevitably also communicates that these actions will *not* lead to their apparent consequences. That the S will in an experiment carry out behaviors that appear destructive either to himself or others reflects more upon his willingness to trust the E and the experimental context than on what he would do outside of the experimental situation.

It can be argued that Ss will carry out behaviors which appear dangerous and that an unscrupulous investigator could utilize this to inflict serious harm on either the S or other individuals. This is, of course, true, but lest we be concerned about breeding a nation of sheep who will unsuspectingly carry out dangerous actions, it is well to remember that in our complex but still basically cooperative society it is impossible to function without trust in reasonable situations. We take our car to have the brakes repaired and assume without personally checking that they have been put back together properly; we take a plane without personally subjecting the pilot to physical examination, trusting in his competence and soundness of mind; when a physician prescribes green pills, we blithely assume that the medication is for our good although, of course, if he had chosen to give us arsenic we would have taken it and died. Therefore, a demonstration that a situation that can legitimately be expected to contain all possible safeguards for the participants could conceivably be perverted cannot at the same time

[2] A secretary would regard this kind of request as intolerable only in the context of her continuing activities but would be relatively untroubled by such a request if it was "episodic" in the sense of Garfinkel (1967) and legitimized in an appropriate fashion, e.g., necessary for science.

be used to prove that man is either gullible or, when on guard, easily deceived. Unfortunately, as important as the problem of obedience is in modern society, it is unlikely to be resolved by using the psychological experiment as a tool in a situation where the S can recognize and define it as such.

CONCLUSION

Ignoring the questions we have raised thus far, one might try to set up a situation where Ss must stop being obedient; for example, having the victim complain of heart trouble and showing signs of having a coronary attack. Certainly no learning experiment would justify continuing at the risk of bringing about the S's death. It is difficult under these circumstances to imagine either an E calmly saying, "Continue—you must go on —the experiment requires that you continue" or a S actually continuing to administer shock to a victim who had passed out after complaining of chest pain. If some other investigator reported such a caricature of the Milgram situation it might be considered a scientific practical joke. A finding that in the face of an apparent coronary by the victim, Ss continued to administer shock would have to be explained by assuming that Ss did not believe in the reality of the events and therefore would most likely be dismissed as a poorly executed piece of laboratory work. Yet it is Milgram himself who reports such findings! The fact that he elicits obedience from a significant proportion of Ss even under the threat of an impending heart attack must throw serious doubt on the manner in which the deception was handled in all of his other studies. Thus, by pushing the psychological deception experiment *ad absurdum*, Milgram forces us to come to terms with issues of ecological validity.

What can be said about the ease with which man can be forced to abuse his fellow man? To show that Milgram's empirical findings do not allow him either to prove or disprove his conclusions does not help us to draw any meaningful inferences about the true nature of man. Rather, the news media, more validly and, alas, more eloquently than any experimental data, attest to the scope of the problem and the urgent need to understand the forces that govern violence. Appropriate ecologically valid techniques must be developed to study this and related problems. The difficulties of research in these areas do not mean that we can afford to abandon either the scientific method or the experimental technique; rather, to attack some problems we will have to devise experiments that are not recognized as such by the Ss.[3] In doing so, moreover, we must make certain that this is in fact the case while being careful to keep in mind the ethical strictures which must govern research in a free society.

Milgram's studies in obedience, though they fail to provide a viable model for the scientific investigation of violence, are nonetheless a milestone in social psychology. By demonstrating that it is possible to stay within currently accepted scientific conventions and yet push the psychological experiment beyond its limits, the obedience studies force us to consider what these limits are and hasten the day when issues of ecological validity will receive the kind of careful attention currently devoted to statistical inference. Finally, Milgram has dared to attempt the systematic scientific study of an urgent problem currently facing our society. While new means will be required for this purpose, by focusing on vital issues Milgram has provided new impetus to an exciting field.

REFERENCES

Asch, S. E. *Social psychology.* Englewood Cliffs, N.J.: Prentice-Hall, 1952.

Brehm, J. W., & Cohen, A. R. *Explorations in cognitive dissonance.* New York: John Wiley, 1962.

Brunswik, E. *Systematic and representative design of psychological experiments with results in physical and social perception.* (Syllabus Series No. 304) Berkeley: Univ. of California Press, 1947.

Garfinkel, H. *Studies in ethnomethodology.* Englewood Cliffs, N.J.: Prentice-Hall, 1967.

Holland, C. H. Sources of variance in the experimental investigation of behavioral obedience. Unpublished doctoral dissertation, Univ. of Connecticut, 1967.

Janet, P. *L'automatisme psychologique: essai de psychologie expéri-*

---

[3] For an extended discussion of these issues, see Orne (1962a); Orne (1969). A particularly elegant example of a method which allows systematic scientific study without the S's recognizing that he is participating in an experiment is the lost-letter technique developed by Milgram (1965).

mentale sur les formes inférieures de l'activité humaine. Paris: Alcan, 1889.

Kelman, H. C. Human use of human subjects: The problems of deception in social psychological experiments. *Psychol. Bull.,* 1967, **67,** 1–11.

Manvell, R., & Fraenkel, H. *The incomparable crime.* New York: Putnam's, 1967.

Milgram, S. Some conditions of obedience and disobedience to authority. *Hum. Rel.,* 1965, **18,** 57–76.

Milgram, S., Mann, L., & Harter, S. The lost-letter technique: A tool of social research. *Publ. Opin. Quart.,* 1965, **29,** 437–438.

Orne, M. T. Antisocial behavior and hypnosis: Problems of control and validation in empirical studies. In G. H. Estabrooks (Ed.), *Hypnosis: Current problems.* New York: Harper & Row, 1962, pp. 137–192. (a)

Orne, M. T. On the social psychology of the psychological experiment: With particular reference to demand characteristics and their implications. *Amer. Psychologist,* 1962, **17,** 776–783. (b)

Orne, M. T. Demand characteristics and quasi-controls. In R. Rosenthal & R. Rosnow (Eds.), *Artifact in social research.* New York: Academic Press, 1969, pp. 143–179.

Orne, M. T., & Evans, F. J. Social control in the psychological experiment: Antisocial behavior and hypnosis. *J. Pers. soc. Psychol.,* 1965, **1,** 189–200.

Riecken, H. W. A program for research on experiments in social psychology. In N. F. Washburne (Ed.), *Decisions, values and groups.* New York: Pergamon Press, 1962, vol. 2, pp. 25–41.

Rosenthal, A. M. *Thirty-eight witnesses.* New York: McGraw-Hill, 1964.

Rowland, L. W. Will hypnotized persons try to harm themselves or others? *J. abnorm. soc. Psychol.,* 1939, **34,** 114–117.

Young, P. C. Antisocial uses of hypnosis. In L. M. LeCron (Ed.), *Experimental hypnosis.* New York: Macmillan, 1952, pp. 376–409.

11

EVALUATING DECEPTION IN PSYCHOLOGICAL RESEARCH

Lawrence J. Stricker, Samuel Messick, and Douglas N. Jackson

The present article reviews studies on the use of deception in psychological research, indicates other directions that such investigations might take, and suggests solutions to the problems posed by this tactic. Deception is widely used, but its efficacy is rarely evaluated. Subjects' suspicion is a useful index of effectiveness and the only aspect that has been investigated so far. Many subjects may be suspicious of the deceptions in a study. This disbelief can be triggered by the experiment itself, operating in conjunction with the subjects' characteristics. Suspicion can affect the level of experimental performance or interact with it. The problems connected with this methodology may be minimized by improving the design of deception studies, by routinely assessing the effectiveness of dissimulations, and by modifying data analyses.

From L. J. Stricker, S. Messick, & D. N. Jackson, *Psychol. Bull.*, 1969, **71**, 343–351. With permission of authors and publisher.

The preparation of this review was supported in part by the National Institute of Mental Health, under Research Grant M-4186; in part by the National Institute of Child Health and Human Development, under Research Grant 1 P01 HD 01762; and in part by the Ontario Mental Health Foundation, under Grant 151. Portions of this article were presented, as part of a symposium on Methodological Issues in the Laboratory Study of Social Influence Processes, at the meetings of the Eastern Psychological Association, Washington, D.C., April 1968. Thanks are due Edward C. Nystrom for locating and abstracting the studies reviewed in this article and Nathan Kogan and Jerome E. Singer for their critical reviews of a draft of the manuscript.

Requests for reprints should be addressed to Dr. Lawrence J. Stricker, Division of Psychological Studies, Educational Testing Service, Princeton, New Jersey 08540.

Deception has a long history in psychological research. In the last few years, however, some of the problems and limitations inherent in this methodology have begun to be recognized. The ethical issues involved in deceiving experimental subjects have been discussed extensively (Baumrind, 1964; Kelman, 1967; Milgram, 1964). The main issues in this inconclusive debate are the potential harm to the participants and the proper balance between this danger and the possible value of the scientific findings obtained through the use of deceit. Quite distinct from the ethical problems posed by deception is the pragmatic question of its effectiveness. In contrast with the concern about the ethics of deception, the practical issues involved in its use have largely been ignored, if only because of the paucity of relevant data. Recently, however, studies that bear directly or indirectly on this tactic have appeared, laying the groundwork for an evaluation of its implications for research outcomes. This article, consequently, focuses on the pragmatics of deception, reviewing these studies, indicating other directions that research might take, and suggesting some tentative solutions to the operational problems connected with this methodology. Throughout, the emphasis is on research in personality and social psychology because of the special importance of deception in these fields, but many of the conclusions and suggestions may be relevant to other areas of psychology, too. Work on verbal conditioning is specifically excluded because of its vastness and its comprehensive treatment elsewhere (Adams, 1957; Greenspoon, 1962; Greenspoon & Brownstein, 1967; Hersen, 1968; Kanfer, 1968; Krasner, 1958, 1967; Salzinger, 1959; Spielberger, 1965; Williams, 1964).

PREVALENCE OF DECEPTION

It is highly likely that the use of deceit has increased through the years, in step with the growth of experimental research in personality and social psychology. Unfortunately, no data exist on this point, but an investigation by Stricker (1967) does provide some estimate of the current prevalence of deception. Studies appearing in 1964 in four journals—*Journal of Abnormal and Social Psychology, Journal of Personality, Journal of Social Psychology,* and *Sociometry*—were examined. These journals, which were chosen because they published the most deception studies, contained 457 studies of human subjects. Nineteen percent (88) of these investigations used deceit. This *percentage* would be lower, of course, if experiments in all psychological journals were included, but the fact remains that dissimulation was involved in a substantial *number* of investigations.

Not surprisingly, deception was employed in 81 percent of the conformity studies, in 72 percent of the studies in cognitive dissonance and balance theory, in 50 percent of the decision-making studies, and in 44 percent of the attitude-change studies. This tactic was also employed in other kinds of investigations, of course, but its use seems to have reached epidemic proportions in these four research areas. And their disproportionately heavy reliance on deceit would remain unchanged, even if studies in all journals were reviewed, for most experiments employing dissimulation were in these fields. Why is deception used so much in these areas? Perhaps their phenomena cannot be investigated in any other way. It seems more likely, though, that the cause is rooted in the scientific culture that flourishes within these fields (Kelman, 1967): There is general agreement that deception is valuable; this tactic is employed by influential investigators and in classic studies, and students are indoctrinated in its use—all in all, this methodology is prestigious and fashionable.

Whatever the reason, in Stricker's (1967) survey of deception studies, distinct patterns of dissimulations characterized different substantive areas, and the same kinds of dissimulations were consistently employed within a field. For example, most attitude-change investigations used deceit about the purpose of the study (82 percent), the apparatus and other experimental conditions (82 percent), and the performance and behavior of the other subjects (64 percent). Few used deception concerning the subjects' own behavior and characteristics (9 percent). Such consistency may mean that the same general research design—perhaps even the identical one—is often used in an area.

ASSESSING THE EFFECTIVENESS OF DECEPTION

An obvious criterion for the effectiveness of deception is the extent to which the dissimulation duplicates in all essential respects the circumstances that it is intended to portray. Two kinds of convergences between the deceptive situation and the real one are important. One is the correspondence between the manifest features of the two situations; this match determines the realism of the deceit. Deception studies undoubtedly differ in their realism, and this variable could be assessed by independent observers. Considerably more relevant are the subjects' own perceptions of realism, for it is they who must be gulled, not the observers. If the dissimulation is not perceived as authentic, the subjects' skepticism will be aroused. Hence, suspicion is a useful index of the effectiveness of deception.

The second kind of convergence is the congruence between subjects' behavior in the deceptive situation and its true counterpart. Such comparisons have limited feasibility, largely because it is difficult to devise a real situation with all the needed experimental controls, such as randomization of subjects' assignment to conditions. It would be both possible and fruitful, however, to obtain comparable data from deceptive and genuine situations that closely approximate each other.

A more indirect approach can also be used. Rather than establishing that the same behavior occurs in the deceptive situation and the real one, one may demonstrate, at the very least, that the deceptive situation elicits different behavior than the same situation stripped of its dissimulations (Vinacke, 1954). A deception study can be compared with the same experiment in which the subjects are correctly informed about the aspects of the investigation that would otherwise be falsified. If different results are obtained in the two studies, the deceptions have had some effect, though it is not certain whether the effect is the intended one or is simply a response to the suspicion engendered by the deceit. The interpretation is unambiguous if the same results are secured: The dissimulations have had no influence.

EXTENT OF SUSPICION

In examining the efficacy of deception, the focus is necessarily on suspicion because no data exist on other aspects of effectiveness. Although the present article is cncerned with studies employing deceit, it should be noted that suspicion of deception may exist about investigations that use no dissimulations. Consequently, much of the subsequent discussion of suspicion in deception studies may also apply to these other investigations.

How common is suspicion among subjects in deception studies? Relatively few investigations report even this basic information. In Stricker's (1967) review of deception experiments, only 24 percent (21) of the 88 studies using deceit presented such data. Failure to report the extent of disbelief existed in all substantive areas. This underreporting is consistent with research on experimenter bias (Rosenthal, 1966), which suggests that investigators may be hesitant to inquire about awareness because of their unwillingness to discard arduously collected data or, at the extreme, to discredit their studies.

In the 16 studies reviewed by Stricker that did report quantifiable data, the median percentage of undeceived subjects was 4 percent, and the range was from 0 percent to 23 percent. The medians were similar in the various substantive areas. Taken at face value, these statistics suggest that suspicion is not a serious problem. However, it is doubtful that the minority of studies reporting these data are representative of all published deception studies, much less unpublished ones. The same kinds of personal and institutional forces working against the publication of investigations with negative results (Sterling, 1959) probably restrain the appearance of deception studies reporting a high degree of disbelief among subjects. In addition, it seems very likely that the overall rate of actual suspicion in these 16 studies was seriously underestimated, in view of the inadequate criteria that were used to evaluate suspicion in some studies (i.e., the investigations employed several distinct deceptions, but the criteria referred to belief about only one of the dissimulations).

Some incidental and unanticipated findings in a conformity study by Stricker, Messick, and Jackson (1967) indicate that suspicion can be massive. The deceptions involved the use of a simulated-group version of the Asch (1956) situation and questionnaires administered with fictitious norms. From 39 percent to 61 percent of the subjects reported that the purpose of these procedures was to determine whether their responses would be influenced by others. Nine percent to 42 percent indicated that they did not hear spontaneous responses by others in the simulated group or that the normative answers reported on the questionnaires were incorrect. The use of two distinct kinds of conformity procedures, each involving a rather different dissimulation, may have elicited somewhat more mistrust than would be encountered otherwise. On the other hand, the subjects were of high school age and, hence, presumably more gullible than the college students used in most studies.

CAUSES OF SUSPICION

Little is known about the causes of suspicion. Several characteristics of the experimental situation may be relevant. Transparent deceptions are one obvious factor, but many studies seem to be extremely ingenious. The use of popular experimental paradigms based on deceit, such as the Asch situation, may also result in suspicion, for publicity is a concomitant of their wide use. This problem is bound to become more serious with the growing discussion of psychological investigations in the communications media (Allen, 1966; Stricker et al., 1967).

Suspicion may also stem from communication among subjects. They may discuss the investigation among themselves as it proceeds and, pooling their information and insights, come to the realization that they are being duped (Stricker et al., 1967). Or, they may learn about the deceptions from subjects who have already been debriefed. Subjects are often asked to promise that they will not discuss the experiment with other actual or potential participants, especially after debriefing, but it is doubtful that these vows are always kept. Wuebben (1967), at the first session of a study using deceit, secured promises from the subjects that they would not discuss the experiment with anyone until it was completed. At the second session, a week later, 64 percent of them reported that they had talked to at least one other person. On the other hand, Aronson (1966) gave subjects an unusually thorough debriefing after their participation in a deception study. The debriefing included "a long and vivid description of the consequences of testing sophisticated Ss [Aronson, 1966, p. 238]." Subsequently, nine subjects were approached by confederates who attempted to get them to reveal the true nature of the experiment. None did, suggesting that the nature of the debriefing may be important. Findings in the Stricker et al. (1967) conformity study are also relevant. These experimenters compared the suspicion of subjects who participated in the Asch situation during the first week of the investigation with those who participated during the second (and final) week. If rumor transmission had occurred, the later run subjects should have been more mistrusting than the early run subjects. In fact, the two groups did not differ in the extent of awareness that they reported. However, the scheduling of subjects was not entirely random.

One characteristic of subjects that may produce suspicion is prior experience in other psychological experiments, particularly those using dissimulation. Disbelief aroused in one study may not generalize to another investigation that also uses deceit, unless the two have something in common. Brock and Becker (1966) found that behavior (petition signing) in a subsequent deception study was affected only for subjects who had performed similar tasks (judging passages ascribed to fictitious authors) in both an earlier experiment and the subsequent one and had been completely debriefed about all the dissimulations in the first study, including those involving the judging task. This finding may explain differences in results obtained by Fillenbaum (1966) and by Stricker et al. (1967). Two distinctly different experimental situations—the first involved impression formation, the second concerned incidental learning—were employed by Fillenbaum in two similar investigations. He consistently found that subjects who were exposed to dissimulations about the first task—and, in one study, debriefed—did not differ from those who were not deceived, either in their suspicions about the subsequent task, which also involved deception, or in their performance on the task. In contrast, Stricker et al. used two kinds of conformity procedures—the Asch situation, followed in a later stage of the study by questionnaires with fictitious norms. Common to both was their reliance on incorrect feedback about the performance of the other subjects. Subjects' suspicions about the purpose of the two conformity procedures were highly and positively correlated, as were their suspicions about the methods that the procedures employed.

Disbelief about a particular study may result from a preexisting suspicion of all situations in general, or of psychological experiments in particular (Stricker et al., 1967). Such generalized suspicion can predispose subjects to seek out evidence of deceit, thereby increasing the likelihood that they will uncover the mechanics of the dissimulations. Anecdotal evidence suggests that psychological experiments are highly suspect

(Orne, 1962). Mistrust may permeate subject populations that have been exposed to deception studies, either through participation in such investigations or by learning about this research in psychology courses (Ring, 1967), the disbelief becoming part of the culture of these groups.

Intelligence should also be linked to suspicion. From the subjects' point of view, the typically ambiguous experiment is a problem-solving situation, and the goal is to discover the study's real nature (Kelman, 1967; Mills, 1962; Orne, 1962; Riecken, 1962). Intelligence contributes to problem-solving success and, hence, would be relevant in this context. Some support for this reasoning comes from the Stricker et al. (1967) study. For both boys and girls, one of the two measures of awareness about the purpose of the conformity procedures correlated positively with an intelligence test. Measures of awareness about the methods used in the procedures, however, were consistently uncorrelated with intelligence.

Passivity or naïveté, insofar as it leads to the unquestioning acceptance of the experiment's legitimacy, may be associated with a lack of suspicion (Stricker et al., 1967). These two traits are apt to be more characteristic of girls than boys, and girls were the least suspicious both in the Stricker et al. (1967) investigation and in Stricker's (1967) review of deception studies. In addition, in the Stricker et al. study, suspicion generally correlated negatively with acquiescence on scales whose content consists of social attitudes, aphorisms, and generalities.

A predisposition toward the use of deceit in the service of manipulating other people, such as investigated by Christie and Geis (1970) in their work on Machiavellianism, probably sensitizes individuals to the use of such tactics by others. Subjects with tendencies of this kind would presumably become suspicious in deception studies. No data exist on this issue at the present time.

Ingratiation in concealing from the experimenter unfavorable things about his study may play an indirect role; subjects characterized by this trait being less likely to report suspicion, even when their doubts are highly aroused (Stricker et al., 1967). To the extent that such ingratiation is more typical of girls than boys, the obtained sex differences in awareness are consistent with this suggestion. However, in the Stricker et al. (1967) investigation, suspicion generally did not correlate with the Marlowe-Crowne (Crowne & Marlowe, 1960) Social Desirability scale, a measure that might tap ingratiation, among other things.

The relationship between suspicion and social desirability response style and other personality traits (ascendance, extroversion, independence-yielding, neuroticism, and self-esteem) was also investigated by Stricker *et al.* (1967). Suspicion was generally uncorrelated with these variables.

CONSEQUENCES OF SUSPICION

In considering the implications of suspicion, its potential effects on experimental performance will be stressed. The logical alternatives that suspicion is a result, not a cause, of behavior in the experiment, or that both the suspicion and the behavior are a function of some third variable seem much less plausible. It is difficult to understand how suspicion can be produced by actual performance in the study, as distinguished from sheer exposure to the experiment and its deceptions. Although it has been persuasively argued that awareness of the reinforcement contingency in verbal conditioning studies is the result of conditioning rather than its cause (e.g., awareness being conditioned at the same time as the reinforced response or representing an a posteriori rationalization of performance—Spielberger & DeNike, 1966), parallel arguments for suspicion, based on its similarity to awareness, are not applicable to the typical study of personality and social psychology. Unlike reinforcements, deception are relatively constant throughout the course of an experiment; in particular, they rarely vary with the subjects' responses; and they commonly are only presented once, at the outset of an investigation. The possibility that suspicion and behavior in the study are a joint product of another variable appears more credible, at least in correlational investigations, but the occurrence of suspicion with a wide assortment of dependent variables raises serious doubts about the generality of such an interpretation.

The effects of suspicion on behavior in an experiment are apt to be extremely varied, depending upon the subjects' perceptions and motivations connected with the study. Perceptions of the nature of the study, the investigator's hypotheses, and the role requirements of the subjects are especially important. Ideas about the study and its hypotheses may be highly diverse, ranging from the veridical to the bizarre, reflecting, in part, the subjects' sophistication (Kelman, 1967; Orne, 1962; Riecken, 1962; Stricker et al., 1967). Some consensus apparently exists among subjects about their role in the experiment. Orne (1962) suggested that they perceive their role as being a "good subject"; this cooperation may be carried to extremes with the subject's behaving in a way that is consciously intended to confirm the study's hypotheses. According to Fillenbaum (1966), many suspicious subjects reported that they felt obliged to follow instructions scrupulously, regardless of their doubts, and to do as good a job as possible. Holmes's (1967) results suggest that these ideas become strengthened with experience in psychological experiments. More of the veteran subjects reported that they "cooperate" in the investigations and do not "try to figure out what the experiment is all about [Holmes, 1967, p. 406]." Equally relevant are the subjects' initial motivations for participating in the study and their motivations after realizing that they have been duped. Subjects may be eager and cooperative, bored, or vindictive and intent on sabotaging the investigation (Allen, 1966; Baumrind, 1964; Brock & Becker, 1966; Fillenbaum, 1966; Goldberg, 1965; Holmes, 1967; Kelman, 1967; MacKinney, 1955; Masling, 1966; Milgram, 1964; Riecken, 1962; Vinacke, 1954). With the many possible differences in the perceptions and motivations of suspicious subjects, the only certainty is that their disbelief increases extraneous variation in a study (Kelman, 1967).

A few investigations—all focused on conformity—have described the actual behavior of suspicious and unsuspicious subjects in an experiment. These subjects differed strikingly in their level of performance in studies by Stricker et al. (1967) and Allen (1966), but not in one by Chipman (1966). All three used a mechanized analogue of the Asch situation, and the Stricker et al. investigation also employed questionnaires with fictitious norms. In the Stricker et al. study, the results were similar for the two kinds of conformity procedures: Suspicion about the purpose of a procedure and suspicion about the mechanics of the deceptions that it employed both correlated negatively with conformity on the device. The correlations for the second kind of awareness were consistently higher —correlations as high as $-.75$ were obtained. The greater impact of disbelief about the mechanics of the deception is not surprising—if a person is to be maximally effective in resisting an influence, he needs to know the form that it will take. In Allen's study, undeceived subjects conformed less than deceived ones, but conformed more than control subjects. The conformity observed in the aware individuals is highly interesting, for it indicates that they were affected, at least to some degree, either despite their disbelief or because of it. In Chipman's study, the two kinds of subjects did not differ in their conformity. This finding is consistent with the point made earlier: Suspicion need not be associated invariably with differences in level of performance.

Suspicion interacted with experimental performance in two investigations by Stricker, Messick, and Jackson (1968, 1969). This work was based on additional analyses of data from their conformity study. In one investigation (Stricker et al., 1968), self-report personality scales correlated with scores on the conformity procedures for the unaware subjects but were uncorrelated for the aware ones, indicating that different processes were involved in the two groups' reactions to the conformity procedures. Disbelief may have largely determined the responses of the undeceived subjects, vitiating any correlation with the personality scales.

In the other investigation (Stricker et al., 1969), factor analyses of scores on the conformity procedures yielded five factors for the unsuspicious subjects and three for the suspicious ones. None of the factors was common to both groups. The relative lack of differentiation in the responses of the undeceived group suggests that reactions to suspicion tend to be relatively general rather than specific to the situation.

The consequences of suspicion may also extend beyond the particular deception study that elicited it. As noted in the previous discussion of the effects of prior experience in other experiments, behavior in later investigations may be affected in subtle and unforeseen ways. Conceivably, these residual effects can have an impact not only on subsequent studies that use deceit but also on those that are free of dissimulation, particularly if the later investigations bear some resemblance to the original one.

POSSIBLE SOLUTIONS

The problems posed by deception can be dealt with at several levels. In choosing research designs, wider recognition is needed of the danger that dissimulation may create more problems than it solves. The prudent investigator will carefully consider all potentially relevant research tactics before opting for deceit (Kelman, 1967).

If deception is used, certain practices may increase its effectiveness. Making the dissimulations as realistic as possible is an obvious necessity. Limiting the different deceptions employed in a study is preferable to using a great variety of them, on the assumption that the more deceptions used, the greater the likelihood of their detection. Using subjects who have not participated in previous studies will help to insure that the investigation begins with minimal suspicion. Drawing subjects from populations of below average sophistication may also lead to a low level of awareness, but their results may not be generalizable to other, perhaps more typical, populations. Completing the study quickly will reduce communication among subjects. And debriefing everyone at the same time, if this is feasible, will eliminate the possibility of contact between the debriefed subjects and the others.

It is essential that experiments using deception establish its efficacy, for such studies cannot be evaluated adequately without this information (Stricker, 1967; Stricker et al., 1967). Effectiveness can be demonstrated in a variety of ways, as indicated earlier, but, at the very least, subjects' suspicions should be assessed—and reported, separately, for each experimental condition. This assessment is peculiarly difficult, but useful procedures have been outlined (Orne, 1962; Riecken, 1962), and some of the solutions developed for dealing with awareness in verbal conditioning studies (Hersen, 1968) may also be applicable (Stricker, 1967).

Several special considerations enter into devising these appraisal procedures. The demand characteristics of the study may affect subjects' reports (Allen, 1966; Orne, 1962): If the subjects believe that the experimenter intended that they be aware of the deceptions, they will report suspicion; if they believe that he intended they be unaware, they will not report it. These effects are apt to be relatively minor, at least among college students, if Rosenberg's (1965) impression is correct that such subjects are motivated to present themselves as sophisticated and, hence, are much more likely to disclose their suspicions than to conceal them. In any event, the influence of demand characteristics may be minimized by emphasizing to the subjects, at the time suspicion is evaluated, that the investigator wants and expects them to uncover the dissimulations.

Cursory questioning may fail to uncover subjects' suspicion, even though it exists and they are willing to admit it. On the other hand, detailed, focused questioning can lead them to suspect deception for the first time, eliciting reports of disbelief that did not exist during the study (Stricker et al., 1967). These problems may be alleviated by the use of fixed-response questions in combination with open-ended ones, arranged in a sequence that goes from broad topics to specific ones. Techniques of this kind are widely used in survey research (Kahn & Cannell, 1957).

A final consideration is that subjects' reports may reflect a mixture of generalized suspicion and mistrust of a particular experiment (Stricker et al., 1967). Inquiries anchored to the details of the study will help to isolate disbelief that is specific to the investigation.

In the event that the dissimulations have not gulled all the subjects in a study, modifications in the data analysis are needed (Stricker et al., 1967). It is crucial that the data for the undeceived subjects be kept separate from those for the deceived ones. Otherwise, differences between these individuals in such variables as suspicion will be confounded with the experimental variables, and interactions between the two sets of variables will be masked. Parallel statistical analyses can be made for the undeceived and deceived subjects, provided that the sample is large enough—if feasible, classifying subjects into several groups, based on the precise extent to which they were duped. Alternatively, suspicion or other indexes of the subject's gullibility in the study can be partialed out of the experimental variables. Both kinds of analyses minimize the interpretive complexity that occurs when subjects are eliminated from an investigation in which they have been randomly assigned to experimental treatments (Chapanis & Chapanis, 1964; Silverman, 1964).

REFERENCES

Adams, J. K., Laboratory studies of behavior without awareness. *Psychol. Bull.*, 1957, **54**, 383–405.

Allen, V. L. Effect of knowledge of deception on conformity. *J. soc. Psychol.*, 1966, **69**, 101–106.

Aronson, E. Avoidance of inter-subject communication. *Psychol. Rep.*, 1966, **19**, 238.

Asch, S. E. Studies of independence and conformity: I. A minority of one against a unanimous majority. *Psychol. Monogr.*, 1956, **70**(9, Whole No. 416).

Baumrind, D. Some thoughts on ethics of research: After reading Milgram's "Behavioral study of obedience." *Amer. Psychologist*, 1964, **19**, 421–423.

Brock, T. C., & Becker, L. A. "Debriefing" and susceptibility to subsequent experimental manipulations. *J. exp. soc. Psychol.*, 1966, **2**, 314–323.

Chapanis, N. P., & Chapanis, A. Cognitive dissonance: Five years later. *Psychol. Bull.*, 1964, **61**, 1–22.

Chipman, A. Conformity as a differential function of social pressure and judgment difficulty. *J. soc. Psychol.*, 1966, **70**, 299–311.

Christie, R., & Geis, F. L. *Studies in Machiavellianism.* New York: Academic Press, 1970.

Crowne, D. P., & Marlowe, D. A new scale of social desirability independent of psychopathology. *J. consult. Psychol.*, 1960, **24**, 349–354.

Fillenbaum, S. Prior deception and subsequent experimental performance: The "faithful" subject. *J. Pers. soc. Psychol.*, 1966, **4**, 532–537.

Goldberg, P. A. Expectancy, choice, and the other person. *J. pers. soc. Psychol.*, 1965, **2**, 895–897.

Greenspoon, J. Verbal conditioning and clinical psychology. In A. J. Bachrach (Ed.) *Experimental foundation of clinical psychology.* New York: Basic Books, 1962.

Greenspoon, J., & Brownstein, A. J. Awareness in verbal conditioning. *J. Exp. Res. Pers.*, 1967, **2**, 295–308.

Hersen, M. Awareness in verbal operant conditioning: Some comments. *J. gen. Psychol.*, 1968, **78**, 287–296.

Holmes, D. S. Amount of experience in experiments as a determinant of performance in later experiments. *J. pers. soc. Psychol.*, 1967, **7**, 403–407.

Kahn, R. L., & Cannell, C. F. *The dynamics of interviewing.* New York: John Wiley, 1957.

Kanfer, F. H. Verbal conditioning. A review of its current status. In T. R. Dixon & D. L. Horton (Eds.), *Verbal behavior and* general behavior theory. Englewood Cliffs, N.J.: Prentice-Hall, 1968.

Kelman, H. C. Human use of human subjects: The problem of deception in social psychological experiments. *Psychol. Bull.*, 1967, **67**, 1–11.

Krasner, L. Studies of the conditioning of verbal behavior. *Psychol. Bull.*, 1958, **55**, 148–170.

Krasner, L. Verbal operant conditioning and awareness. In K. Salzinger & S. Salzinger (Eds.), *Research in verbal behavior and some neurophysiological implications.* New York: Academic Press, 1967.

MacKinney, A. C. Deceiving experimental subjects. *Amer. Psychologist*, 1955, **10**, 113.

Masling, J. Role-related behavior of the subject and psychologist and its effect upon psychological data. *Nebr. sym. Mot.*, 1966, **14**, 67–103.

Milgram, S. Issues in the study of obedience: A reply to Baumrind. *Amer. Psychologist*, 1964, **19**, 848–852.

Mills, T. M. A sleeper variable in small groups research: The experimenter. *Pac. sociol. Rev.*, 1962, **5**, 21–28.

Orne, M. T. On the social psychology of the psychological experiment: With particular reference to demand characteristics and their implications. *Amer. Psychologist*, 1962, **17**, 776–783.

Riecken, H. W. A program for research on experiments in social psychology. In N. F. Washburne (Ed.), *Decisions, values, and groups.* Vol. 2. New York: Pergamon Press, 1962.

Ring, K. Experimental social psychology: Some sober questions about some frivolous values. *J. exp. soc. Psychol.*, 1967, **3**, 113–123.

Rosenberg, M. J. When dissonance fails: On eliminating evaluation apprehension from attitude measurement. *J. Pers. soc. Psychol.*, 1965, **1**, 28–42.

Rosenthal, R. *Experimenter effects in behavioral research.* New York: Appleton-Century-Crofts, 1966.

Salzinger, K. Experimental manipulation of verbal behavior: A review. *J. gen. Psychol.*, 1959, **61**, 65–94.

Silverman, I. In defense of dissonance theory: Reply to Chapanis and Chapanis. *Psychol. Bull.*, 1964, **62**, 205–209.

Spielberger, C. D. Theoretical and epistemological issues in verbal conditioning. In S. Rosenberg (Ed.), *Directions in psycholinguistics.* New York: Macmillan, 1965.

Spielberger, C. D., & DeNike, L. D. Descriptive behaviorism versus cognitive theory in verbal operant conditioning. *Psychol. Rev.*, 1966, **73**, 306–326.

Sterling, T. D. Publication decisions and their possible effects on inferences drawn from tests of significance—or vice versa. *J. Amer. statis. Ass.*, 1959, **54**, 30–34.

Stricker, L. J. The true deceiver. *Psychol. Bull.*, 1967, **68**, 13–20.

Stricker, L. J., Messick, S., & Jackson, D. N. Suspicion of deception: Implications for conformity research. *J. pers. soc. Psychol.*, 1967, **5**, 379–389.

Stricker, L. J., Messick, S., & Jackson, D. N. Desirability judgments and self-reports as predictors of social behavior. *J. exp. Res. Pers.*, 1968, **3**, 151–167.

Stricker, L. J., Messick, S., & Jackson, D. N. Conformity, anticonformity, and independence: Their dimensionality and generality. *Res. Bull.* 69–17 Princeton, N.J.: Educ. Testing Ser., 1969.

Vinacke, W. E. Deceiving experimental subjects. *Amer. Psychologist*, 1954, **9**, 155.

Williams, J. H. Conditioning of verbalization: A review. *Psychol. Bull.*, 1964, **62**, 383–393.

Wuebben, P. L. Honesty of subjects and birth order. *J. pers. soc. Psychol.*, 1967, **5**, 350–352.

12

THE HUMAN EXPERIMENTAL SUBJECT IN CONTEXT

Ralph Sasson and T. M. Nelson

Abstract

Safety, comfort, privacy and personal dignity are the ethical dimensions which have dominated discussions about the role of humans in experimentation. These dimensions are reviewed from a psychological perspective. However, research conducted within educational settings alters ethical problems greatly. Decisions can be made which permit experimentation to be a device promoting methodological education. Suggestions concerning the role human experimentation should play within the University context, discussion of the relevance of issues such as deception to proper educational experimentation, and scrutiny of the traditional laboratory concept of experimentation, are made.

Disciplines gathering data among humans are just now attempting to revise or form new functional codes out of past experimental practice. Several related issues seem implied in the present ferment over human subjects. Basically, controversy revolves around concepts of either safety, comfort, privacy, self-concept or dignity. In addition, there are legal aspects since, obviously, experiments must not violate legal interpretation of laws governing human relations.

To these questions, even the last, there are few concrete answers. This has not inhibited public controversy, however. Ferry (1968), for example, has gone so far as to insist that the U. S. Constitution must be rewritten to "control technology."

From R. Sasson & T. M. Nelson, *Canad. Psychologist*, 1969, **10**, 409–437. With permission of authors and publisher.

Bills aimed to restrict the activity of psychological testing have been appearing in the states' legislature in the U.S.A. from time to time (Lovell, 1967), and Conrad (1967) points to a more pervasive danger when he warns that "social science must not become identified in the public mind with snooping and prying. . . . [p. 359]"

This review summarizes positions with respect to these six issues. It is offered here because it may prove of value to committees having responsibility for welding a code of ethics covering use of humans in all experimental settings.

Aside from the general desirability of having a review of the various sides of experimentation, it should be borne in mind that a great amount of psychological research, particularly in university settings, is undertaken for educational as well as scientific purposes. Curiously enough, this has been generally overlooked. The ethical issues are altered by the presence of this feature and are examined in this light in the final portions of this paper.

THE ISSUE OF SAFETY

Safety has been defined as freedom from exposure to danger or as exemption from hurt or injury.[1] Subjects in experimental investigations have not always been free from possibility of injury. As McGuire (1967) points out, several experimental manipulations include the use of noxious conditions, dangerous physiological treatments, and anxiety-producing manipulations. The problem of safety is a very serious ethical concern, according to McGuire (1967), Katz (1967), and Smith (1967). The American Psychological Association (1968) Code on ethics has this to say on the issue of safety and harmful after-effects:

(1) When a reasonable possibility of injurious after-effects exists, research is conducted only when the subjects or their responsible agents are fully informed of this possibility and agree to participate nevertheless.

(2) The psychologist seriously considers the possibility of harmful after-effects and avoids them, or removes them as soon as permitted by the design of the experiment.

[1] Unless otherwise indicated, all definitions will be taken from *Webster's Third New International Dictionary*.

(3) Investigations of human subjects using experimental drugs (for example, hallucinogenic, psychotomimetic, psychedelic, or similar substances) should be conducted only in such settings as clinics, hospitals, or research facilities maintaining appropriate safe-guards for the subjects.

Smith (1967) asks how big a probability is a "possibility" of serious after-effect and "how much does the experimenter have to hurt people for it to be serious?" He mentions the Public Health Service regulations which require that every institution receiving a grant have the experimenter's judgment reviewed by a committee of his institutional associates (associates inside and outside the scientists' own field). Smith heartfully espouses this answer to the above question in that (a) judgments are not left to the researcher alone but become a matter of shared public responsibility, and (b) there will be assurance that the safety of human subjects is sufficiently protected.

Writing in the context of psychopharmacologic research Katz (1967) reasonably points out that the crucial question is not how to eliminate all breaches of ethics (since this is at times very difficult and certain designs require that subjects be misinformed about drug effects). Instead he suggests that the experimental gains be weighed against the possible ethical infractions. He also asserts that it is scientists who must develop solutions before legislators intervene and apply their formulae to human experimentation problems. Wolfensberger (1967) writing in a similar vein formulates the principle that the more deleterious an experimental effect may be to a subject, the more precautions the investigator should take. One can ask here at what point is an experimental effect negligibly deleterious, very deleterious, extremely deleterious, and so forth, and what are the corresponding precautions to be taken. But this question is unanswered by Wolfensberger.

In closing this section, we mention two more stipulations of the APA Code which bear on the safety question:

(1) Care must be taken to ensure an appropriate setting for clinical work to protect both client and psychologist from actual or imputed harm and the profession from censure.

(2) In the use of accepted drugs for therapeutic purposes special care needs to be exercised by the psychologist to assure him-

self that the collaborating physician provides suitable safe-guards for the client.

THE ISSUE OF PRIVACY

Threats to individual privacy posed by behavioral research has been the most burning of all issues and has led to numerous congressional hearings as well as extensive discussion by the scientific community generally. Conrad (1967) shows why when he indicates that some items analogous to those that have appeared in personality questionnaires are the following (the last two being in the form of True-False statements):

Are you an illegitimate child?

Does your father or mother drink to excess?

I am no good at anything.

My father is really pretty stupid, like my mother.

The matter of privacy is also brought forth in another context. Lovell (1967) strongly objects to the "strong personnel contract," a personality test upon which decisions about hiring, promoting, terminating, etc., are made and the score of which is sent to other persons such as administrators, teachers, and prospective employers. He asserts that this test "proposes that kind of total surveillance of the individual which is characteristic of police states . . . (that it) reeks with paternalism . . . (and) creates . . . mutual suspicion and distrust. . . ." On the other hand, Lovell espouses the use of the "client contract," a personality test which guarantees confidentiality and which could be declined by the respondent. Even more important is Ferry's (1968) question concerning whether there will be any privacy left to the individual should the proposal for a National Data Center (U.S.A.), a computerized bank capable of storing every conceivable piece of information on the American citizenry, be realized.

What then is to be done concerning the privacy issue?

The Panel on Privacy and Behavioral Research (of the President's office of Science and Technology) attacked the problem seriously. This group defines the right to privacy as the right to decide for oneself how much we will share with others our thoughts, feelings, and personal facts. The Panel points out that since the root of the conflict between the right to privacy and the right of discovery is the research process which seeks to ascertain men's feelings, actions, and the qualities of their mind, the absence of the subject's informed consent represents an invasion of privacy. In case, however, an informed consent is difficult to obtain, the relationship between scientist and subject must be one of mutual trust, and all measures to ensure the confidentiality of the information obtained must be put into effect. Further comments are made to the effect that (a) should intrusion on privacy be a necessary part of the experiment the scientist should proceed with the research only if he and his colleagues have decided that the benefits to be acquired from the successful experiment outweigh the costs of the ethical breach; and (b) the major responsibility for the use of ethical procedures should rest with the scientist.

Relevant to the last point is the Panel's opinion that legislation to control research methods is not appropriate since it might prove too inflexible to apply to the individual idiosyncracies of research and to the "sensitive conflicts of (scientific progress versus the right to privacy) values under consideration." Instead of direct legislation, the group suggests that the institution employing the investigator be required to accept full responsibility to appoint appropriate persons (from within the area *and* related ones) to review the experiment with respect to the ethical aspects.

The Panel also makes the following recommendations:
(1) that institutions in which government-supported research is being carried out be left free to determine independently the procedures needed to review research;
(2) that scientists and institutions be aware of the importance of consent and confidentiality as ethical requirements of their research procedures;
(3) that the (government) agency under which research is *directly* undertaken be entirely responsible for the protection of privacy;
(4) that universities and professional organizations be encouraged to stress the ethical facets of behavioral experimentation.

These recommendations form only a part of the opinions voiced in regard to the privacy issue. Bennett (1967) also thinks that restraints are needed to prevent people from misusing private communications and other privileges. He insists, though, that there are secrets one has no right to withhold (such as income, education, sex, etc.). In addition, he maintains that it is imperative to promote an atmosphere of confidence and trust within which secrets can be treated with respect and used constructively. This is a very sensible point. However, Bennett also suggests that one should examine first how important those secrets are to the subject, how damaging would their disclosure be and what would be the effects of their disclosure or silence on other persons than the subject.

These suggestions seem questionable. Does not examining the importance of the secrets to the subject and the subsequent effects of their disclosure entail the use of personality analyses, tests, and interviews? If so, then are we not back full circle to the same problem since the methods used to fulfill Bennett's suggestions may themselves contain questionable items with respect to the privacy issue?

Other writers have stressed different points. Anastasi (1967) contends that the solution to the privacy matter must be worked out in individual cases in terms of (a) the purpose of the investigation (whether it is for counseling, selection and classification, or research) and (b) the relevance of the information sought to the testing objective (greater relevance being cause for greater justifiability of the test's presence). She also submits that from an ethical standpoint the transmittal of test results to other persons should not take place unless the respondent is warned at the test outset. Speaking of transmittal of test results, it has been pointed out (Berdie, 1960, 1965; Brown, 1961; Goslin, 1963) that since there is a likelihood of misinterpreting them the question of how much test result information is communicated, in what form and under what circumstances are of basic importance.

In other than the strictly behavioral field, interesting views have also been aired; we shall review these because they might prove valuable in stimulating similar ideas which could be applicable in the behavioral area. Gans (1967) suggests including in the law provisions for ensuring that data collected for social-economic accounting purposes[2] be used only for statistical tabu-

---

[2] Social accounting is a method to help public officials formulate social programs to achieve a certain social objectives (e.g., urban renewal) with maximum efficiency.

lations and methods that analyze the behavior of groups, not of individuals. In addition, access to confidential data must be prohibited as should also (in social-economic accounting studies) the obtaining of the individual's name directly or indirectly. Hauser (1967) makes a similar point but like Bennett adds that the rights of privacy do not include the right to withhold crucial information (such as age, income, education, etc.) which the government might need to determine policy and programs vital to social and economic progress. Here, one might argue that this same principle could be applied to behavioral research— i.e., no subject has the right to withhold information that is crucial to an important experiment and hence to the progress of theory or science. It should be noted, however, that this principle is in reality again that of weighing the importance of an experiment against the cost of intruding on the privacy of the individual.

Another facet of the privacy issue has been recognized. In a thoughtful book entitled *Privacy and Freedom*, Westin (1967) discusses man's basic desire for privacy. He mentions that this is related to the well-known territorial behavior of many animals. And although he acknowledges the necessity for society to exercise certain controls over the individual, he also points out that a certain minimum of privacy is indispensable to the health of individuals. Abelson (1967) who takes many arguments from Westin's book, emphasized in *Science* that since many modern means (hidden cameras, wire-tapping, etc.) for invading privacy have been made available, "It is clearly desirable to seek technical and legal means of curtailing the use of what might otherwise become instruments for the destruction of our freedom."

Although one may agree in principle with Abelson's argument, it is not thought that, for behavioral studies in particular, legislation delineating very specifically the procedures to be followed in research or instituting specific rules to be followed would be an appropriate solution. Experiments in behavioral science vary enormously in their nature and in their aims and purposes. It is doubtful, therefore, that one rule (or set of rules) could be easily applied to all experiments.

The reason for some "tough stands" on the privacy matter is not all due to the prying of some behavioral investigations. Kosa (1968), for instance, indicates that agencies other than academic ones (governmental, civic, legal, bureaucratic) are employing a great number of questionnaires, many of which represent an undeniable intrusion of privacy—to an extent even greater than that of academic institutions. He is thus of the opinion that, importantly, means of curtailing the invasion of privacy must be aimed at nonacademic institutions as well. This, it is noted, could be taken as another reason for our attitude that tough measures should not be applied to the behavioral field. What would be appropriate for behavioral science, though, are general principles like those propounded by the Panel on Privacy and Behavioral Research [p. 5].

Before concluding this section, the second privacy issue— confidentiality—will be given additional attention. Ruebhausen and Brim (1966) outline ways by which confidentiality of the data collected on a person may be maintained. They are as follows:

(1) To design the research such that the subject's responses remain anonymous; if, however, anonymity is not possible then the following possibilities are open:
(2) the integrity of the scientist must be assumed,
(3) use can be made of control techniques—e.g., the subject's identity can be coded and separate from his response except for the code number,
(4) the research data can be destroyed or the consent of the subject to preservation of the data can be obtained,
(5) the research data need not be made available to others.

The same writers also advance principles for a code of ethics for behavioral research. The ones relevant to the issue of privacy are, briefly (a) the claim to private personality should be recognized, (b) subject anonymity should be actively pursued when designating a study, (c) the research data should be destroyed as soon as possible, and (d) the research data should not be used for other than the original purpose without the subject's consent.

THE ISSUE OF SELF-CONCEPT

As defined by Snygg and Combs (1949) the self-concept ". . . includes those parts of the phenomenal field (i.e., the actor's personal frame of reference or universe as it appears to him at any moment) which the individual has differentiated as definite and fairly stable characteristics of himself." The maintenance in the experiment of the subject's self-concept then would be the maintenance of those phenomena which he attributes, or which he thinks are relevant to himself. In several experiments, however, this maintenance of subject's self-concept is not retained and more frequently than not the subject emerges from the experiment with a self-concept lower than the one he had initially. An example of this type of research is Milgram's (1963, 1965) work mentioned on p. 18. As Kelman (1967) asserts, there is good reason to believe that in these studies the obedient subjects came away with a lower "self-esteem, having to live with the realization that they were willing to yield to destructive authority to the point of inflicting extreme pain on a fellow human being.

There is another case in point. Sato (1965) indicates that sensory deprivation experiments result in a change of the self-concept. His results on the "Who am I?" test showed that (a) past tense description on the self decreased, (b) self-evaluation responses increased, and (c) behavior description responses increased while motivation description ones decreased. One can go on citing many examples of experiments where subjects' self-concepts are lowered (and Evans, 1962 does); however, it is clear from the preceding ones that the issue of self-concept is both a relevant and a real one.

In searching for a solution that would resolve the problem of self-concept and that would not prove an obstacle for research efforts, Stollak (1967) raises the following questions with respect to whether subjects should be debriefed (or informed about the nature of the experiment after it is over) and to the effects this might have:

(1) Should all subjects in such research necessarily be debriefed by revealing to them the nature of the experiment, or should they necessarily be debriefed in the same way?

(2) What does it mean to a subject who has performed obediently and ignobly to be informed, however benevolently, of this fact?

(3) Does informing such subjects of their behavior increase the probability that they will emerge from the experience with lower self-esteem, perhaps specifically because they and

others (including the experimenter and his accomplices) now know this fact?

(4) Is it possible that we could produce less side-effects, and is it perhaps more kind and ethical to either have no debriefing, or a specific kind of debriefing which does not inform subjects of the true nature of the experiment?

(5) Should debriefing which includes informing subjects of the true nature of the experiment only be given to those who performed disobediently and nobly to reward such action?

(6) Does the truth always set out subjects free?

(7) Is truth always more important than compassion?

Baumrind (1964) is also seriously concerned with the issue of self-concept. She thinks that from the subject's point of view "procedures which involve loss of self-esteem are probably most harmful in the long run and require the most thoughtfully planned reparations if engaged in at all."

A topic of some controversy within the general issue of self-concept has been that of deception in human experimentation. Smith (1967) states that some of the questions that have arisen (by persons inside and outside the behavioral sciences including U.S. congressmen) are whether it is permissible for investigators to deceive their subjects as to the nature and purpose of the experiment (Kelman, 1967), and if they do use deception, how can "informed consent" be obtained (Ruebhausen & Brim, 1966).

The question of permissibility of using deception arises especially when the deception has potentially harmful consequences for the subject. The studies of Bramel (1962, 1963) provide a good case in point. In the Bramel studies, males were induced to believe that they were homosexually aroused by photographs of men. Although, after the experiment, the deception was explained, one wonders whether the explanation did in fact remove the subjects' fears about their homosexuality. The ethical question of central concern then is as Kelman (1967) put it whether "we, for the purpose of experimentation, have the right to provide such potentially disturbing insights to subjects (insights which Milgram [1964] said subjects would have an opportunity to learn in deception experiments). . . ." In other words does the importance of our experiment outweigh the potential risks that are possible?

To deal with the problem of deception, particularly in social psychological experiments, Kelman suggests three steps as follows:

(1) That we ask ourselves whether the use of deception is necessary and justified. This active awareness of the problem means that we will try to weigh the value of an experiment using deception against its possible harmful consequences.

(2) That we take measures to counteract and lessen the harmful effects of deception. Specifically, Kelman suggests that subjects who are particularly susceptible to the risks of deception be discarded; that potentially harmful manipulations be kept at a moderate intensity level; that the experimenter be sensitive to danger signals in his subjects' reactions, and that at the conclusion of the session he take time to carefully explain the deception to the subject and reassure him.

(3) That we explore alternative experimental techniques that do not involve deception. Kelman suggests techniques (e.g., role-playing) which evoke the subject's positive motivations to cooperate in the study; these techniques would involve the subject as "an active participant in a joint effort with the experimenter."

Writing in connection to the use of children as subjects, Smith (1967) argues that the solution of debriefing used with adults is undesirable and, at any rate, rarely possible with children subjects—even if matters were so contrived that by the end of the experiment the child would have an experience of success. For rejecting the experience of success solution, Smith gives the reason that far too much trust would have to be put in the biased scientist that the child did in fact experience success. But what solution does Smith argue for? He contends that the way out of the deception issue lies in the 1966 USPHS regulation that PHS supported research be reviewed by an inter-disciplinary committee of institutional associates. As previously mentioned, in his opinion this will apportion diffuse responsibility to many persons and will assure that the problem is carefully considered.

The same writer also mentions a relevant statement of the previously referred to APA Code on ethics: "Only when a problem is significant and can be investigated in no other way is the psychologist justified in giving misinformation to research subjects. . . ." To the question of what determines when a problem is significant, Smith also finds that the above PHS regulation will provide the answer (i.e., the review committee will establish when a problem is significant and when it is not).

THE ISSUE OF DIGNITY

The dictionary defines dignity as the quality or state of being worthy or esteemed, and an indignity as something that offends against one's personal self-respect.[3] One can ask, therefore: have subjects always been treated with respect or with the worth that corresponds to that inherent in every individual human being? Several writers do not think so.

One person who has approached the issue of dignity has been Smith (1967) who distinguishes between the ethically desirable and the ethically permissible. Smith criticizes the predominant cast of much permissible behavioral research for too often adopting a "manipulative and condescending" attitude toward its subjects. This ethical undesirability, he asserts, will not be redressed by review committees and codes of ethics because the latter will inevitably be concerned only with ruling out what is not permissible. On the other hand an attitude of respect towards subjects (which is particularly important with children subjects) will be an outgrowth of continuous discussions in the professional societies, in academic settings and of resultant changes in graduate training. Smith also says that as scientists come more characteristically to accord respect to their subjects, the state of the public mind will create a more favorable atmosphere for behavioral research; importantly, he states that "the styles of research that prevail may be more important than skill in public relations in creating a favorable 'image' of behavioral science." Kelman (1967) also comments on the prob-

---

[3] Dignity differs from self-concept in that dignity is a part of the self-concept. A person who attributes worthiness to himself (or who feels worthy) is differentiating a *part* of the phenomenal field as a characteristic of himself.

lem of dignity. For him, serious ethical issues arise by the use of deception per se and the "kind of use of human beings that it implies." He goes on to comment as follows:

> In our other interhuman relationships, most of us would never think of doing the kinds of things that we do to our subjects —exposing others to lies and tricks, deliberately misleading them . . . , making promises or giving assurances that we intend to disregard. We would view such behavior as a violation of the respect to which all fellow humans are entitled and of the whole basis of our relationship with them. Yet we seem to forget that the experimenter—subject relationship—whatever else it is—is a real interhuman relationship, in which we have responsibility toward the subject as another human being whose dignity we must preserve.

At this point, one may argue that a specific investigation where subjects have been treated with indignity has not yet really been discovered. But Baumrind (1964) cites Milgram's (1963, 1965) studies where subjects were required to administer increasingly intense electric shocks to a victim who was an accomplice of the experimenter and who was not in reality receiving any shocks. Baumrind asks what happens to the dignity of the subjects when, embarrassingly, the deception (or the fact that they have been lied to) is finally revealed? Are they not treated with disrespect here? She goes on to state that "it has become more commonplace in sociopsychological laboratory studies to manipulate, (and) embarass . . . subjects. At times the insult to the subject's sensibilities extends to the journal reader when the results are reported."

Although, as we have seen, dissatisfaction and protest has been aired, recommendations to safeguard against the possibility of subjects being treated with less dignity than they deserve have not yet been made.

THE ISSUE OF COMFORT

In many studies subjects are whirled in a Barany chair, electrically shocked, subjected to days of starvation, or quizzed about their sex practices. If the definition of comfort is being at ease physically, mentally and socially and feeling no pain or urgent, unsatisfied wants, then it is safe to say that in many investigations subjects are not comfortable but undergo mental and physical stress.

Berg (1954) has attempted to resolve the comfort (as well as other) issues. He writes: ". . . where the experiment involves some pain, discomfort, or risk, the subject should be made fully aware of what he is consenting to, at least in a general way." This should also apply, according to Berg, to cases where the discomfort may be negligible or trivial for after all, "Kidd (1953) was correct" when he said that ". . . the law does not regard trifles—*de minimis non curat lex;* the public however, often does."

Sinick (1954) holds different views. He submits that experimenters should be free to induce emotional stress and let general discomfort exist when there is some justification for it. In his opinion, the progress of knowledge outweighs in importance the value of the (justified) discomfort. Incidentally, Sinick points out a disadvantage in solely using volunteers in an experiment, namely that volunteers may differ from non-volunteers in ways germane to hypotheses and conclusions. He, therefore, suggests that experimenters take into account this factor.

The APA Code of ethics has at its core the same conception as that of Sinick. The relevant statement is as follows:

> Only when a problem is of scientific significance and is not practicable to investigate it in any other way is the psychologist justified in exposing research subjects, whether children or adults, to physical or emotional stress as part of an investigation.
>
> (Principle 16a)

In concluding this section, it is worthy to mention the contentions of McGuire (1967) who is quite concerned with the comfort (and other) issues. McGuire thinks that the comfort problem will be largely eliminated when theorists decide to test their hypotheses out in the real world and take advantage of natural manipulations.

THE LEGAL ASPECTS OF EXPERIMENTATION

In discussing the legal aspects of human experimentation emphasis shall be directed mainly (although not totally) to

Canadian legal questions and to what Canadian attorneys have had to say about these questions. It should be noted, however, that legal problems in the United States and Great Britain are frequently similar to the ones in Canada.

Section 14 of the (Canadian) Criminal Code states that:

> No person is entitled to consent to have death inflicted upon himself, and such consent does not affect the criminal responsibility of any person by whom death may be inflicted upon the person by whom consent is given.

One can see then that if the charges are appropriate consent (or his guardian's if the subject is a child) provides no defense against a charge of murder or manslaughter. As Freund (1967) put it: "Man shall not play God with human lives." The same applies to a charge of causing death by criminal negligence. Criminal negligence is defined by the Code as follows: "Everyone is criminally negligent who (a) in doing anything, or (b) in omitting to do anything that is his duty to do, shows wanton or reckless disregard for the lives or safety of other persons." In the case, however, where there has been no negligence on the part of the investigator but still the subject is harmed, Mackintosh (1959) indicates that here the law would in all probability require (a) that the volunteer had been informed of the purpose of the study and of the results that it might lead to, (b) that the study had been performed not only without negligence but also with extreme care to avoid disaster, and (c) that the experimenter could have been trusted with the undertaking of the study.

In connection to assault, section 230 of the Code defines it as follows:

> A person commits an assault when, without the consent of another person or with consent, where it is obtained by fraud, he applies force intentionally to the person of the other directly or indirectly. . . .

It is clear, therefore, that if an acquiescing subject is deceived as to the nature of the experiment his consent is not valid; if, on the other hand, he understands the nature of the experiment his consent is valid. In addition, it is held by the Law of Tort that even a fully informed and free consent would not constitute a defense if, for instance, animal experiments have not previously been undertaken or if the experiment is badly designed from a statistical point of view so that it did not lead to any fruitful results. It seems then, that before carrying out an experiment the scientist is required to do his utmost to provide an adequate reason for going ahead with the study.

But the situation may arise where there is no contractual agreement between investigator and subject. Should this occur the court (under the Law of Contract) may probably demand or imply conditions which are in harmony with the above ethical principles. If, however, the experimenter is employed full time by a hospital or university, then these institutions could be made liable for the experimenter's torts.

Waddams (1966) has written at some length about medical experiments on human subjects. He suggests that a doctor administering a novel therapeutic treatment should, if "there is no reason against it," ask the patient's consent, consider the gravity of the patient's condition, his capacity to make a judgment, and the subsequent effects on him of knowing the attendant risks. One might ask how is the subject to give a meaningful consent if knowledge of the technicalities of the experiment is required first? Waddams' reply is that what should be made is a disclosure of the treatment's nature that is as complete and candid as circumstances allow and also a truthful estimation of the risks involved. Furthermore, in the case where it is not therapeutic treatment that is involved but experimentation (stricto sensu) nondisclosure of the risks inherent in the experiment has no justification and the investigator may be liable.

Other requirements that must be fulfilled before an experiment can be called ethical are neatly expressed in a body of principles advanced at the trial of physicians for war crimes in Nuremberg in 1947. The Nuremberg Code is as follows:

(1) The voluntary consent of the human subject is absolutely essential . . . there should be made known to him the nature, duration and purpose of the experiment . . . (and) all inconveniences and hazards reasonably to be expected. . . .

(2) The experiment should be such as to yield fruitful results

for the good of society, unprocurable by other methods or means of study, and not random or unnecessary in nature.

(3) The experiment should be so designed and based on the results of animal experimentation and a knowledge of the natural history of the disease or other problem under study that the anticipated results will justify the performance of the experiment.

(4) The experiment should be so conducted as to avoid all unnecessary physical and mental suffering and injury.

(5) No experiment should be conducted where there is an *a priori* reason to believe that death or disabling injury will occur; except, perhaps, in those experiments where the experimental physicians also serve as subjects.

(6) The degree of risk to be taken should never exceed that determined by the humanitarian importance of the problem to be solved by the experiment.

(7) Proper preparations should be made, and adequate facilities provided to protect the experimental subject against even remote possibilities of injury, disability or death.

(8) The experiment should be conducted only by scientifically qualified persons. The highest degree of skill and care should be required through all stages of the experiment of those who conduct and engage in the experiment.

(9) During the course of the experiment the human subject should be at liberty to bring the experiment to an end if he has reached the physical or mental state where continuation of the experiment seems to him to be impossible.

(10) During the course of the experiment the scientist in charge must be prepared to terminate the experiment at any stage, if he has probable cause to believe, in the exercise of the good faith, superior skill and careful judgment required of him that a continuation of the experiment is likely to result in injury, disability, or death to the experimental subject.[4]

It is interesting to note that the Nuremberg Code does not

[4] Sinick (1954) pointed out that the Nuremberg principles have been formulated mainly in connection to medical science. He asserts that these principles could be beneficially applied to psychological research if they are first translated into psychological terms through an accumulation of illustrative incidents.

deal with subjects who are children, abnormal, or in any other special groups. Waddams, however, deals with this and mentions some important legal points. When the experiment is for the child's benefit, parental consent can justify the treatment; when the experiment, though, is for the advancement of knowledge and involves considerable risk, parental consent does not necessarily justify the experiment, but can justify it if the experiment involves very small risks (such as the weighing of a baby). Furthermore, experiments ought not be carried out on abnormals if the individual involved is so unstable as to lack the capacity to comprehend and consent. Waddams' further comments on laboratory assistants and medical students are also illuminating. In the ordinary case, one must ensure that acquiescence to experimentation is voluntary and does not occur because of a fear of losing a job. In the case of students, consent to experimentation is a condition of admittance to medical studies, but must only be sought in teaching experiments. Furthermore, if a teacher wishes to experiment on his students he ought to refrain because of his power to influence the students' progress toward their goals. The experimenter ought to recruit students other than his own.

On the question of rewarding volunteers, Waddams points out that offering a substantial reward to a "needy subject may detract from the freedom of his consent." Thus, subjects ought not to be paid more than out-of-pocket expenses and an hourly rate equivalent to the one of an unskilled worker. Importantly, though, the institution financing the study should be ready to compensate in full the subject if he is harmed in the course of the investigation.

Also writing on the subject of reward is Moore (1960). He holds that subjects who are scientifically competent to judge the nature of the study, to participate in it as scientists, and co-author its publication, should not be paid. On the other hand, for subjects who derive "no scientific, personal, intellectual or biologic" information from the study, there should be some reward.

At this point, one should note that the above discussion has been largely devoted to the legal aspects of *medi*cal experimentation on human subjects (since little has been said in connection with behavioral experiments). However, as Wolfe (1960) points out, medical experiences cannot always serve as an adequate guide. In a medical situation it is customary to explain the nature and possible dangers of the experiment and to secure the patient's consent before the study is tried—without there being the possibility as in behavioral research of vitiating the results. Furthermore, a new medical treatment is ordinarily tried out on ill patients who may themselves be directly benefited. In psychological research, however, this is usually not the case. What then is to be done regarding experiments in behavioral science? The Duke Law Journal (1960) offered a partial solution with the concept of "liability without fault." Under this concept, if a subject is damaged during the experiment he would be entitled to be made whole, through treatment or rehabilitation, or to receive compensatory damages. Thus the subject would be protected. The investigator would also be protected. He would not be considered to be at fault, but rather to have acted in the interests of society. Although this solution is very helpful, we note that some practical problems remain—how, for instance, would psychological damage be assessed? And which investigators would be protected?

Wolfensberger (1967) is also aware that knowledge of the experiment's nature and subsequent consent may, in behavioral research, vitiate the results. He suggests that there is no need to explain the nature of the experiment to the subject nor to tell him of all the possible dangers that may ensure. What one can do, though, that is, consent can be considered informed, when the subject understands the nature of the "rights" he has surrendered to the scientist. The subject may yield any of four rights: (a) invasion of privacy, (b) donation of personal resources (e.g., time, energy), (c) surrender of autonomy (as in drug studies, for instance), (d) exposure to discomforting procedures that may prove harmful in the long run. Wolfensberger also suggests that the more serious the right to be surrendered, the more consideration and effort should be devoted to the question of consent.

Other writers have made different suggestions. Ruebhausen and Brim (1966) have held that if consent is impossible without invalidating the research, then before the research is undertaken, the responsible officials of the institution financing, administering and sponsoring the study should be satisfied with the social good in the proposed research outweighs the social value of the ethical breaches. The actions of the National Advisory Health Council also have been made in the same spirit or with the same idea as that of Ruebhausen and Brim. In 1965 the Council passed a resolution (later accepted by the Surgeon General, U.S. Department of Health, Education and Welfare) to the effect that the Public Health Service will not subsidize research involving human subjects unless the grantee institution has, through a panel of the scientist's associates, taken the following steps:

(1) Assured itself that the subject's rights and welfare are protected.
(2) Determined the risks and benefits of the study.
(3) Made certain that the methods used to secure informed consent are appropriate.

These procedures became operative on November 1, 1966. In the same article USPHS stressed that to deal adequately with the ethical issues involved it is best to consider each study individually and to ensure that ethical matters are resolved in the study's design and procedures. It should also be clear that the USPHS is opposed to the type of legislation with large numbers of controls over the carrying out of research.

This matter of the kind of legislation that should be established to deal with the ethical issues in human experimentation has caught the attention of many individuals. It would be interesting to mention the views of a few of them. Recently, the APA Committee on Legislation reaffirmed the policy that "legislation governing the practice of psychology should be so written that the official code of ethics of the APA be adopted. . . ." In addition the Committee emphasized that too much restriction in the laws might impede evolution and development in psychological techniques and practices. Even less pro-legislative is Freund (1967). Freund does not think that the law is ready for human experimentation because it cannot at the present time yield precise answers to the ethical problems involved. He contends that a wider exchange of ideas between science and the law on these problems is needed.

Before concluding this section, we would like to mention the discussions of two writers who have written specifically in connection to two types of experiments involving human beings—questionnaire tests and tests of new drugs on patients. As regards the first type of test, Conrad (1967) indicates that the legality of questionnaire items can be called into question when they have the following characteristics:

(1) They deal with an area which—either through custom or through constitutional or statutory protection—is generally regarded as highly personal.

(2) They seem likely to have an adverse psychological effect upon a significant number of respondents.

(3) They might lead to "self-incriminating or self-demeaning admission or confession."

(4) They refer to excessively abnormal behavior, feelings, attitudes, etc. (when they seem heavily psychiatric).

(5) They unduly recognize or countenance behavior which is considered reprehensible, immoral, or illegal.

(6) They request confidential information about a person other than the subject (without the other person's permission).

(7) They could be interpreted by the subject as propaganda for or against one side of a highly emotional and controversial issue.

(8) They enter a politically sensitive area from the standpoint of the person who may be affected.

Since the above set of criteria (which overlap with one another) cannot be applied routinely, certain factors would be taken into account. Some of them are (a) purpose(s) of the study, (b) the nature of the respondent (e.g., age, color, sex, religion, etc.) and (c) voluntariness of response.

For experiments involving the testing of drugs, Bowker (1963) is of the opinion that should the drug prove harmful the scientist (the person carrying out the testing) is protected from liability if he has disclosed the experiment's risks and if he has obtained the volunteer's free consent. The point is also made that since the risks are not all known the scientist can further protect himself by making a statement of the "fact of unknown risks" and even of the possibility of fatal risks. Dean Bowker makes additional remarks on other important legal issues.

(1) If the subject is a married woman and has given an "effective consent" the husband's consent is unnecessary.

(2) Only if the physician who referred the subject to the scien-

tist participated in an experiment which was conducted
negligently would he be liable.

(3) Only if the drug maker was negligent in the preparation of
a drug and gave incorrect information would he be liable.

(4) If the subject is a child or a mentally ill person, the scientist
is not necessarily protected from liability if he has the
guardian's consent.

EDUCATIONAL DIMENSIONS

This new tinge to modern minds is a vehement and passionate
interest in the relation of general principles to irreducible and
stubborn facts. All the world over and at all times there have
been practical men, absorbed in "irreducible and stubborn facts":
all the world over and at all times there have been men of
philosophic temperament who have been absorbed in the weav-
ing of general principles. It is this union of passionate interest
in the detailed facts with equal devotion to abstract generalization which forms the novelty in our present society. Previously
it had appeared sporadically and as if by chance. This balance
of mind has now become part of the tradition which infects
cultivated thought. It is the salt which keeps life sweet. The
main business of universities is to transmit this tradition as a
widespread inheritance from generation to generation.

A. N. Whitehead, *Science and
the Modern World*, 1930.

While educators sometimes find themselves in sympathy with
the intent of critics, at the same time they find it difficult to
interpret their research within this context. Perhaps this is because so many critics conceive research too narrowly.

First we may recognize that most arguments have been directed against investigations undertaken to increase *administrative efficiency*. Certainly it can be argued that filed test data
work to the disadvantage of the individual who provided them.
It can be argued that any interpretation of test behavior which
deprives the individual of a coveted position or advancement, or
change which is personally considered an improvement over his
present condition—economically or for whatever reason—is not
totally consistent with the individual's self-interest. In the case
of governments and corporative agencies where such data are

made a part of a personnel file, test interpretations can fix prejudice and serve as a permanent barrier to advancement. Whether this is a justifiable prejudice or barrier is not at issue; social values are not to be treated as always identical with self-interest.

The other class of research criticized is that designed to increase the *resources of human knowledge*. Unlike administrative research, this is undertaken for disinterested purposes. Again, one can argue that some procedures employed to this end are deleterious from the participant's standpoint. There is no reason *a priori* that some one group of persons should be arbitrarily selected out to suffer reduction of self-esteem, anxiety, deception, etc. The fact that society presumably wants to know about such matters is not the entire issue. The question is, "Who should provide such data?" And as a popular placard proclaims "Why me?"

Granted that ethical issues can arise in the above contexts, some principle which weighs benefits to be acquired from an experiment against social cost of disregarding or approaching some assumed or stated ethical desiderata must doubtless influence methodological decisions. This is the one principle constantly reoccurring in papers devoted to analyzing ethical issues in human experimentation. In whose hands such decisions should be is the important matter which has been addressed by those referred to in the prior sections.

However, now let us consider another very common type of research which has *not* become a matter of issue. This is research undertaken for purposes of *experimental education*. We should like to suggest that many of the ethical problems touched upon in the previous section are extraneous to research conducted within properly administrated educational contexts.

All departments of psychology worthy of the name offer some type of laboratory course. We have offered such courses at the University of Alberta since 1909, and this is probably not atypical for most well-established universities. Undergraduate laboratories where sensory processes, sensory deprivation, perception, learning, motor skills, sleep, small group interactions, psychophysiology, reaction time, cognition, and work efficiency are studied immediately come to mind. In these courses, it is almost always necessary for the student enrolled to assume the role of subject. It is universally assumed that first-hand familiarity with methods employed to measure response and to produce statements of fact and theory is indispensable to the education of the "student-experimenter-subject" in all instances. There is no other reason for offering such courses that we know of. Typically, in a year's time, it is common for the student to put in upwards of 100 hours as a subject.

Similar educational benefits should be provided the student enrolled in an introductory course in psychology. Almost all departments having a sufficiently active research program do provide such education. The educational demands placed upon the student are somewhat different, however. They are much more minimal in general, because of the great difficulties in adequately serving the educational requirements of such large numbers. Customarily, less than 10 hours of experimental exposure per year is the rule.

Another significant difference is the fact that the introductory student does not usually serve as experimenter but merely as subject, i.e., he is a "student-subject." Because of his or her low levels of sophistication, it is necessary for the student-subject to rely upon briefings and explanations given after the experimental sessions by staff, graduate or senior honors students if his or her experience is to be made intelligible.

The chief ethical problem occurring within the educational contexts is therefore rarely, if ever, touched upon by those dealing with experimental ethics. The ethical problem within this setting is the old one and very familiar to educators; that of providing a level of education commensurate with the time expended by the student.

Mass experimental education poses some unique educational problems. In the experimental context the student is dependent upon educational staff in an unfamiliar way. In lecture situations the responsibility for education is more largely his own since he is free to listen or not listen, take notes or not take notes, review or not review materials, participate in class discussion, or not, etc. The lecture is not designed to maintain his naïveté. Similar analysis applies to meeting reading assignments. Ordinarily, one can say that the instructor is attempting to reduce rather than maintain his naivete.

But most experimental sessions, as a matter of course, and in contrast, attempt to hide from the student-subject the purposes of experimentation. This is for the very good reason of reducing experimental effects. Anyone reading Rosenthal's book, *Experimental Effects in Behavioral Research* (1966), cannot but consider prior knowledge a serious threat to valid experimentation. Many experiments, in fact, must go so far as to engender what are carelessly labeled as "deceptions" if valid results are to be obtained. In perceptual and sensory experiments, this often amounts to showing people things or scenes that exist differently than they naively presume. For example, one can produce a false impression of luminance or wave length sheerly through intermittent presentation of photic stimuli (light timing). We see a "deceptive" scene since it appears to most students-subjects as a moon and buildings, but in reality is toys (buildings), an illuminated piece of opal glass (sky), and a projected light spot (moon). We are, of course, deceiving the student-subject, for in our effort to hold a mirror to nature in the laboratory, we must deceive.

The same is true when social interaction is studied in the laboratory. But here one sometimes finds deceit intolerable. It seems, generally, that we expect nature to be deceptive but we will not condone this when the environment is our fellow man. Although geared to the same pragmatic ends as all experimentation, social deceit is seen as an unacceptable form of methodological education. This is in opposition to the fact that virtually everyone agrees that people should indeed be educated concerning the role that belief and opinion exert upon behavior and experience. Whether the experimental study of belief, for example, is based upon a true situation or not is not really to the point.

The difference between sensory-perceptual and social deception or simulation probably rests on implicit assumptions guiding everyday behavior. We take it for granted the physical world about us is not what it often seems to be. This does not upset us because it is simply a matter of nature which we are *not* free to alter as we desire. On the other hand, language communications (words and sentences) are structured by humans entirely and have, as one of their chief functions, the conveying of knowledge from one individual to another. If the truthful intent of another individual cannot be assumed, then the possibility of vicarious experience and satisfying human relationships is much reduced. This is probably the basis for the general repugnance for Hitler's "big lie," communist indoctrination procedures, advertising techniques, and propaganda generally, but this does not alter the fact that virtually all laboratory experimentation is necessarily "deceptive" to the same extent.

The problem is partially semantic. Deceit has as synonymous "fraud," "hypocrisy," "insincerity" and "duplicity"—all emotionally loaded terms, their use may be possibly defensible in descriptions of research undertaken for non-educational reasons. It is clearly possible to avoid these connotations in educational settings, however, by substituting the term "simulate." It is a more accurate reflection of what we do since it carries with it connotations of "feigning," "mock," and "sham." It is also a superior usage because simulator is specifically defined in *Webster's Third New International Dictionary* as "a device in a laboratory that enables the operator to reproduce under test conditions phenomena likely to occur in actual performance." In some respects it might be preferable to abandon the term "laboratory" in educational settings in preference for the term "simulator." Instead of scheduling hours in the psychological laboratory we might better arrange times at the "environmental simulator" or Psychological Simulation Laboratories." This would be a concrete move in the direction of joining the activities of pure science with those of education.

The problem is partially attitudinal also. For, in fact, as we all know, staff and graduate students consider themselves to derive the principal benefit from experimentation with undergraduates. This is unfortunate since it probably tends to depress the adjustment of educational procedures to the requirements of our age. It does not, however, alter the validity of the preceding analysis, since this was made from an educational and not a personal perspective.

But what of the educational problems? How are they to be dealt with effectively? We honestly do not know for certain. At the University of Alberta, we think that effective experimental education at all levels must include at least two stages: what we call the "Briefing" and "Debriefing" stages.

The Briefing Stage consists initially of one exercise preliminary to enrollment. As said, educational standards demand that the psychology student become familiar with methods employed by modern society in order to produce knowledge, to increase efficiency, or to achieve desirable social control. Since matriculation constitutes the acceptance of standards prevalent at the institution, it is unethical to inaccurately or incompletely describe the requirements for courses being offered, particularly when such courses have this as one of the primary aims. Certainly, the issue here is somewhat different from that of assigned reading requirements because the latter can be assumed to constitute common knowledge. If we omit this in our descriptions, methodological education sometimes comes as an unpleasant surprise. Thus, the tendency of universities to publish simply course titles, eliminating descriptions to save money, is deplorable and should be acted against wherever course requirements of a research character are excessive to those listed under conventional headings of Lecture and Laboratory.

The ethics of education also recommend a secondary briefing stage. In this stage the general ground rules for experimental education are set forth. These must also be made clear beforehand to the student who is to be educated through services as a subject. He should be told that it is obviously impossible for us to bring him in direct contact with situations in the real world. Since we cannot educate him by taking advantage of natural manipulations,[5] we must simulate. It should be made clear that simulation always involves substituting artificial for real conditions.

It should be emphasized that most psychologists are empiricists, and because of this they do not feel free to make up an ideal world to rationally investigate. They therefore attempt to create a realistic model in order to investigate the world as it appears to exist. This interpretation should be stressed so that the subject will not construe experimental settings as personal deceptions.

The third stage of briefing takes place as continuing education during the year. This aspect is necessarily the most time-consuming and difficult. The student must be thoroughly educated as to the character of fact, theory and method. Method

[5] This, incidentally, is all but impossible for other scientific departments as well. Let us take two examples—one from botany and the other from geology. Glacier action is not easily studied by the student at the University of Florida. *Genus Palmae* is not readily studied at the University of Alberta. And in neither of these two cases do we have the complexities that interfering with active lives in natural settings would entail.

is particularly important because it contains notions of control, measurement, classes of variables, operational thinking, stimulus control, hypotheses, etc. Needless to say, many introductory textbooks of psychology as well as specialized undergraduate level texts already treat this general subject extensively.

The final Debriefing Stage of experimental education requires a consideration of the actual experiments undertaken during the period of enrollment and service as a subject. Here the student should be told the background of the problem in terms of contemporary theory, hypothesis being tested, methodology employed, difficulties experienced during administration, and, if possible, a brief summary of the outcome. It is likely that this final stage cannot be adequately accomplished within the compass of the lecture room, but requires special arrangements such as experimental tutorials.

There are other ethical problems, but these seem so obvious as to require only brief treatment. The following might be outlined in connection with short, common-sense recommendations:

(1) Procedures to assure the subject's safety must be rigidly adhered to. There is generally little mystery as to what safe education entails. Just as we would not endanger a student by holding classes in an unsafe location, we must not conduct method education with unsafe instruments. We must be just as willing to assume the legal responsibilities for experimental education as for classroom education.

The major problem in psychology so far as safety is concerned is now perhaps associated with the use of drugs. All drugs are potentially lethal and all harbor the risk of side effects of a sensory or affective character. Any drug should be given only on medical advice and only after the participating subject has been directly seen by the physician-advisor. The medical advisor should be prepared to consider not only the possibility that the drug may be deadly to this individual but also the possibility of side effects endangering his later efficiency as a student, driver, or in his supporting employment. If this procedure is too expensive or too cumbersome the experiment should, of course, not be attempted.

(2) The legal requirements for experimentation ought to be established. Great care must be taken, however, not to mislead the university or student into thinking that they are embarking upon a terrible or bizarre new adventure. Laboratories have been an integral part of university education for many decades. The

introduction of experimental education in the earliest exposure of the student to a discipline is a logical extension of a trend that has been an accumulating force over a number of years.

(3) The educators must be quite explicit in stating that no self-revealment is intended to be the product of any experiment. Ruebhausen and Brim's (1966) suggestions regarding ways in which confidentiality of data may be maintained should be adhered to. More to the point, the aims of experimental education are inconsistent with the needs of the International Data Center and, indeed, with those of any local data center. The educator-experimenter must not stockpile human data in case it is needed on some future occasion. Experimentation must be planned so far in advance as to make all group testing pertinent to a specific methodological experience. This requirement has been commonly violated. Violation is in the form of conduct of massive testing of groups of students on a great number of psychological measures without any specific intent of using the data obtained. It is difficult to justify such a profligate waste of student time on an educational level.

(4) The lack of interest in the student-subject on a personal level should be made quite clear. Science is impersonal.

(5) Honesty with respect to the validity of psychological testing is helpful. Psychologists have been possibly guilty of over-stressing the favorable side of psychological measures. It has never been made sufficiently clear that results have a low degree of individual prediction in criterion situations. We, in fact, find out very little about the person under the very best of circumstances using psychological instruments. Frank pathology often proves difficult to adequately describe.

SUMMARY

Arguments in "The Human Experimental Subject in Context" covering (a) the issue of safety, (b) the issue of privacy, (c) the issue of comfort, (d) the issue of self-concept or dignity, and (e) the legal aspects of experimentation are made.

The review showed a restricted view on human experimentation dominating the writing of critics. Human experimentation was viewed either as the design to assess the individual for social or engineering purposes or to provide data increasing the resources of human knowledge. Neither of these ends need to be consistent with the self-interest of the individual.

Much human experimentation, however, is undertaken for the purpose of education as well as for scientific reasons. In such circumstances, the ethical issues shift. Ethics governing teaching should be applied. Some unique ethical issues arise in a student-subject educational setting and these are discussed.

REFERENCES

Abelson, P. H. Privacy. Editorial in *Science*, 1967, **156**, 3800, p. 433.
American Psychological Association. Ethical standards of psychologists. *Amer. Psychologist*, 1968, **23**, 357–361.
Anastasi, A. Psychology, psychologists, and psychological testing. *Amer. Psychologist*, 1967, **22**, 297–306.
Baumrind, D. Some thoughts on ethics of research. *Amer. Psychologist*, 1964, **19**, 421–423.
Bennett, C. C. What price privacy? *Amer. Psychologist*, 1967, **22**, 371–376.
Berdie, R. F. Policies regarding the release of information about clients *J. counsel. Psychol.*, 1960, **7**, 149–146.
Berg, I. A. The use of human subjects in psychological research. *Amer. Psychologist*, 1954, **9**, 108–111.
Bowker, W. F. Legal liability to volunteers in testing new drugs. *Can. med. Ass. J.*, 1963, **88**, 745–751.
Bramel, D. A. A dissonance theory approach to defensive projection. *J. abnorm. soc. Psychol.*, 1962, **64**, 121–129.
Bramel, D. Selection of a target for defensive projection. *J. abnorm. soc. Psychol.*, 1963, **66**, 318–324.
Brown, D. W. Interpreting the college student to prospective employers, government agencies, and graduate schools. *Personnel Guid. J.* 1961, **39**, 576–582.
Conrad, H. S. Clearance of questionnaires with respect to "invasion of privacy," public sensitivities, ethical standards, etc. *Amer. Psychologist*, 1967, **22**, 356–359.
Duke Law Journal 1960.
Evans, G. C. The influence of "fake" personality evaluations on self-description. *J. Psychol.*, 1962, **53**, 457–463.
Ferry, W. H. Must we rewrite the Constitution to control technology? *Sat. Rev.*, 1968 (March), 50–54.
Freund, P. A. Is the law ready for human experimentation? *Amer. Psychologist*, 1967, **22**, 394–399.
Gans, H. J. Testimony before the Senate Subcommittee on Govern-

ment Research of the Committee on Government Operations: Full Opportunity and Social Accounting Act. *Amer. Psychologist,* 1967, **22,** 983–991.

Goslin, D. A. *The search for ability: Standardized testing in social perspective.* New York: Russell Sage Foundation, 1963.

Hauser, P. Testimony before the Senate Subcommittee on Government Research of the Committee on Government Operations: Full Opportunity and Social Accounting Act. *Amer. Psychologist,* 1967, **22,** 991–994.

Katz, M. M. Ethical issues in the use of human subjects in psychopharmacologic research. *Amer. Psychologist,* 1967, **22,** 360–363.

Kelman, H. C. Human use of human subjects: The problem of deception in social psychological experiments. *Psychol. Bull,* 1967, **67,** 1–11.

Kidd, A. M. Limit of the right of a person to consent to experiment on himself. *Science,* 1953, **117,** 211–212.

Kosa, J. Who invades privacy and why? *Amer. Psychologist,* 1968, **23,** 138.

Lovell, V. R. The human use of personality tests: A dissenting view. *Amer. Psychologist,* 1967, **22,** 383.

Mackintosh, J. M. Ethical and legal aspects of medical research on human beings. *J. pub. Law,* 1959, **3,** 467–479.

McGuire, W. J. Some impending reorientations in social psychology: Some thoughts provoked by Kenneth Ring. *J. exp. soc. Psychol.,* 1967, **32,** 124–139.

Milgram, S. Behavioral study of obedience. *J. abnorm. soc. Psychol.,* 1963, **67,** 371–378.

Milgram, S. Some conditions of obedience and disobedience to authority. *Hum. Rel.,* 1965, **18,** 57–76.

Moore, F. D. Part II. Symposium on the study of drugs in man. *Clin. Pharm. Therap.,* 1960, **1,** 149–155.

Privacy and behavioral research: Preliminary summary of the report of the Panel on Privacy and Behavioral Research. *Amer. Psychologist,* 1967, **22,** 345–349.

Rosenthal, R. *Experimenter effects in behavioral research.* New York: Appleton-Century-Crofts, 1966.

Ruebhausen, O. H., & Brim, O. G., Jr. Privacy and behavioral research, *Amer. Psychologist,* 1966, **21,** 423–437.

Sato, I. Studies on sensory deprivation: IV, Part 5. Changes of self-concept under sensory deprivation. *Tohoku Psychologica Folia,* 1965, **24** (1–2), 18–23.

Sinick, D. Comments on the "use of human subjects in psychological research." *Amer. Psychologist*, 1954, **9**, p. 589.

Smith, J. The use of children subjects in psychological research. *Amer. Psychologist*, 1967, **22**, 282–298.

Snygg, D., & Combs, A. W. *Individual Behavior; a new frame of reference for psychology*. New York: Harper & Row, 1949.

Stollak, G. E. Obedience and deception research. *Amer. Psychologist*, 1967, **22**, 678.

Waddams, S. M. Medical experiments on human subjects. *Fac. Law Rev.*, 1966. Univ. of Toronto, 25–54.

Westin, A. F. *Privacy and freedom*. New York: Atheneum, 1967.

Wolfensberger, I. Ethical issues in research with human subjects. *Science*, 1967, **155**, 48–59.

Wolfe, D. Research with human subjects. *Science*, 1960, **1321**, p. 189.

INDEXES

NAME INDEX

SUBJECT INDEX

71 72 73 74   7 6 5 4 3 2 1